# Catering Solutions

## For the culinary student, foodservice operator, and caterer

*Ed Sanders*

*Chef Larry Lewis*

*Nick Fluge*

*Prentice Hall, Upper Saddle River, New Jersey 07458*

**Library of Congress Cataloging-in-Publication Data**

Sanders, Edward E.
    Catering solutions : for the culinary student, foodservice
operator, and caterer / by Ed Sanders, Larry Lewis, Nick Fluge.
        p.    cm.
    ISBN 0-13-082900-5
    1. Caterers and catering Handbooks, manuals, etc.    I. Lewis,
Larry (date)  II. Fluge, Nick (date).  III. Title.
TX921.S32  2000
642'. 4—dc21
                                                          99-32443
                                                             CIP

Acquisition Editor: Neil Marquardt
Editorial Assistant: Sue Kegler
Managing Editor: Mary Carnis
Project Manager: Linda B. Pawelchak
Prepress and Manufacturing Buyer: Ed O'Dougherty
Cover Director: Marianne Frasco
Cover Design: Maria Lange
Cover Art: Farida Zaman
Marketing Manager: Shannon Simonson
Copy Editing: Lynn Buckingham
Proofreading: Nancy Menges

This book was set in 10/12 Bookman by Pine Tree Composition
and was printed and bound by The Courier Companies.
The cover was printed by Phoenix Color Corp.

©2000 by Prentice-Hall, Inc.
Upper Saddle River, New Jersey 07458

Printed in the United States of America
10  9  8  7  6  5  4  3  2  1

**ISBN 0-13-082900-5**

Prentice-Hall International (UK) Limited, *London*
Prentice-Hall of Australia Pty. Limited, *Sydney*
Prentice-Hall Canada Inc., *Toronto*
Prentice-Hall Hispanoamericana, S. A., *Mexico*
Prentice-Hall of India Private Limited, *New Delhi*
Prentice-Hall of Japan, Inc., *Tokyo*
Pearson Education Asia Pte. Ltd., *Singapore*
Editora Prentice-Hall do Brasil, Ltda., *Rio De Janeiro*

# Contents

# List of Figures

# Foreword

What a book! From setting a date to setting the table, *Catering Solutions: For the Culinary Student, Foodservice Operator, and Caterer* caters to every whim, taking the reader step by step through the rigorous process of catering a gourmet event, even advising on such things as appropriate background music and proper napkin folding.

I particularly enjoy the book's imaginative recipes, which complement each other so well, and also the beverage suggestions. Even experienced culinary professionals are often at a loss as to just which wine or other beverage to serve with a gloriously prepared meal, and *Catering Solutions* removes the guesswork.

This book offers valuable information not only to the catering professional, but also to all chefs and operators for whom a catered event is a value-added part of a foodservice program. With increasing competition for the customer's food dollar, and with the lines separating the various foodservice segments becoming more and more gray, an on-or-off-site catering program can be the point of distinction between a moderately successful venue and a wildly successful one.

I would recommend this book not only to an established, successful catering operation, but also to anyone who cannot allow one detail of his or her occasion to be less than absolutely perfect.

Brent T. Frei, Editor in Chief
*Chef Magazine*

# Acknowledgments

The authors would like to acknowledge the following people for their help in bringing the book to production:

Neil Marquardt, acquisitions editor, Prentice Hall, who shared the authors' enthusiasm from the time of the book's conception.

Randall Towns, product development leader, the Education Foundation of the National Restaurant Association, for thoroughly reviewing and offering helpful suggestions for Chapter 1.

Jim Cook, vice president of marketing, Boxer Northwest, foodservice equipment supply and design, for sharing ideas and contacts for many of the equipment examples used throughout the book.

Tom Ohling, chef and consultant, for the critical attention to detail in reviewing the first five chapters.

Donna Caputo, who provided the initial editorial review at the time of the book's conception, and Vicky Rafn for developing the menu theme graphics.

The staff at Western Culinary Institute: Greg Ogdahl, president, and Eric Stromquist, administrative dean, whose creativity and editing assistance helped make the beverage sections engaging for our readers. Marsha Parmer, director of graduate services, and Ramsey Hamdan, director of restaurants, who added unique concepts as well as helped proof the first draft of the beverage references. Chef Darrell Puckett and the students for preparing all of the recipe items for photographing. Joe Gonzales, director of public relations and corporate training, who directed the photo shoots and took the pictures; and James Reichstadt, resource director, who provided technical assistance and coordinated the software implementation.

Jay Sanders, who carefully edited and provided an orderly flow and logical direction to the text material. Mark Sanders, who always questioned the details and along with Katie Sanders taste-tested and objectively monitored all of the recipe items as they were being reviewed for accuracy and cooking times. Dad genuinely appreciated the help. Linda Sanders, who patiently supported, provided superb suggestions and ideas, and survived yet another of her husband's projects. Nick and Dorothy Drossos, lifetime restaurateurs, who were a continual source of inspiration to the developing career of Ed Sanders.

The dedicated staff at the *Hospitality News Group,* who made it a team effort to get the book done and to the publisher on time. Lori Smith, production manager, who was quick to point out when something didn't look right or could be presented better; Earlene Naylor, data entry, design, and production, who helped keep the developing ideas and material in a logical order; and Brenda Carlos, publisher of the *Hospitality News Group* of newspapers, who consistently shared her enthusiasm for the book's promotion.

Linda Pawelchak, who supervised editorial production; and Lynn Buckingham, who thoroughly edited every detail of the book, which exceeded the authors' expectations in every way.

# Introduction

This book is written so that the chapters are self-contained, allowing the reader to go directly to any chapter for specific information. The text allows the culinary student to gain an understanding and knowledge of the fundamental basics of successful on- and off-premise catering. It can also be used as a guide and quick reference source for anyone involved with professional catering.

Chapter 1, "Always Serving Safe Food," covers the critical areas of laws and codes, causes of foodborne illnesses, food temperatures, cross-contamination, HACCP, ServeSafe® training, and the latest in safe food-handling equipment.

Chapter 2, "Catering Details," references a catering contract that identifies all the possible catering options that are typically available to customers. Explanations with appropriate examples are provided for each detail. Also included are examples of an entertainment contract and of catering management software.

Chapter 3, "Serving the Food," discusses types of service; service rules; examples of dinnerware, flatware, and holloware; as well as various napkin presentations and buffet setups.

Chapter 4, "Kitchen Production," introduces menu cost, food production and portion control, the operation of a dish-up serving line and service table, areas of emphasis for off-premise catering, and methods of scaling recipe quantities.

Chapter 5, "Beverages," reviews beverage functions and alcoholic beverage license requirements and provides a basic description of wine, beers, ales and lagers, distilled spirits, coffee, espresso, and tea as well as pairing beverages with food.

Chapter 6, "Catering Menus and Recipes," provides twenty-five theme menus with complete detailed recipes that would be appropriate for a wide variety of catered events.

Appendix A, "ChefTec Software," demonstrates the function of scaling recipe quantities, recipe and menu costing, and recipe nutritional analysis.

Appendix B, "Blank Forms," includes the Catering Contract, Entertainment Contract, Food Production and Portion Control Chart, and Order Sheet. They may be photocopied and used to complete chapter exercises, or they can be used in an actual foodservice or catering operation.

The reader should not expect to be able to immediately jump into the catering business upon reading this book or completing it as part of an academic course. Additional courses of study in cost controls that would include purchasing, measuring product yield, pricing, labor scheduling, and human resource management, along with training in sales, marketing, and promotion, would be helpful. Those skills coupled with the opportunity to work with experienced professionals in the field would provide the basics to becoming a successful caterer.

# About the Caterer

The caterer is a person who

- Has the skills and ability to plan, organize, direct, execute, and control an event.
- Has the spirit of adventure that welcomes challenges and risks associated with every new circumstance.
- Focuses a great deal of attention on details.
- Courteously listens and promptly responds to the wants and needs of every guest.
- Maintains a polite and positive attitude in every situation.
- Knows his or her catering capacity in size and nature of event.
- Recognizes problems or emergency situations and solves them promptly, professionally, and efficiently.
- Understands how to be cost-efficient and financially profitable.
- Is imaginative with food and beverage presentations and creates "something special" for every event.
- Knows when to be prepared with contingency plans.
- Knows how to assign responsibilities.
- Can control stressful situations and still maintain a sense of humor.
- Delivers on all commitments.
- Continually develops new skills and advances his or her professional qualifications.
- Inspires all of these attributes in his or her staff.

# About Professional Catering Associations

**The National Association of Catering Executives (NACE)** is the world's oldest and largest organization for professional caterers and related suppliers. NACE offers a comprehensive agenda of national and local chapter programs that emphasize continuing education, professional certification, and networking and career support. Founded in 1958, NACE represents more than 3000 members in forty-six chapters that embrace all aspects of the vast catering industry.

NACE members who wish to demonstrate advanced skill and competence may seek the designation of Certified Professional Catering Executive (CPCE). This status may be achieved by sitting for a comprehensive examination that covers all aspects of the catering profession including on- and off-premise catering, sales and marketing, food and wine knowledge, safety, sanitation, legal liabilities, and many other related topics. Caterers with the CPCE designation stand out as the best of the best in this highly competitive industry. For information about NACE membership, services, and certification, contact the administrative director at NACE, 60 Revere Drive, Suite 500, Northbrook, IL 60062, or call 847.480.9080. You may also visit the NACE Web site at www.nace.net.

**The National Caterers Association (NCA)** is a leader in educational programs, including seminars, workshops, and product presentations. The NCA hosts a successful annual conference, at which members from all over the world network with others and discover new ideas. Founded in 1981, the NCA serves its members as a resource by providing help with all aspects of the catering industry. Membership is expected to exceed 2,000 members by the year 2000.

The NCA has a working alliance with the National Restaurant Association in Washington, D.C. For information about NCA membership and services, contact the executive director at the NCA, 1200 Seventeenth Street NW, Washington, D.C. 20036, or call 202.973.3964. You may also visit the NCA Web site at www.ncacater.org.

# About the Authors

*Photo by Richard Stefani*

**Ed Sanders, Chef Larry Lewis, Nick Fluge**

**Ed Sanders**
**Editor in Chief**
***Hospitality News***
***Group***

ED is the founder and editor in chief of the *Hospitality News Group*, which publishes regional foodservice industry newspapers. He is a Certified Food Executive and a Certified Purchasing Manager; his professional career has included being chief operating officer for a regional chain of restaurants, an associate professor of business, and procurement director of a large-volume foodservice operation. He has a master of science degree in international management from the American Graduate School of International Management and a doctor of business administration degree in management and organization. He was the co-founder and director of industry relations for the Hotel, Restaurant, and Resort Management Program at Southern Oregon University. He is also the co-author of *Foodservice Profitability: A Control Approach* (Prentice Hall, 1998).

**Chef Larry Lewis**
**Educational Manager**
***Le Cordon Bleu***
***Schools North***
***America***

LARRY is the educational manager for Le Cordon Bleu Schools North America. He had previously served as executive chef and academic dean of Western Culinary Institute. He is a Certified Executive Chef and Certified Culinary Educator. Chef Lewis attended the California Culinary Institute in San Francisco and graduated with honors; his career has encompassed all aspects of the culinary profession, including being executive chef of Harvey's Resort Hotel in South Lake Tahoe for seven years. He has served as chairperson for the American Culinary Federation Educational Institute, reviewing various culinary programs throughout the United States, and he currently serves as a commissioner of the American Culinary Federation Educational Institute Accrediting Commission.

**Nick Fluge**
**Managing Director,**
**Culinary Division**
***Career Education***
***Corporation* & Chief**
**Operating Officer**
***Le Cordon Bleu***
***Schools North***
***America***

NICK is the managing director of the culinary division of Career Education Corporation, with responsibility for culinary programs in the United States and Canada, and is chief operating officer for Le Cordon Bleu Schools North America. He has previously served as president of Western Culinary Institute for nine years. He is a Certified Culinary Educator, and his many years of experience have included being a sommelier, captain, and maitre d' in leading hotels, restaurants, and private clubs. Nick is a Master Knight of the Vine and has received the prestigious Commanders Award. His wine columns in *The National Culinary Review* and his position as chairperson of wine fiestas and culinary salons have earned him regional and national acclaim.

# From the Authors

Catering is a business that can be increasingly fulfilling as the caterer's knowledge and capabilities grow and expand through successful experiences. The people who enjoy success in catering are universally driven by one common goal: the desire to achieve 100 percent customer satisfaction. They are totally focused on identifying their customers' wants and desires, and in delivering the results that will meet and typically exceed customer expectations. This achievement provides them with an intense feeling of satisfaction as each catered event offers new challenges and opportunities for creativity, flair, innovation, and above all showmanship.

This book introduces the culinary student to the hands-on mechanics of catering and provides the foodservice operator with a checklist of details, tips, and ideas. The experienced caterer will find creative menu themes paired with beverage and wine selections along with unique recipes.

The number of caterers and foodservice operators expanding into the catering business is growing as demand within the hospitality industry for catered events increases. Therefore, it is our goal to produce a text that can be used in a competency-based academic program and as a guide and reference book for the professional caterer.

While there are many factors involved in training and preparing to become a caterer, what clearly separates the exceptional from the average is the desire to continually learn something new with every experience, along with the ability to consistently deliver a pleasing event to the customer.

This book is designed to provide accurate and authoritative information with regard to the subject matter covered. It is provided with the understanding that the authors are not engaged in rendering legal, accounting, or other professional services. If legal advice or other expert assistance is required, the services of a competent professional should be sought.

Ed Sanders

Larry Lewis

Nick Fluge

# 1

# Always Serving Safe Food

## Learning Objectives

After reading this chapter and completing the discussion questions and exercises, you should be able to

1. Understand the reasons for serving safe food.
2. Recognize the importance of knowing the laws and codes that deal with safe food handling and food safety.
3. Know the common causes of foodborne illnesses.
4. Discuss safe food temperatures.
5. Identify and describe the use of thermometers.
6. Define good personal hygiene.
7. Explain cross-contamination.
8. Recognize that the kitchen should always operate according to a safety and quality-control plan.
9. Understand dishwashing procedures.
10. Explain a Hazard Analysis Critical Control Point (HACCP) program for safe food handling.
11. Know what is required for safety in off-premise catering.
12. Know how to handle leftover foods.

**Introduction**

The first and most critical responsibility for all foodservice operators and caterers is serving safe food in order to prevent foodborne illnesses. A foodborne illness is carried or transmitted to humans by food containing harmful substances. When safe food-handling procedures are established, accompanied by simple instructions for easy understanding and followed by attentive supervision, their objective can be consistently achieved.

For the foodservice operator and caterer, this responsibility begins with a personal commitment to always serve safe quality food. This commitment should then translate into an all-employee commitment to maintaining a safe food kitchen and serving environment. A set of safe food policies and procedures should be established that clearly supports the following pledge:

*"We always serve safe quality food prepared in a clean and sanitary kitchen."*

## Laws and Codes

The laws and codes that specifically govern safe food handling and food safety issues may have certain variations according to city, county, and state health departments. In certain situations, federal regulations may also be applicable. For example, an airline catering kitchen may be subject to federal codes.

The foodservice operator and caterer should thoroughly understand these laws and codes before identifying and setting forth the operational policies and procedures that will ensure serving safe food. As a result, the foodservice/catering operation will comply with all the laws and codes that apply to the given community in which it is operating.

When off-premise catering is provided for a private party or public event, specific laws and codes must be followed that relate to mobile food facilities, rented facilities, customers' facilities, portable equipment, and food transportation, along with any unique situation or circumstance. Certain events may require a permit issued by the city, county, or state health department to operate as a temporary restaurant. The permit is issued upon the approval of the foodservice operator's application (see Figure 1–1 as an example) and may include specific date and time restrictions along with limits on the types of food that can be served. This is often the case for outdoor events that require a permit. Figure 1–2 is an example of a temporary restaurant license and inspection report.

## Causes of Foodborne Illnesses

The most common causes of foodborne illnesses are

1. Improper food temperatures
2. Poor personal hygiene
3. Cross-contamination

## Food Temperature

The easiest rule to remember is: KEEP HOT FOOD HOT AND COLD FOOD COLD.

Remember that food is safe when it is kept at temperatures below 41°F (5°C) and above 140°F (60°C). Foods are at risk while passing through the temperature danger zone (between 41°F and 140°F). Foods are often at risk within your facility during purchasing/receiving, storing, thawing, preparing, cooking, holding, serving, cooling, and reheating.

# Oregon Health Division

TEMPORARY RESTAURANT LICENSE APPLICATION

**This application must be returned prior to the event. All portions of the application must be completed.**

Submit the proper fee with the application prior to the event. (Nonprofit tax ID No. _____ )

1. RESTAURANT/ORGANIZATION: ———————————————————————

   Applicant: ————————————————— Day Phone: ———————————

   Mailing Address: ———————————————————————————————
   (include City, State & Zip)

   Hours of Operation: ————————————— Date(s): ———————————

   Person in Charge of Operation: ————————————— Day Phone: —————————

2. ADVANCE PREPARATION: For any foods prepared before the event, describe how the food will be cooked and rapidly cooled (include container type, food depth, and equipment). Some foods requiring extensive cooling and reheating may be prohibited.

   Describe: ————————————————————————————
   —————————————————————————————————————
   —————————————————————————————————————

3. FOOD TEMPERATURE CONTROL: How will you provide for proper food temperature control in booth?

   a)   Cold-holding devices **(provide spirit-stem thermometers)**

   Describe: ———————————————————————————

   b)   Hot-holding devices (e.g., warmer, steam table, heat cabinet)

   Describe: ———————————————————————————

   c)   Rapid-heating devices (e.g., stove, oven, burner)

   Describe: ———————————————————————————

4. LEFTOVERS: What will you do with leftover food?

   Describe: ———————————————————————————
   —————————————————————————————————————

5. HANDWASHING: **Handwashing facilities must be set up inside booth before any food preparation takes place.**

   Describe: ———————————————————————————

6. CLEANING AND SANITIZING **(provide test kit)**

   Describe: ———————————————————————————

7. BOOTH CONSTRUCTION:

   Type of Overhead Protection Provided: ————————————————————

   Type of Floor Provided: ————————————— Type of Screening Provided: ———————————

8. FOOD HANDLER CARDS: Yes ——————— No ———————      (Must get before event.)

9. THERMOMETER: Probe Thermometer provided to check food temperature, (RANGE OF 0° - 220°F): Yes ——————— No ———————

*10. WATER SUPPLY: ———————————————————————————

*All water utilized by your temporary restaurant must be obtained from an approved public water supply.

Comments:

———————————————————————————————————————
Signature of Applicant                                             Date

MENU (list all food items, including toppings):

| Food Item | How Served | | Made to Order | | Off-Site Prep | | On-Site Prep | | Describe Cooking Method |
|---|---|---|---|---|---|---|---|---|---|
| | Hot | Cold | Yes | No | Yes | No | Yes | No | |
| | | | | | | | | | |
| | | | | | | | | | |
| | | | | | | | | | |
| | | | | | | | | | |
| | | | | | | | | | |
| | | | | | | | | | |
| | | | | | | | | | |
| | | | | | | | | | |
| | | | | | | | | | |
| | | | | | | | | | |
| | | | | | | | | | |
| | | | | | | | | | |
| | | | | | | | | | |
| | | | | | | | | | |
| | | | | | | | | | |
| | | | | | | | | | |
| | | | | | | | | | |

FOOD PREPARATION:    All food must be prepared in a facility approved by the Health Department or the Department of Agriculture. **No home prepared foods are allowed**.

FACILITY USED FOR (**OFF-SITE**) FOOD PREP, STORAGE, AND UTENSIL WASHING

Facility Name: _____

Address: _____   Phone: _____

_____
Signature of Facility Operator

B:\Tmpapplc.frm                                                    #34-1C  5/98

FIGURE 1–1 **TEMPORARY RESTAURANT LICENSE APPLICATION**
*Courtesy of Oregon Department of Human Resources, Health Division*

Within the temperature danger zone of 41°F (5°C) to 140°F (60°C), bacteria can rapidly grow. High-protein foods present a greater risk than other foods because they are moist, allowing for a rapid growth of bacteria if not correctly handled. Any foods consisting of or containing the following are potentially hazardous: milk and milk products, shell eggs, poultry, fish, shellfish, meats, cooked rice, cooked beans (and other heat-treated plant foods), baked and boiled potatoes, tofu and other soy-protein foods, raw seeds and sprouts, garlic and oil mixtures, and sliced melons. Also, packaged ready-to-eat foods that are refrigerated or frozen and require additional cooking at specific internal temperatures are at risk.

To ensure safe food, the temperatures that follow starting on page 6 must be reached and held for internal cooking, cooling, reheating, and holding. Also see Figure 1–3.

| EVENT | | AUDIT/LICENSE NO. | 02925 T |
|---|---|---|---|
| Business/Organization | | Phone | |
| Applicant/Contact Name | | Phone | |
| Mailing Address | | | |
| Location | Menu | | |
| Dates of Operation | | Hours of Operation | |

☐ Benevolent

☐ Non Benevolent       MAKE CHECK PAYABLE TO:

Fee Paid _____

Approved by _____       *   Date _____

## VIOLATION CHECKLIST

### Public Health Hazards

☐ 1 Food, ice, potable water from unapproved source (159-120, 010, 040)
☐ 2 Potentially hazardous food at improper temperature (45-140°F) for unacceptable length of time (159-130, 135)
☐ 3 Potentially hazardous food not rapidly reheated to 165°F, not rapidly cooled to 45°F (151-120, 050)
☐ 4 Potentially hazardous food inadequately iced (159-130)
☐ 5 Hand washing facilities not provided or maintained (159-070)
☐ 6 Poor hygienic practices; unclean hands, eating, smoking, unrestrained hair (159-140)
☐ 7 Toxic items improperly used, stored, labeled (156-250, 240, 230)
☐ 8 Improper disposal of solid and liquid waste (159-060, 100)

### Food Protection

☐ 9 Food not protected during transport, display, storage; packaged food in undrained ice or water; cooling food in drinking ice (151-250; 159-120, 050, 010)
☐ 10 Improper handling of food; scoops/tongs not used (159-120, 010)
☐ 11 Unwashed fruits/vegetables (151-080)

### Equipment And Utensils

☐ 12 Food contact surfaces not clean and sanitized (154-000)
☐ 13 Food contact surfaces not protected (159-110)
☐ 14 Non-food contact surfaces not clean (154-000)
☐ 15 Equipment and utensils not in good repair; not easily cleanable (159-110, 020)
☐ 16 Single service items not protected (154-080)
☐ 17 Extra utensils not provided (159-110)

### Miscellaneous

☐ 18 Spirit-stem/probe thermometers not provided (159-130; 151-140)
☐ 19 Sanitizing clothes not provided; maintained (154-010)
☐ 20 Garbage disposal inadequate; absorbent liner used (159-060)
☐ 21 Booth area not clean (159-090)
☐ 22 Floors, walls, ceiling inadequate (159-080, 090)
☐ 23 Unauthorized personnel in booth (156-280)
☐ 24 Operating without a license (ORS 624.025)
☐ 25 Personnel lacking food handler certificates

| ITEM/OAR | SPECIFIC PROBLEM & REQUIRED CORRECTION |
|---|---|
| | |
| | |
| | |
| | |
| | |
| | |
| | |
| | |
| | |

Operator                                                                      Sanitarian

B:\TempLic3.CL                White - Licensing Agency;  Green - Operator                34-1E (3/97)

FIGURE 1–2 **TEMPORARY RESTAURANT LICENSE & INSPECTION REPORT**
*Courtesy of Oregon Department of Human Resources, Health Division*

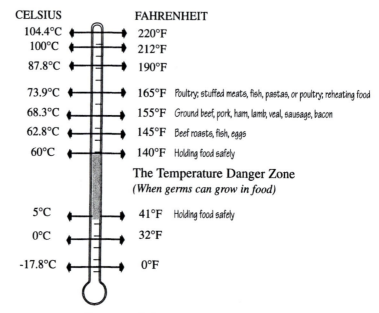

FIGURE 1–3 **SAFE FOOD TEMPERATURES**

---

## MINIMUM SAFE INTERNAL COOKING TEMPERATURES

Temperature reached and held for at least 15 seconds. For additional safety, cook at a higher than minimum temperature, being careful not to compromise food quality.

| | |
|---|---|
| 165°F (73.9°C) | Poultry; stuffed meats, fish, pastas, or poultry (stuffing and food item should be cooked separately first); reheating food. |
| 155°F (68.3°C) | Ground beef, pork, ham, lamb, veal, sausage, bacon. |
| 145°F (62.8°C) | Beef roasts, fish, eggs. |

## COOLING FOOD SAFELY

| | |
|---|---|
| 41°F (5°C) | Internal temperature should drop from 140°F to 70°F within 2 hours and from 70°F to 41°F within 4 hours. |
| Quick Chill* | Put food into shallow (2- or 3-inch) stainless steel pans (large food items and batches should be reduced to smaller sizes). Place pans into larger pans of ice, stirring frequently. When the temperature is significantly reduced, dry the bottom of the food pans and place on the top shelves in the refrigerator. Loosely cover the pans with a lid, foil, or plastic wrap. Another method is to use rapid cool aids for liquids and semisolids such as soups, stews, and chili (see Figure 1–4). |
| Label and Date | Place a tag with the date, day, and time that the food was prepared. Use within 7 to 10 days or throw it out. |

*Large foodservice operations would use a blast chiller unit first, then place pans in a refrigerator.

FIGURE 1–4
**Rapi-Kool™** allows for a quick and cost-effective method to cool cooked soups, stews, chili, and other liquids and semisolids. A container filled with tap water, which has been frozen solid, is placed in cooked liquids and semisolids to accelerate cooling. An application and use chart details procedures. NSF listed, which meets industry and regulatory standards.
*Courtesy of KatchAll Industries International, Inc.*

## REHEATING FOOD SAFELY

| | |
|---|---|
| 165°F (73.9°C) | Internal temperature must be reached and held for at least 15 seconds. The reheating should be completed within 2 hours. If not, toss the food out. |
| | Reaching internal temperature when reheating with a microwave oven: Cover the food and leave in the microwave for 2 to 5 minutes after reheating to allow the heat to spread evenly throughout the food. Check temperatures in at least two places. |
| | Reheat food only once. |

FIGURE 1–5
**Coldmaster®** standard
food pans are filled with
nontoxic refrigerant gel
that can hold prechilled
foods at or below 41°F for
approximately 8 hours.
The pans need to be
charged by placing them in
a freezer for 8 hours prior
to use. NSF Listed
*Courtesy of Carlisle
FoodService Products*

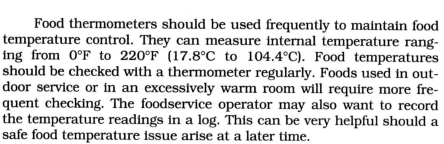

| HOLDING FOOD SAFELY | |
|---|---|
| 140°F (60°C) | Internal temperature for hot foods can be maintained with heat-holding equipment such as steam tables, heated cabinets, double boilers, and chafing dishes. |
| 41°F (5°C) | Internal temperature for cold cooked and raw foods can be maintained with cold-holding equipment such as refrigerators, refrigerated cold tables, iced buffet tables, and freezer-charged food pans (see Figure 1–5).<br><br>Check food temperatures frequently (at least every 2 hours). |

*Food Thermometers*

Food thermometers should be used frequently to maintain food temperature control. They can measure internal temperature ranging from 0°F to 220°F (17.8°C to 104.4°C). Food temperatures should be checked with a thermometer regularly. Foods used in outdoor service or in an excessively warm room will require more frequent checking. The foodservice operator may also want to record the temperature readings in a log. This can be very helpful should a safe food temperature issue arise at a later time.

The following are the most commonly used thermometers:

**Bimetal-Instant Read** (Figure 1–6)

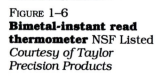

FIGURE 1–6
**Bimetal-instant read
thermometer** NSF Listed
*Courtesy of Taylor
Precision Products*

| | |
|---|---|
| Speed: 15 to 20 seconds | Placement: 2 to 2 1/2 inches just past the dimple mark deep in the thickest part of the food. |
| Usage Considerations: | 1. Can be used in roasts, casseroles, and soups. |
| | 2. Use to check the internal temperature of a food at the end of cooking time. |
| | 3. Can be calibrated. |
| | 4. Cannot adequately measure thin foods. |
| | 5. Cannot be used in an oven while food is cooking. |

### Bimetal-Oven Safe (Figure 1–7)

Speed: 1 to 2 minutes

Usage Considerations:

Placement: 2 to 2 1/2 inches just past the dimple mark deep in the thickest part of the food.

1. Can be used in roasts, casseroles, and soups.
2. Can be placed in food while it is cooking.
3. Not appropriate for thin foods.
4. Heat conduction of metal stem can cause false high reading.

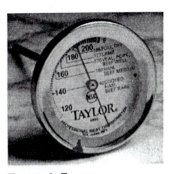

FIGURE 1–7
**Bimetal-oven safe thermometer** NSF Listed
*Courtesy of Taylor Precision Products*

### Digital (Figure 1–8)

Speed: 1 second

Usage Considerations:

Placement: At least 1/2-inch deep in the food.

1. Gives instant reading.
2. Can measure temperature in thin foods.
3. Digital face is easy to read.
4. Cannot be used in an oven while food is cooking.

FIGURE 1–8
**Digital thermometer**
NSF Listed
*Courtesy of Taylor Precision Products*

### Infrared (Figure 1–9)

Speed: 1/2 second

Usage Considerations:

Placement: Laser-aiming beam.

1. Can measure grill surface and cooking surface temperatures.
2. Can measure food surface temperatures during delivery.
3. Can measure hot and cold holding cabinet temperatures.
4. Can measure refrigerated and freezer storage temperatures.
5. Cannot measure internal temperatures.
6. Cannot measure ambient air temperature.

FIGURE 1–9
**Infrared thermometer**
NSF Listed
*Courtesy of Taylor Precision Products*

FIGURE 1–10
**Thermocouple thermometer** NSF Listed
*Courtesy of Taylor Precision Products*

**Thermocouple** (Figure 1–10)

Speed: 1/2 second

Placement: 1/4-inch deep in the food or deeper as needed.

Usage Considerations:
1. Fast.
2. Can quickly measure even thin foods.
3. Digital face is easy to read.
4. Can be calibrated.

*Oven and Grill Thermometers*

Precise temperature control assuring consistent cooking results can be further supported by oven and grill thermometers.

FIGURE 1–11
**Oven thermometer**
NSF Listed
*Courtesy of Taylor Precision Products*

**Oven Thermometer** (Figure 1–11)

Usage Considerations:
1. Can be placed in any oven.
2. Temperature range is 200°F to 500°F.

### Grill Guide Thermometer (Figure 1–12)

Usage Considerations:

1. Magnetic back keeps thermometer in place on grill.
2. Temperature range is 50°F to 600°F.

FIGURE 1–12
**Grill Guide thermometer**
NSF Listed
*Courtesy of Taylor
Precision Products*

When food items require refrigeration, freezing, or dry storage, the following temperature rules and safety guidelines should be followed:

*Storage Temperatures
and Safety Guidelines*

**Refrigeration.** An air temperature of 38°F to 40°F should be constantly maintained. Even if the refrigeration unit has an exterior temperature readout panel, a thermometer should be placed at the back of the unit and another thermometer placed by the door (Figure 1–13). The readings should be checked on a daily basis.

When possible, the use of two or more refrigerators for different applications is convenient. For example, one could be used for cooked foods and the other for raw foods. When using only one refrigerator, place the cooked foods on the top shelves and the raw foods on the bottom shelves. This prevents the raw food from dripping onto the cooked food. Caution should also be exercised to not overload a refrigeration unit. Overloading taxes its ability to maintain the 38°F to 40°F temperature range and reduces the air circulation.

FIGURE 1–13
**Freezer-Refrigerator
thermometer** NSF Listed
*Courtesy of Taylor
Precision Products*

Large foodservice operations are typically equipped with one or more walk-in refrigeration units, allowing for a greater capacity to refrigerate meat, produce, and dairy products, as well as cooked and prepared foods. In all foodservice operations, square food containers will maximize refrigeration space, and clear containers will allow prepared food to be easily identified. See Figure 1–14.

**Freezing.** A 0°F temperature should be maintained and checked daily by the use of a thermometer if the unit does not have an exterior readout panel. Freezer units that require defrosting should be defrosted on a scheduled basis, for example, every 3, 4, or 6 months. Usage will be the determining factor. Foods should be rotated for use and not stored in the freezer for long periods of time. Extended freezing can result in diminished food quality. Also, food that has thawed should never be refrozen until it has been completely cooked.

FIGURE 1–14
**Cam Square® Food
Containers** NSF Listed
*Courtesy of Cambro
Manufacturing Company*

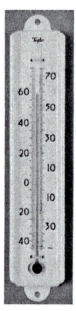

FIGURE 1–15
**Wall thermometer**
for storage room use.
*Courtesy of Taylor
Precision Products*

***Good Personal
Hygiene***

Thaw frozen food by the following methods:

—Place in a refrigerator on the lower shelves. Be sure to allow larger items such as roasts and turkeys enough time to thaw completely.
—Thaw in a microwave oven and immediately cook either in the microwave oven or with another type of cooking equipment.
—Place in a large, clean, and sanitized sink and run cold water over the food item, being careful not to splash on other food items or contact other surfaces. This process should not exceed 2 hours. When thawed, the food item should be promptly removed and be ready for preparation and cooking. The sink should immediately be cleaned and sanitized. This method is not effective for large items and is the least preferred method for thawing food.

**Dry Storage.** The temperature range for dry storage items should be maintained between 50°F and 70°F with low humidity and good ventilation. A thermometer should be hung onto or built into the wall to accurately measure the room's temperature (see Figure 1–15). To allow for adequate air circulation, slatted shelves should be used with the lowest shelf at least 6 inches off the floor. Nothing should be stored on the floor. This allows for easy cleaning and pest control. Also, the room should not receive any direct sunlight and should be cleaned and inspected for pests on a scheduled basis.

The foodservice operation should always maintain the highest standards for employee grooming, personal cleanliness, and hygiene. Employees should strictly adhere to the following basic grooming guidelines:

• Employees should bathe daily, ideally just before preparing to go to work.
• Hair should be clean and restrained.
• Strongly scented perfume or cologne should be avoided.
• Jewelry and loosely fitting items should not be worn.
• Fingernails should be short, clean, and neatly trimmed. Nail polish should not be used.
• Uniforms or work clothes should be clean and pressed and should fit properly.

Personal cleanliness and hygiene begins with frequent hand-washing. Hands must be thoroughly washed each and every time after

—Using bathroom
—Handling raw food
—Sneezing or coughing
—Smoking
—Chewing gum or tobacco
—Touching hair, face, or body

—Using a handkerchief or tissue
—Eating or drinking
—Using a toothpick
—Clearing away used dishes, glasses, or utensils
—Touching anything that may represent a potential danger to safe food handling

**Frequent handwashing is critical for safe food handling.** A handwashing sink should be conveniently located in the kitchen area, specifically designated for handwashing use with a convenient soap dispenser and single-use paper towels and/or air-blowing hand dryer. A portable hand sink, as shown in Figure 1–16, would be recommended for off-premise catering. The availability of a fingernail brush may be appropriate for certain situations, such as following the handling of raw meat, fish, or poultry. The brush needs to be kept in a sanitizing solution between uses. A sanitizing lotion or dip may also be used after handwashing when added protection is desired.

When an employee is sick, he or she should not be allowed to work with food.

Figure 1–16
**CamKiosk™ Hand Sink Cart** for handwashing any time, anywhere. Provides approximately 70 handwashings.
*Courtesy of Cambro Manufacturing Company*

## Cross-Contamination

Cross-contamination occurs when harmful substances, such as chemicals, bacteria, or other microorganisms, are transferred to food while storing, preparing, cooking, or serving. Cross-contamination typically occurs under the following conditions:

—Food contact surfaces such as knives, cutting boards, and countertops touch raw foods, such as meats or poultry, and are not cleaned and sanitized after use. Then they touch food that is cooked and ready to be served. For increased safety, separate cutting boards should be designated by category and identified by a color code (see Figure 1–17). The high-density polyethylene cutting boards are the easiest to wash and sanitize.
—Hands that have touched raw food have not been properly washed and then touch food that is cooked and ready to eat.
—A cloth, towel, or sponge touches raw food, cooking equipment, utensils, or contact surfaces that have not been cleaned and sanitized and then touches surfaces, equipment, or utensils to be used for food ready to be served and eaten.
—Raw food touches, drips, or splashes onto cooked or ready-to-eat foods.
—Ice is scooped with a glass, paper cup, or scoop that is dirty or ice is transported in buckets or containers that have not been sanitized. See Figure 1–18 and accompanying discussion on safe ice handling.
—A pesticide, cleaning solution, or other compound comes into direct contact with food.
—Any type of foreign matter, such as hair, dust particles, or packaging material, touches or gets into food.

Figure 1–17
**Kolor-Cut™ cutting boards** offer six color-coded boards for key food groups: poultry, raw red meats, cooked foods, fish, vegetables, and dairy. Selector chart and sanitary guide provide quick and easy reference. NSF listed, which meets industry and regulatory standards.
*Courtesy of KatchAll Industries International, Inc.*

Follow these procedures to handle ice safely:

1. Store the ice scoop outside of the ice machine bin and in a separate container to keep the scoop safe from bacteria and dirt when not in use.

2. Use an ice funnel to provide a fast, safe, and efficient way to fill a tote bucket for transporting ice from the ice machine to holding bins.

3. Use a safe tote 6-gallon bucket designed to be sanitary and clearly marked for transporting ice only.

FIGURE 1–18
**SAFE ICE HANDLING**
*Photos courtesy of KatchAll Industries International, Inc.*

The kitchen should always operate according to a safety and quality control plan that functions as follows:

—A detailed scheduled work flow should be instituted that allows for tasks to be completed quickly, eliminating crisscrossing and backtracking by employees. This will help to avoid collisions and spills.

—The work areas and equipment should be clean and sanitary and ready for immediate use when food is brought out of storage.

—At the completion of every task, all food contact surfaces, equipment, and utensils should be cleaned and sanitized with either hot water or safety-approved chemicals.

***Sanitizing: hot water.*** The temperature of the food contact surfaces must reach at least 165°F (73.9°C) to kill harmful microorganisms.

***Sanitizing: chemicals.*** The solutions are effective, easy to use, and affordable. A product label must clearly state directions for use, contents, and any warnings regarding use and possible danger to health. See Figure 1–19 for an example of an all-purpose sanitizing wiper.

Dishwashing procedures should always be controlled and frequently checked while in progress. Depending upon the size, volume, and specific needs of the foodservice facility, dishwashing can be accomplished by any of the following safety-approved methods:

—High-Temperature Dishwasher: Hot water cleans and sanitizes. These machines are designed to handle the needs of fast-paced, large-volume foodservice operations. Built-in thermometers measure temperatures during the wash and rinse cycles and should be checked often during use. Final rinse cycle is 180°F.

—Chemical Sanitizing Dishwasher: A chemical sanitizing solution is part of the final rinse water. Water temperatures and chemical concentrations need to be checked periodically during use.

—Manual Dishwashing: This is accomplished with the use of a three-compartment sink and should function according to the following procedure: There should be an area to the left of the first sink to scrape, soak, and pre-rinse; wash and clean with a detergent solution at 110°F in the first sink; thoroughly rinse with clear water at 120°F in the second sink; sanitize in the third sink with a chemical sanitizing solution at the manufacturer's recommended water temperature, or sanitize in the third sink with 170°F to 180°F water for at least 30 seconds. Use a rack to lower dishes into the hot water. Thermometers should be placed in all three sinks to measure water temperatures (see dishwasher thermometer, Figure 1–20). As items are removed from the third sink, they should be placed in racks to air dry.

FIGURE 1–19
**Simple Solutions**™ is a pretreated wiper that instantly creates one (200 ppm) gallon of no-rinse food contact surface sanitizer.
*Courtesy of Atlantic Mills, Inc.*

FIGURE 1–20
**Dishwasher thermometer**
Temperature range is 0°F to 200°F. NSF Listed
*Courtesy of Taylor Precision Products*

## Taste Testing

It is often necessary to taste-test food during preparation and cooking. When this occurs, it should always be done safely. A small amount of food can be sampled by slicing, spooning, or ladling it into a small dish, then tasting it with a clean fork or spoon. The dish and utensils should then be placed for washing and sanitizing.

## Setting and Serving

The person who is setting tables and serving food should never touch the contact areas of cups, glasses, flatware, or plates. Also, whenever possible a separate individual should be assigned to removing dirty dishes, wiping tables, and cleaning up after customer use.

## HACCP Program

A Hazard Analysis Critical Control Point (HACCP) program for safe food handling can be an effective method to prevent or reduce the risks of foodborne illness by identifying potential food hazards and monitoring critical control points. A critical control point is an operational step or procedure in a process, production method, or recipe at which control can be applied to prevent, reduce, or eliminate a food safety hazard.

Foods are at risk during the following conditions: purchasing/receiving, storing, thawing, preparing, cooking, holding, serving, cooling, and reheating (refer to Figure 1–21). Therefore, a food safety system can help to ensure food safety by

—Identifying potentially hazardous foods and conditions that could jeopardize food safety. A potentially hazardous food can be served either individually or as an ingredient in a recipe. For example, chicken can be an entrée or an ingredient in a pasta salad.

—Establishing procedures that will keep the food safe at all times.

—Developing time and temperature checkpoints for each food item and recipe.

The following are examples of procedures that deal specifically with food temperatures, time, and conditions:

—Hold temperature at 165°F at least 15 seconds when cooking poultry.

—Hold hot food at 140°F or higher.

—Do not mix new food with old food.

—Cool in a shallow pan; internal temperature should drop from 140°F to 70°F within 2 hours and from 70°F to 41°F within 4 hours; label and date cooking time.

—Reheat to 165°F or higher for at least 15 seconds. If reheating takes longer than 2 hours do not use; toss food out.

## HACCP PROGRAM

### Hazard Analysis Critical Control Points

| FUNCTION | HAZARD | CRITICAL CONTROL PT. | MONITOR |
|---|---|---|---|
| Purchasing/ receiving | Bacteria growth and contamination | Inspected, temperatures, approved source of supply | Manager |
| Storing | Bacteria growth and cross-contamination | Temperatures, separate raw from ready-to-eat food | Manager |
| Thawing | Bacteria growth and cross-contamination | Temperatures | Chef |
| Preparing | Bacteria growth and cross-contamination | Recipe steps, temperatures, separate raw from ready-to-eat food, control bare hand contact | Chef |
| Cooking | Bacteria growth and cross-contamination | Temperatures | Chef |
| Holding (hot or cold) | Bacteria growth and cross-contamination | Temperatures: 140°F or above for hot, 40°F or below for cold | Manager |
| Serving | Bacteria growth and cross-contamination | Temperatures | Manager |
| Cooling (leftover food) | Bacteria growth and cross-contamination | Temperatures, separate raw from ready-to-eat food, control bare hand contact | Chef |
| Reheating | Bacteria growth and cross-contamination | Temperatures | Chef |

FIGURE 1–21 **FOOD SAFETY SYSTEM**

Procedures must be rechecked when any of the following occurs:

—Recipe changes.
—Cooking equipment changes.
—Kitchen changes for off-premise catering.
—Preparation changes for quantity adjustments.

The preparation function has the greatest variety of activities that must be controlled and monitored. There is an extremely wide range of tasks along with variances in recipes, employee skills, and kitchen facilities. Therefore it is extremely important that the manager, chef, line-supervisor, or designated employee has the knowledge, skill, and commitment to follow preparation procedures, monitor critical control points, and take corrective action when procedures are not being followed or critical limits are not met. The proper use of gloves in food handling is important. Gloves establish a barrier against pathogens that may be on a worker's hands from poor personal hygiene or cross-contamination. Figure 1–22 is an example of gloves used in foodservice. This control point is easy to monitor: Workers are either wearing gloves or they are not. You can see in chapter 6 that the detailed preparation and serving steps for each recipe have been noted with symbols for attention to the use of gloves as well as safe food temperatures.

An HACCP program, when effectively implemented and fully supported by management through proper training, can successfully reduce the risk of foodborne illness. Refer to Figure 1–23 for an example of an HACCP Inspection Data Sheet provided courtesy of the Food and Drug Administration.

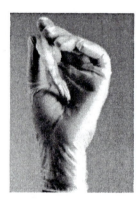

**Vinyl gloves** for foodservice tasks where tactile sensitivity is important.

**Elbow length poly gloves** for light tasks that require changing gloves often, such as mixing salads.

FIGURE 1–22 **GLOVES USED IN FOODSERVICE**
*Courtesy of FoodHandler®*

***Off-Premise Catering***

Off-premise catering can service many occasions, including weddings, anniversaries, birthdays, religious affairs, charity events, special parties, and business-related meetings and promotions.

The food can be prepared on-site in the customer's kitchen (home or office); in a rented facility that has a kitchen (e.g., church or fraternal organization); or in the caterer's kitchen, which typically represents the safest and most efficient choice as it allows for greater control. When using a customer's kitchen, it is important to check the laws and codes that regulate the use of the facility, specifi-

# HACCP INSPECTION DATA

| EST. NAME: | | PERMIT NO. | | INSPECTOR: | |
|---|---|---|---|---|---|
| DATE: | | TIME IN: | :AM / PM | TIME OUT: | :AM/ PM |

Record all observations below - transfer violations to Inspection Report

## FOOD TEMPERATURES / TIMES / OTHER CRITICAL LIMITS
### Use Additional Forms If Necessary

| FOOD STEP | 1. | CRITICAL LIMIT | 2 | CRITICAL LIMIT | 3 | CRITICAL LIMIT | 4 | CRITICAL LIMIT |
|---|---|---|---|---|---|---|---|---|
| A. SOURCE | | | | | | | | |
| B. STORAGE | | | | | | | | |
| C. PREP BEFORE COOK | | | | | | | | |
| D. COOK | | | | | | | | |
| E. PREP AFTER COOK | | | | | | | | |
| F. HOT/COLD HOLD | | | | | | | | |
| G. DISPLAY/ SERVICE | | | | | | | | |
| H. COOL | | | | | | | | |
| I. REHEAT | | | | | | | | |

| OTHER FOOD TEMPERATURES OBSERVED | | | Use steps from above for location | | | | | |
|---|---|---|---|---|---|---|---|---|
| FOOD | TEMP. °C/F | STEP | FOOD | TEMP. °C/F | STEP | FOOD | TEMP. °C/F | STEP |
| | | | | | | | | |
| | | | | | | | | |
| | | | | | | | | |

Page 1 of 2

FIGURE 1–23 **HACCP INSPECTION DATA SHEET**
*Courtesy of Food and Drug Administration*

cally whether the kitchen is licensed for the designated use. If not, the use of the kitchen may be prohibited or limited to serving purposes only. Outdoor catering may require a permit for operation as a temporary restaurant, and specific restrictions may exist depending upon the individual situation.

Transporting food from the catering kitchen to the catering event must be accomplished in a manner that retains the quality of the food while maintaining safe food-holding temperatures. Therefore, it is important to select the most appropriate type of portable equipment that will accomplish that goal, such as that shown in Figure 1–24.

## MANAGEMENT / PERSONNEL OBSERVATIONS

| | |
|---|---|
| | |
| | |
| | |
| | |

## OTHER FOOD OBSERVATIONS

| | |
|---|---|
| | |
| | |
| | |
| | |

## EQUIPMENT, UTENSILS, AND LINEN OBSERVATIONS

| | |
|---|---|
| | |
| | |
| | |
| | |

## WATER, PLUMBING, AND WASTE OBSERVATIONS

| | |
|---|---|
| | |
| | |
| | |
| | |

## PHYSICAL FACILITIES

| | |
|---|---|
| | |
| | |
| | |

## POISONOUS OR TOXIC MATERIALS OBSERVATIONS

| | |
|---|---|
| | |
| | |
| | |

*HACCP Inspection Data  Page 2 of 2*

**Leftover Food**

The caterer should establish a policy regarding the handling of leftover food. As a general rule, the customer has contracted for a specific number of people to be fed versus a given quantity of food. Therefore the caterer is under no obligation to provide or make available leftover food. Although certain situations and circum-

**CamServer®** for coffee, decaf, tea, and hot water.

**Ultra Camtainer®** for hot or cold beverages with interlock stacking for easy transportation and storage.

**Camcarts®** have a large capacity to hold a variety of food pans in a variety of combinations and, with thermobarriers, can store hot and cold foods together.

Tough polyethylene outer shell and thick foamed-in-place polyurethane insulation maintains hot or cold temperatures for hours.

**Ice caddies** roll ice to where it is needed and keeps it frozen for days.

**Camcarriers®** accommodate a variety of hot and cold food transporting needs.

FIGURE 1–24 **FOOD AND BEVERAGE TRANSPORT SYSTEMS**
All of the above equipment is NSF listed, which meets industry and regulatory standards.
*Courtesy of Cambro Manufacturing Company*

stances may predicate being responsive to a customer's request for the leftover food, that will require the professional judgment of the caterer.

When providing leftover food to the customer or customer's guests, that food should be properly wrapped, labeled, dated, and marked with the proper handling instructions (e.g., refrigerate, reheat to a certain temperature, and use by a certain date). Another alternative may be to give the food away to a local church or agency that has a meal program for the needy and homeless.

**Garbage/Trash Disposal**

Garbage and trash should be removed as soon as possible and must always be kept away from food contact surfaces. The containers and/or dumpsters should be regularly cleaned and sanitized after each use and must remain free of odor and insects.

**Pest Control**

Effective pest control begins with a clearly defined program. The foodservice operator should be able to recognize the signs of a beginning or reoccurring problem with pests, such as flies, insects, birds, or rodents. The safest way to guard against possible pest control problems and protect the foodservice facility is to recruit the services of a professionally licensed and certified pest control company that will regularly inspect and spray the possible problem areas.

**Safety Risk Will Vary with Individuals**

Some people, such as children, the elderly, and immunocompromised individuals, are at a higher risk for being susceptible to food-related illnesses. Other people may physically react to certain foods or food ingredients. Therefore, it is important to know recipe ingredients in the event someone asks. With so many varying circumstances and situations for food-related illnesses to occur, the foodservice facility must always maintain a total commitment to serving safe food.

**Key Points**

The constant focus on always serving safe food can be summarized by the following key points:

—Keep hot food hot and cold food cold. Hot food should be kept above 140°F (60°C) and cold food below 41°F (5°C). Frequently check temperatures.
—Quickly cool food and refrigerate in shallow stainless steel pans.
—Reheat food only once and ensure an internal temperature of 165°F (73.9°C) for at least 15 seconds. When using a microwave oven, heat the food to 165°F, cover it, and keep it in the oven for 2 to 5 minutes after reheating to allow the heat to spread evenly throughout.
—Properly thaw frozen food in the refrigerator, microwave oven, or under cold running water and cook immediately.
—Make personal cleanliness and hygiene that includes frequent handwashing a conscious commitment on the part of all employees.
—Strictly follow sanitary procedures to avoid any possibility of cross-contamination.
—Always operate the kitchen according to a safety and quality-control plan.
—Control and frequently check dishwashing procedures.
—Establish an HACCP program for safe food handling. Critical control points should be identified with every recipe.
—Maintain garbage and trash removal as well as pest control with a scheduled program of safety and prevention.

ServSafe® is a food safety program developed by the Education Foundation of the National Restaurant Association. The program has a well-designed coursebook used in approved seminars, college courses, and workshops and is offered nationally through culinary schools, community colleges, four-year colleges, and university hospitality programs. It is sponsored by professional industry associations, regulatory agencies, and organizations.

The ServSafe® training course is followed by a comprehensive written examination. Those who successfully complete the course and pass the examination receive certification, which is accepted in most jurisdictions that require food safety training.

For more information about ServSafe® training, contact the Education Foundation of the National Restaurant Association at 800.765.2122 or www.restaurant.org.

The material presented in this chapter serves as an introduction to serving safe food for the culinary student as well as a review for the experienced foodservice operator and caterer. It is also designed to be a quick reference for on-the-job use, as temperature points and safe food handling procedures may need to be quickly checked.

To always serve safe food, there must be constant monitoring through all phases of purchasing/receiving, storing, thawing, preparing, cooking, holding, serving, cooling, and reheating.

The safe checkpoints include the following:

| | |
|---|---|
| Food | Food handlers |
| Storage | Preparation |
| Kitchen | Cooking |
| Equipment | Serving |
| Utensils | Clean-up |

Managing for food safety must be fully integrated into every aspect of the foodservice and catering operation as an active and ongoing system.

## Discussion Questions and Exercises

1. What is a foodborne illness?
2. List and explain the most common causes of foodborne illnesses.
3. What are the laws and codes that specifically govern and deal with safe food handling and food safety issues within your community?
4. What are the laws and codes for off-premise catering within your community?

**Note:** To answer questions 3 and 4, the student will need to check with city, county, and state health departments.

**5.** Fill in the boxes with the correct temperatures.

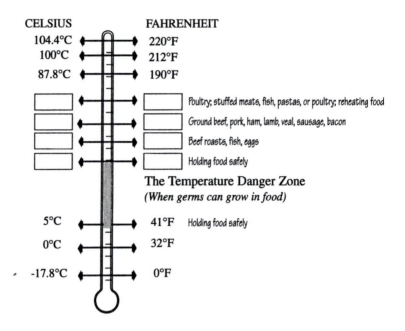

CELSIUS          FAHRENHEIT
104.4°C ←→ 220°F
100°C ←→ 212°F
87.8°C ←→ 190°F

[ ] ←→ [ ] Poultry; stuffed meats, fish, pastas, or poultry; reheating food
[ ] ←→ [ ] Ground beef, pork, ham, lamb, veal, sausage, bacon
[ ] ←→ [ ] Beef roasts, fish, eggs
[ ] ←→ [ ] Holding food safely

The Temperature Danger Zone
*(When germs can grow in food)*

5°C ←→ 41°F  Holding food safely
0°C ←→ 32°F
-17.8°C ←→ 0°F

**6.** Explain two different methods for cooling food safely.

**7.** Name several types of thermometers and describe their use.

**8.** Explain the three different methods of thawing frozen food.

**9.** List ten examples of when hands should be thoroughly washed.

**10.** Explain cross-contamination and describe situations when it could occur.

**11.** How is food safely taste-tested during preparation and cooking?

**12.** Define and explain the primary areas that allow a kitchen to operate according to a safety and quality-control plan.

**13.** Explain the three safety-approved methods for dishwashing.

**14.** How does an HACCP program for safe food handling function?

**15.** List several areas of concern and importance when dealing with off-premise catering.

**16.** How should a caterer deal with leftover food?

**17.** What is the safest way to guard against possible pest control problems?

**18.** Why is it important to know the ingredients of food being served?

# 2

# Catering Details

## Learning Objectives

After reading this chapter and completing the discussion questions and exercises, you should be able to

1.  Recognize the importance of providing a complete list of catering options to the customer.
2.  Understand the purpose of a catering contract.
3.  Know that a time schedule is a critical factor in allowing a catered event to flow smoothly.
4.  Understand the terms *approximate guest count, guaranteed guest count,* and *confirmed guest count* and know the relevance of each to the caterer.
5.  Know how to calculate a room's capacity for comfortable seating and how to prepare a floor plan diagram that meets the customer's needs, while still allowing for good traffic flow and safe, efficient service.
6.  Recognize the most typically used tables, table sizes, and table configurations.
7.  Know the guidelines for seating arrangements.
8.  Understand how to create a menu featuring foods and portions that will be comfortable for the customer and his or her guests.
9.  Recognize that an awareness of wines and other specialty beverages is an important part of the caterer's role in helping the customer select the right beverages for the event.
10. Be aware of the many choices in tablecloths, napkins, table skirting, and chair covers.
11. Discuss the various options available for floral decor and table and room decorations.
12. Know how to select appropriate background music.
13. Recognize what is involved when printing menus and invitations.

14. Know what to look for in ice sculptures and ice carvings.
15. Understand how to use a beverage fountain.
16. Know how to coordinate with valet parking and limousine service companies.
17. Recognize what to look for in entertainment and in signing or preparing an entertainment contract.
18. Understand the importance of always keeping up with what is available in computer applications.
19. Know how to set up a head table, registration desk, or speaker podium.
20. Know how to use table numbers.
21. Understand the procedure for coatroom checking using double theater tickets.
22. Know how to place a lectern and arrange for a portable stage, dance floor, or piano.
23. Know the correct placement when arranging the United States flag with another flag on display.
24. Know how to set up a display with tripods and easels.
25. Recognize the wide range of audio and video equipment for presentations and state-of-the-art shows.
26. Recognize the importance of lighting in creating the desired atmosphere and enhancing the food presentation.
27. Know what is involved with invitation collection.
28. Be aware when to use tents and what to look for in companies that provide tent rental service.
29. Recognize that room temperature can be an important issue for guests' comfort.
30. Explain the specific conditions that affect pricing.
31. Understand how to deal with cancellations, gratuities, and deposits.
32. Understand the importance and functions of catering software for event management and financial control.

**Introduction**

The success of any catered event is the direct result of a good operational plan, which begins the moment the event is identified. A well-constructed plan can result in an event being executed with style and swiftness. The plan should start with a detailed catering contract, which serves as a checklist to effectively identify a customer's needs. The customer may not be fully aware of the many accessory details that can further enhance the catered event. Therefore, a complete listing of options that the caterer is capable of providing should be set forth in contract form, as shown in Figure 2–1. This also serves to reduce the risk of any possible misunderstandings that could later arise as a result of what a customer might assume. For example, the customer may expect that coatroom

# CATERING CONTRACT

*(Name, address, phone, fax, and e-mail of catering company)*

Name of Organization _____

Name of Contact Person _____

Phone _____ Fax_____ E-mail _____

Address _____

## Menu Details

Menu Theme _____ ❏ Full Service    ❏ Buffet

Menu Selection _____

_____

_____

_____

_____

Special Cake _____

_____

Beverage Selection *(Alcoholic/Non-Alcoholic)* _____

Portable Bar:    ❏ Open    ❏ Cash    ❏ Combination

### Time Schedule

| | |
|---|---|
| Arrival time | _____ |
| Cocktails served | _____ |
| Hors d'oeuvres served | _____ |
| Food served | _____ |
| Bar time | from _____ to _____ |
| Entertainment | from _____ to _____ |
| Speaker(s) | from _____ to _____ |
| Dancing | from _____ to _____ |
| Photography | from _____ to _____ |
| Videography | from _____ to _____ |
| Departure time | _____ |

## Accessory Details

❏ Linen

    Tablecloths _____

    Napkins _____

    Skirting _____

    Chair Cover(s) _____

❏ Floral Decor *(real or artificial silks)*

    Centerpieces _____ Sprays _____

    Baskets _____ Canopy _____

    Plants _____ Trees _____

❏ Decorations

    Table _____

    Room _____

❏ Sound System

    Microphone(s):  ❏ Cordless  ❏ Lavaliere (neck)

    ❏ Standing  ❏ Lectern  ❏ Table

❏ Background Music _____

❏ Printing

    Menus_____

    Invitations_____

❏ Ice Sculpture(s) _____

❏ Beverage Fountain(s) _____

❏ Valet Parking _____

❏ Limousine Service _____

❏ Other_____

❏ Entertainment *(Band, solo instrumental, singer, etc.)* _____

❏ Head Table

❏ Table Numbers/Names

❏ Candles

❏ Coatroom Checking

❏ Registration Desk

❏ Speaker Podium

❏ Lectern

❏ Notebook & Marker

❏ Stage

❏ Flags

❏ Exhibits

❏ Tripod

❏ Easel

❏ Projector, Screen, VCR

❏ Lighting Effects

❏ Invitation Collection

❏ Dance Floor

❏ Piano

❏ Costumes

❏ Balloons

❏ Photography

❏ Videography

❏ Tenting

❏ Room Temperature

_____

❏ Computer Requirements_____

### Guest Count

| | |
|---|---|
| Approximate number | _____ |
| Guaranteed number | _____ |
| *Date for final guarantee* | _____ |
| Confirmed number | _____ |

### Floor Plan

Table Arrangements _____

_____

_____

Seating Assignments _____

_____

_____

*Diagram Space*

*(See attached if needed)*

### Special Instructions

_____

_____

_____

_____

## Agreement of Charges

Date _____

Guaranteed guest count of _____ at a $_____ per guest for a total of . . . . . . . . . . . . . . $ _____

*(The final charge will be for the guaranteed guest count or confirmed guest count, whichever is greater.)*

Accessory Charges: _____   _____

_____   _____

_____   _____

**48 HOUR NOTICE REQUIRED ON CANCELLATIONS**

Caterer will be prepared to accommodate _____ % over the number of guaranteed guest count.

_____   _____
*Customer's Signature*   *Date*

_____   _____
*Caterer's Signature*   *Date*

| | |
|---|---|
| Gratuities | _____ |
| Subtotal | _____ |
| Tax | _____ |
| Total | _____ |
| Due Date _____ Deposit  (-) | _____ |
| Due Date _____ Balance  $ | _____ |

FIGURE 2–1 **CATERING CONTRACT**

checking is automatically provided by the caterer at no additional charge. This could potentially lead to a dispute over final payment or become a source of frustration and disappointment during the catered event. For example, if coatroom checking is needed because of weather conditions, coatracks may be provided by the caterer and be conveniently available for guests to use at no additional charge. That would not be the case, however, if the caterer had to rent the coatracks or transport them to an off-premise catering site. There would also be an additional charge if the customer wanted the caterer to provide one or two people to personally check in and check out guests' coats. Whatever the situation or circumstances may be, the caterer should clearly present the options to the customer prior to the event, thereby providing the customer with the opportunity to understand the costs involved and make the choice that will best fit his or her needs and budget. A thorough and complete catering contract will provide the caterer with all the necessary instructions to do the job and will provide the customer with a detailed list of what was actually ordered or could have been ordered for the event.

The information listed in the catering contract is described in the sections that follow.

## The Caterer

The name, address, phone, fax, and e-mail address of the catering company should be clearly printed at the top of the catering contract. Some companies may also list their federal tax identification number for the convenience of their customers who will need that number for tax reporting purposes.

## The Customer

The name of the customer's organization, contact person, phone, fax, e-mail, and address must be recorded accurately. Many events require frequent communication between the caterer and the customer, particularly as the event draws closer.

## Function Information

The first step in the planning process is to identify and schedule the date, day, time, and location of the catered event as well as the type of function, such as a birthday party, wedding reception, anniversary party, Christmas or New Year's Eve party, bar or bat mitzvah, company picnic, office party, business awards luncheon, retirement dinner, charity fundraising dinner, summer barbecue, or any other special event.

## Time Schedule

The caterer must be prepared to deliver according to a planned time schedule. That schedule becomes a critical factor in allowing the catered event to flow smoothly. The arrival time and the time for cocktails and hors d'oeuvres, if served, followed by the time for the food to be served are extremely important. When the food is served on time, prepared and cooked to quality standards and perfection, the guests are bound to be pleased. The experienced caterer knows the preparation, cooking, and serving times, as well as the amount of time needed to do the overall catering job.

The time allowed for such things as a bar, entertainment, speaker(s), dancing, photography, and videography should be identified with a beginning and ending time. Although specific times might be difficult to establish for certain activities, at least an approximate time frame should be given for when activities are to happen, including the guests' departure time.

The caterer must be prepared with a contingency plan to deal with any unexpected time surprises. For example, some of the guests may be delayed by bad weather or traffic conditions. In that case, the caterer must quickly verify with the customer and confirm a decision to hold the dinner and perhaps offer the guests who have arrived some additional hors d'oeuvres, if served, or other light refreshments. The caterer must always remain flexible when the unexpected occurs.

**Guest Count**

Most catered events are initially planned with an anticipated number of guests who will attend. Thus an approximate guest count is established, which serves as the basis for planning the details and estimating the costs. The guaranteed guest count is the minimum number that the customer is committed to pay for and is the number that the caterer will be preparing to accommodate. That number is typically requested no later than 2 to 7 days prior to the event, depending upon how large the event may be and/or the complexity of the menu and accessory details.

The confirmed guest count is the actual number of guests served. This number may be more or less than the guaranteed count. The customer is responsible for paying for whichever is greater, the guaranteed guest count or the confirmed guest count. This is set forth in the agreement of charges section of the catering contract.

Although some catered events control the number of guests attending, often through the use of invitation cards or tickets that must be presented at the entrance prior to admittance, most events do not. Therefore, there are usually a few less or a few more people attending than were actually planned for. The caterer covers the situation by preparing a given percentage over the guaranteed number, and that percentage is also identified in the agreement of charges section of the contract.

The caterer has to determine a reasonable percentage amount to prepare for over the guaranteed guest count. That percentage will typically average between 5 and 20 percent, depending upon the size of the guaranteed number. For example, when the guaranteed number is 25, then 20 percent over would be appropriate, resulting in preparing for 30 possible guests. When the guaranteed number is 300, then 5 percent over would be appropriate, resulting in preparing for 315 possible guests. The smaller the guaranteed number the larger the percentage, and the larger the guaranteed number the smaller the percentage. Also, it is important for the caterer to inquire of the customer whether any unusual circumstances may exist that could influence a greater number of guests attending over the guaranteed number, thus determining the percentage to use. For example, a well-known guest speaker at a lunch or dinner event might attract more guests than anticipated.

The final confirmed guest count can be verified according to a method that is appropriate for the type of service being offered. That is, a full-service menu would be counted by the portion number actually served to guests taken from a Food Production and Portion Control Chart (see Figure 4–1). A buffet menu would be counted by the actual number of dinner plates used.

When the confirmed guest count is significantly less than the guaranteed number, there will be leftover food. Therefore, the caterer should have a clearly defined policy in dealing with leftover food. Refer to chapter 1, which discusses possible options for leftover foods.

The cost to the caterer for the percentage amount over the guaranteed guest count number is initially calculated into the cost of the guaranteed number. This protects the caterer from having to absorb that cost should the confirmed number be close to or less than the guaranteed number.

## Floor Plan

The table arrangements should be clearly identified according to a floor plan diagram. The maximum person capacity for the facility is typically posted near the entrance by order of the local fire marshall. The seating arrangements and traffic flow should be carefully set forth for the comfort of the guests and for safe, efficient service.

The facility or catering site should be surveyed by taking the measurements of the room and calculating the room's capacity for comfortable seating. This is accomplished by recording the measurements on layout or graph paper and calculating the total square footage of the room, then dividing by 12 square feet for banquet seating (long tables lined up in a row) or 15 square feet for traditional seating (individual or round tables). Allowances should be made for any unusual room design along with adequate space for any accessory items, such as a bar, hors d'oeuvre buffet table, piano, and so forth. Figure 2–2 illustrates a room that is 50 feet by 70 feet; using our earlier calculation method, 50' X 70' = 3500 square feet, divided by 15 square feet for traditional seating = 233.3 square feet, or a seating capacity of 233.

The room could accommodate 233 for traditional seating, however, the figure shows the customer had requested a bar, hors d'oeuvre buffet table, and a piano, along with a full-service menu to follow. Therefore, allowing adequate space for these items as drawn on the floor plan diagram would reduce the seating capacity to 160 persons. This would translate into 2400 square feet for seating and 1100 square feet to accommodate the bar, hors d'oeuvre buffet table, piano, and guest gathering area.

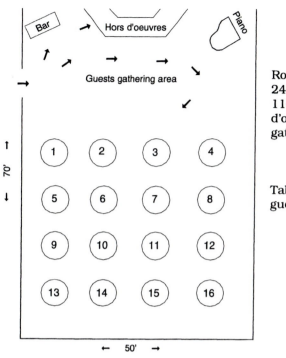

Room size: 3500 square feet, 2400 square feet for seating, 1100 square feet for bar, hors d'oeuvres, piano, and guests gathering

Tables are each set for 10 guests

FIGURE 2-2 **FLOOR PLAN DIAGRAM**

If the seating needed to be increased, banquet seating (long tables lined up in a row) could be used instead of the 72-inch round tables set for 10. This would increase seating by 40 (2400 square feet for seating divided by 12 square feet equals 200 square feet, or a seating capacity for 200 versus 160). If the customer had guaranteed the guest count number to be 145, and had requested the caterer to be prepared to accommodate 10 percent over the guarantee, then seating for 160 would be adequate; 145 x 10% = 14.5 rounded to 15; 145 + 15 = 160 total seating.

As the caterer's experience grows, he or she will be able to quickly produce a floor plan diagram with these measurements, calculations, and details. Larger events will require the use of several sheets of layout or graph paper; diagrams should be attached to the catering contract with a copy also attached to the customer's copy of the catering contract. There are also computer building and design software programs that can complete the calculations and draw a layout with visual enhancements.

**Table Sizes**

The banquet, round, and conference table sizes shown in Figure 2-3 are examples of the most typically used table sizes because of their flexibility for dining, buffets, and food stations. They are also the most convenient sizes for handling, storing, and transporting.

**Table Arrangements**

Tables can be arranged in a variety of configurations, as shown in Figure 2-4. Banquet tables along with quarter-round and trape-

## Banquet Tables

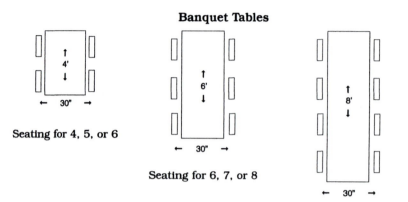

Seating for 4, 5, or 6

Seating for 6, 7, or 8

Seating for 8, 9, or 10

**Note:** Seating would be increased by adding additional chairs to opposite ends of the table.

## Round Tables

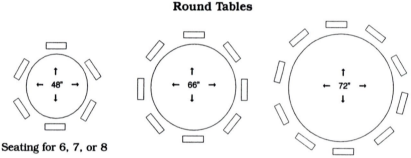

Seating for 6, 7, or 8

Seating for 8, 9, or 10

Seating for 10, 11, or 12

## Conference Tables

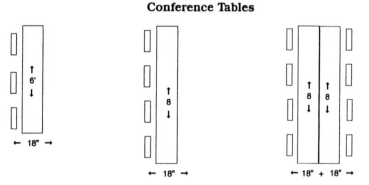

**Note:** Conference tables will typically be 18 inches in width and 6 or 8 feet in length. They are primarily used for conference meetings or as seminar or exhibit display tables. When used for meal service they are put together side by side and covered with linen.

FIGURE 2–3 **TABLE SIZES**

## Banquet Tables

6' & 8' × 30" tables lined in rows

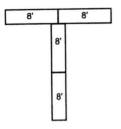

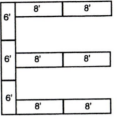

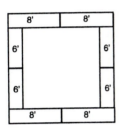

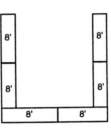

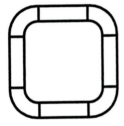

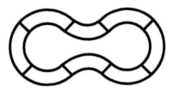

## Quarter-Round Tables

60" × 30" size

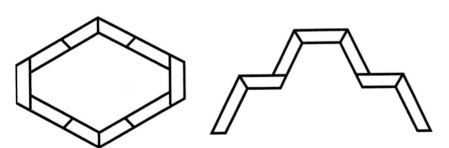

## Trapezoid Tables

60" × 30" size

FIGURE 2–4 **TABLE CONFIGURATIONS**

zoid tables can be used for dining, buffets, food stations, and elaborate food presentations. Unique table arrangements add interest and appeal to any catered event.

## Seating Arrangements

The following guidelines should be considered when making seating arrangements:

—Each table setting should be approximately 24 inches wide and 15 inches deep. This will allow a comfortable space for guests' seating and dining as well as adequate serving room.

—Tables and chairs should be arranged so that guests can be conveniently seated and served. Chairs, when in use, will normally extend 18 to 20 inches from the table edge and are 18 inches in width. Allow 24 to 30 inches from back to back (when in occupied position) for comfortable service between tables.

—When a head table is being used, arrange the other tables so that the majority of the guests will be able to view the head table.

## Menu Details

The type of function, location, time schedule, guest count, and the customer's budget will provide the guidelines for the menu details. The type of service, full-service or buffet, will be discussed in chapter 3. A menu theme may evolve into a total theme experience depending upon the customer's budget and the nature of the event. The theme should be compatible with the event and the guests, and the food and beverages being served should conform to the theme. Chapter 6 presents twenty-five menu themes complete with easy-to-follow recipes, and beverage and wine selections.

## Menu Selection

When creating a menu, the caterer should focus on finding a food comfort level with the customer, which may involve innovative or traditional foods or a combination of both, as well as small or large food portions. Therefore, it is important to inquire as to the profile of the average guest, which would include the following information:

—The percentage of men and women, and if children are attending, their approximate ages.

—The economic and employment status of the guests.

—Their tastes and preferences for different foods, such as ethnic or regional. Also, if there are any diet restrictions.

The goal is to create a memorable experience that offers something unique in presentation and serving, resulting in an experience that will be favorably remembered.

## Special Cake

The nature of the occasion, such as a birthday party, wedding reception, or anniversary party, may require a special cake. The cake will be a focal point of the event and must be prepared and presented exactly to the customer's request. The caterer should have at least two or three specialty bakeries as sources that could be called upon to fulfill the order. Many specialty bakeries require a two- to four-week advance order date depending upon the time of the year and the complexity of the cake. The caterer should be very familiar with each bakery's capabilities and pricing.

**Beverage Selection**

The beverages should always complement the food and theme of the event, and the caterer should be knowledgeable in being able to recommend appropriate alcoholic and nonalcoholic beverage choices. An awareness of wines and other specialty beverages is an important part of the caterer's role in helping the customer to select the right beverages for the event. Beverages are further discussed in chapter 5.

**Portable Bar**

The caterer should always be prepared with an attractive portable bar that can quickly be set up and in place to service guests at any location (Figure 2–5). The bar has to be versatile, adequate in size, and fully functional to meet the customer's beverage needs for on-premise and off-premise catering.

The bar can function as follows:

**Open bar**—hosted by the customer whereby the guests do not have to pay for drinks.

**Cash bar**—also referred to as a no-host bar where guests pay for their drinks.

**Combination open bar/cash bar**—where the customer may pay for the first one or two drinks with drink tickets that are given to the guests prior to or upon arrival. The guests pay for drinks after their tickets have been used.

The time that the bar will be functioning should be established, for example from 6:00 P.M. to 7:00 P.M., just prior to dinner being served. Also, the customer will need to decide how well he or she would like to have the bar stocked with drink choices and specific brands that guests may request. Once this is determined, the caterer will know how to be prepared as well as how to charge for the bar service.

FIGURE 2–5
**PORTABLE BAR**
*Courtesy of Cambro Manufacturing Company*

**Accessory Details**

The accessory details are the available options that the customer may request. These are items that are individually priced and can represent a significant portion of the total catering cost.

**Table Linen**

The caterer can choose from a number of possibilities when it comes to color, fabric, and weave in table linen. Some manufacturers offer several thousand standard and custom color choices. The primary concern is to select table linen that will either blend with or provide an appropriate accent to the catering atmosphere. Figure 2–6 shows an example of table linen. Tablecloths are available in a number of sizes that will fit most tables. The rule to follow is that the

FIGURE 2–6
**TABLE LINEN**
*Courtesy of Artex International*

tablecloth should fit the table and drape to approximately 1 inch above the chairs where guests will be seated.

*Linen rental.* Tablecloths, napkins, skirting, and chair covers are available in a variety of sizes and colors from local rental stores and from national linen rental companies. The national companies are often a division of a linen manufacturing company and, therefore, are usually able to meet any size and quantity requirement within short notice and will promptly ship to any location. Napkins are an essential part of the table linen presentation and should be selected with equal concern. Napkin folds will be presented in chapter 3.

### Table Skirting

FIGURE 2–7
**TABLE SKIRTING**
*Courtesy of Artex International*

Buffet tables and head tables should be draped. This can be accomplished with tablecloths or table skirting. When tablecloths are used, at least three will be needed for a buffet table and two for a head table, depending upon the size of the table. One is draped over the front of the table reaching approximately 2 inches above the floor. A second is draped over the back, again reaching 2 inches above the floor. The tablecloths are best secured in place with masking tape. A third tablecloth is draped in the usual manner, covering part of the first and second tablecloths. (A head table does not have a tablecloth draped to the floor in back where people are seated.)

Table skirting (see Figure 2–7) is quicker to install and allows greater flexibility in use and application than draping tablecloths. The skirting is secured and held in place with Velcro® clips, tape, or T-pins. Pleat styles include wedding, accordion, box, and shirred pleats. Patterns can range from elegant and understated to festive and bold. Also, valances can add a dramatic look and are available in a number of styles.

### Chair Covers

FIGURE 2–8
**CHAIR COVER AND BOW**
*Courtesy of Artex International*

Whether it be for the bride and groom, distinguished guests, or a special person being honored, tailored chair covers with bows add an elegant touch to any event. Figure 2–8 shows a chair cover and bow application.

**Floral Decor**

The floral arrangements are often coordinated with the caterer and a local florist or floral designer. The extent to which floral arrangements are used is in direct relationship to the nature of the event and the budget. Typically, wedding receptions will use the most floral arrangements. Fresh flowers are the preferred choice, but occasionally customers request artificial silks or in some cases a combination of both: fresh flowers for certain arrangements, such as table centerpieces, and artificial silks for others, such as by a speaker podium. The artificial silks allow for tremendous flexibility in selecting some colorful and/or exotic flowers and best of all will not emit any scent. This is particularly important when a potential allergy problem may exist for some guests.

Baskets of fresh flowers or colorful sprays often add decorative accents to a room when appropriately placed by an entrance or near a stage. A floral canopy will add a formal touch to a wedding reception or for the grand entrance to any festive event. Plants and trees such as palms and ficus trees, real or artificial, are excellent choices to accent parts of a room or to create an aisle that will serve to guide guests' movement.

The cost of flowers will fluctuate during the year according to seasons, holidays, and general availability. Therefore flowers should be priced for the time when they will actually be purchased and should be ordered well in advance of the event, depending upon the complexity of the order.

**Table and Room Decorations**

Craft and gift stores offer many unique and unusual items that could be used to tastefully decorate any table and complement a given theme, such as red hearts for Lovers' Night/Valentine's. The items selected should not require too much table space or distract from the food being served. Table centerpieces and decorations should not cramp the table and should be at a comfortable height without obstructing anyone's view.

Room decorations can create any atmosphere and enhance every occasion. Balloons, mobiles, portable lighting, pictures, and floral decorations can all be used. Good judgment is the key factor in selecting the right items to complement the occasion. Party supply and rental stores are excellent sources for ideas and materials.

**Sound System**

Microphones may need to be available for speakers and/or entertainers. The microphones could be either cordless, lavaliere (neck), standing, attached to the lectern, or placed on a table. The caterer should be experienced and familiar with the types of sound systems that will provide the best quality sound and functions for each specific use.

**Background Music**

Soft background music may add a nice touch to the dining atmosphere. A good selection of tapes, CDs, or records enhances the excitement and enjoyment of the occasion. When the dinner theme is chosen, select the appropriate music. For example, for "Evening in Paris," some Maurice Chevalier songs, or for "Mardi Gras," a jazz band.

**Printing Menus and Invitations**

Special occasions may require some printing, either computer generated or photocopied. Some menus may need to have a specific design, graphic, or logo for a commemorative event, such as a golden anniversary party. Remember, printing requires advanced planning and preparation. Desktop publishing allows for a wide range of flexibility in format, graphics, type style, and presentation. It is essential to check and then double check the accuracy of all the information that is to be printed. ***Thoroughly review the proof copy.***

***Menus.*** Menus should be descriptive enough to create a mental picture of what is to be served, such as "Oysters Rockefeller" or "Chicken Kiev with Citrus Champagne Sauce."

***Invitations.*** The invitations should indicate the type of function, such as a birthday or holiday party, and the theme (if any), and should state the date, day, time, place, mode of dress, and RSVP information.

**Ice Sculptures**

Ice sculptures add a definite touch of elegance and are often used for buffets. Figure 2–9 shows several examples of ice sculptures. Sculpture molds are filled with water, placed in a freezer, and removed when ready to use. The molds are cut along a marked bead, peeled away, and discarded. The result is a decorative ice sculpture. For a larger original work of art done by ice carving, a competent professional should be hired and can often be found listed in the yellow pages of the local telephone directory. Also, the local affiliate of the American Culinary Federation (chefs) could be contacted for referrals. People who do original ice carvings typically have a photo album of their work for prospective customers to review.

An ice sculpture or carving should be placed in a large pan with a drain hose attached to a 5-gallon bucket to control the flow of water as the ice slowly melts. The base of the pan is often covered with parsley or other greens. For small sculptures or carvings placed in an appropriate size pan, the water can be absorbed with a convenient supply of dry bar towels.

Bride and Groom

Grecian Bowl

Horn of Plenty

Swan

FIGURE 2–9 **ICE SCULPTURES**
*Courtesy of Carlisle FoodService Products*

Beverage fountains like the one in Figure 2–10 add a beautiful display effect as guests are able to quickly fill or refill their cups or glasses. The caterer would assign a staff member to maintain the necessary beverage quantity for the fountain to adequately function. The beverage should be chilled before pouring into the fountain. Champagne fountains are very popular, but the champagne cannot remain in the fountain too long or it will become flat. Also, exercise caution when using fruit with pulp that may restrict the fountain's flow.

The fountain should be placed to a side of the room near an electrical outlet and the cord taped to the floor to avoid any possibility of a guest tripping. These units are available at most full-service rental stores. The fountain should be thoroughly washed and rinsed before actual use as well as after each use.

## *Beverage Fountains*

FIGURE 2–10
**BEVERAGE FOUNTAIN**
*Courtesy of Floware*

## *Valet Parking and Limousine Service*

Valet parking and limousine service are specialized functions that the customer would normally be responsible for contracting directly with licensed and bonded companies offering these services. The caterer, however, must coordinate the time schedule of these services with the customer.

The time schedule for valet parking is an important factor in determining the number of attendants to schedule for the event. For example, if guests will be arriving within a short period of time, say between 7:00 and 7:30 P.M., more attendants would be needed. The same is true for the departure time. But if the nature of the function allows guests to trickle in, say between 6:30 and 8:00 P.M., and depart with the same type of schedule, then fewer attendants would be needed. Experienced valet parking service companies would evaluate the site prior to the event and are accustomed to working with catering companies.

Limousine services are often recruited to chauffeur the bride and groom at a wedding or to provide transportation from the airport for arriving guests. When transportation is provided for a number of guests, more than one limousine would be needed. Again, the need for coordinating time schedules is obvious.

## *Entertainment*

The entertainment will help to determine the success of any event. Although guests may enjoy excellent food and superb service provided by the caterer, if the music or entertainment is unpleasant or inappropriate, the party will be remembered negatively. When music or any form of party entertainment is involved, it must fit the nature of the function and meet with the customer's approval in price and presentation. That is why in most cases it is recommended that the customer deal directly with the people providing the music or entertainment. However, the caterer is occasionally asked to arrange for the entertainment or coordinate the details of it. In that case, some basic steps should be followed, such as checking references and taking the time to see a performance, an audition, or a performance video.

Most professional entertainers have a contract that details the terms and conditions under which they will perform, including the price they charge for a performance. That contract should be thoroughly reviewed and acceptable to the caterer's customer before the caterer signs it. If the entertainers do not have a contract or if the contract they do have lacks some specific details, then the caterer should be prepared to provide a contract that will cover those details, as shown in Figure 2–11.

Entertainment can range from a full orchestra to a one-person band and can represent a wide spectrum of musical specialties, such as contemporary, country and western, Dixieland, disco, Greek, Italian, Polish, Mexican mariachi, oompah, rhythm and blues, or jazz. A piano, harp, or violin (accordion for Italian or German themes) played before and perhaps during dinner can add a touch of class to any type of catered occasion. The entertainer(s) should be appropriately dressed and have a suitable selection of music. There might be an occasion where the guests can sing along with the musician when provided word sheets. Also, magicians, mimes, comedians, impressionists, clowns, DJs, caricature artists, belly dancers, and so on are all possibilities. The list of entertainment options can be endless, and the right choice or combination of choices will make an event most memorable.

**Computer Requirements**

The technological advances in computer applications continue to produce amazing results each year. Computers are used with laser lights and with various types of audio and video presentations. Therefore, the caterer should always be aware of the latest technology available and be able to answer questions and know where to direct customers desiring professional computer services. Events requiring a registration desk are usually equipped with computers and printers, and speaker podiums may have a computer connection for audio and video presentations. Caterers should be familiar with these options as well.

**Head Table**

When a head table is needed, it should be set apart from and face the other tables as shown in Figure 2–12.

The front of the head table should always be covered with a second tablecloth or skirting, described earlier (see Figure 2–7). Some events may require the head table to be placed on a stage that is raised 6, 12, 24, or 36 inches above the main floor. The head table is usually reserved for honored guests, speakers, or the bride and groom, parents, and wedding party.

# ENTERTAINMENT CONTRACT

*(Name, address, phone, fax, and e-mail of catering company)*

Name of band/entertainer(s)_____

Name of contact person  _____Federal Tax ID _____

Phone  _____Fax  _____E-mail _____

Address_____

The band/entertainer(s) and catering company agree
to the following terms set forth in this contract:

Date  _____Day  _____Time _____

Location  _____

Type of function_____

Type of music or songs that will be played or sung _____

_____

_____

_____

Mode of dress *(entertainers)* _____*(guests)* _____

### Time Schedule

| | |
|---|---|
| Arrival Time | _____ |
| Start Time | _____ |
| Break Times | _____ |
| Length of Breaks | _____ |
| *Designated Break Area* | |
| _____ | |
| End Time | _____ |

### Requirements

| | |
|---|---|
| Stage | _____ |
| Seating | _____ |
| Lighting | _____ |
| Electrical | _____ |
| Sound System | _____ |
| Microphone(s) | _____ |
| Other | _____ |

### Special Instructions

_____

_____

_____

_____

**Authorized:**  ❑ Photos  ❑ Videotaping  ❑ Audiotaping

### Food & Beverages

The band/entertainer(s) may be provided with food and beverages at break time according to the following schedule:  _____

_____

_____

*The band/entertainer(s) further agree that no alchoholic beverages
will be consumed or drugs used during the event.*

### 30 Day Notice Required on Cancellations

Total   $ _____

Overtime charge will be billed at a rate of $_____ per hour
for each additional hour beyond contracted time . . . . . . . . . . . . Overtime charge   _____

Subtotal   _____

Tax   _____

_____
*Entertainer's Signature*          *Date*

Total   _____

Due Date _____  Deposit  (-) _____

_____
*Caterer's Signature*          *Date*

Due Date _____  Balance  $ _____

FIGURE 2–11 **ENTERTAINMENT CONTRACT**

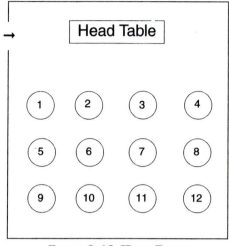

FIGURE 2–12 **HEAD TABLE**

**Table Numbers/ Names**

Guests will often be assigned seats according to table numbers or names. This is usually the case for functions that may have several distinguished guests who would need to be seated near a head table or speaker podium. Assigned seating is also common for events that sell tickets, whereby a group of individuals or a business may purchase tickets for one complete table. Table numbers or names are printed on small cards and placed in the center of the table or clipped to a centerpiece and removed after the guests are seated.

**Candles**

Candles often add just the right accent to a catered event. When candles are used, they should be unscented and placed at a height that will not distract guests. Table and floor candelabras can be rented and must be placed and used with caution. Dripless candles are a wise choice, as candle wax can be difficult to remove from linens or carpet and may cause permanent damage.

**Coatroom Checking**

A place for the guests' coats, hats, raincoats, or umbrellas is important. For small groups, a conveniently located coatrack or table will do, depending upon weather conditions. When groups of 50 or more are attending an event and all of the guests have coats, then the caterer could be asked to have one or more attendants assigned to coatroom checking. This is efficiently accomplished with the use of double theater tickets: One ticket is hung on the hanger with the coat, and the other is given to the guest. The coats are hung on the rack in the order of the ticket numbers. When the event is over, the coatroom attendant will be able to quickly return guests' coats.

**Registration Desk**

Certain events require guests to turn in or fill out a registration form, pick up a name badge, or possibly pay a fee. A registration desk may be equipped with a computer and printer, along with welcome bags filled with complimentary gift items for guests. The caterer usually sets up the registration desk according to the customer's request, that is, with banquet tables or stand-up counter, chairs or stools, skirting for the tables or counter, and the necessary electrical requirements for computers and printers.

**Speaker Podium**

A speaker podium may need to be set up with a microphone, computer connection for audio and video presentation, floral display, or anything else relevant to a speaker's presentation.

**Lectern**

A lectern for a speaker's use will normally be placed on top and at the center of a banquet table that has been prepared as a head table. Lecterns can be small and simple, with folding sides and top for easy portability, or large and equipped with a microphone, reading light, and perhaps the name and logo of the restaurant or hotel prominently displayed on the front.

**Notebook and Marker**

Business luncheons are often followed by meetings that require a large stand-up notebook or flip chart and marker pen for recording information provided by the group and its leaders. There are various versions of this type of system, including a chalkboard, chalk, clean eraser, and pointer.

**Stage**

A stage, as it is used in catering, is usually a platform that is available in 6-, 12-, 24-, and 36-inch heights with 4-by-4- or 4-by-8-foot adjoining sections. The height is determined by the size of the room: The bigger the room the higher the stage. Most stages are portable and can be adjusted to meet the needs of the function (e.g., as a speakers' stand, to support a head table, or as a stage for a band). The part of the stage that faces the guests should be covered with skirting from the edge of the stage to the floor. Stages are readily available to rent.

**Flags**

The United States flag is often displayed with the flags of states, schools, colleges, universities, clubs, and various organizations on a speaker podium or stage or as part of a room display. The United States flag should be placed to the right of any other flag and slightly higher than the flag of another country. When a speaker is addressing an audience, however, and flags are beside or behind the podium, the United States flag should be placed to the speaker's right as he or she faces the audience. Other flags should be to the speaker's left.

**Exhibits, Tripods, and Easels**

The customer may request the caterer to set up a display area using skirted tables, tripods, and easels on which to display business products, family memorabilia, an individual's accomplishments, art objects, and so forth. Special lighting may also be necessary for the display. If the exhibit requires more than what the caterer is capable of providing, the caterer should advise the customer to seek the services of a company that specializes in creating exhibit and booth displays.

**Projector,
Screen, VCR**

There is a wide range of audio and video equipment capable of producing anything from the simplest presentation to the latest state-of-the-art show. Therefore, many caterers choose to contract with the professionals in that field, who can provide everything from slide and overhead projectors to big screens, VCRs, and rear-screen projectors.

**Lighting Effects**

Lighting plays an important role in creating the desired atmosphere. Soft lighting can create a relaxed mood as food and beverages are served. Buffet displays will be further enhanced with the right degree of lighting. A stage or speaker podium may need spotlights. Whatever the lighting requirements, all the lights must be adjusted to the desired levels before guests arrive. There are professional lighting consultants available through local utility companies who can provide helpful information and tips on specific lighting needs.

**Invitation Collection**

The caterer may be asked to assign a person, possibly in costume, to collect invitations at the door as guests arrive, allowing only invited guests to attend. To add a bit more mystique to the catered event, invitations may include some additional activity, such as the following:

1. Ask guests to write on the back of the invitation a brief statement about some unusual occurrence that has happened to them during their life. As they arrive, have them drop the invitations into a basket to be read later by the host. The fun is guessing who belongs to which situation.

2. Make the invitations part of a puzzle. If the dinner theme happens to be "Everyone Loves a Mystery," find a photo or drawing of a Sherlock Holmes type character (see page 118), perhaps a computer graphic. Then cut the picture into puzzle pieces to include with the invitation, along with a reminder to bring the puzzle piece to the event. As guests arrive, have a small table set aside where they can place their pieces of the puzzle. When the puzzle is complete, the party can begin. For a Valentine's theme use the Queen of Hearts; for a Christmas or holiday party, a picture of Old Saint Nick.

**Dance Floor**

When the catered event requires a dance floor and the facility is not adequately equipped for dancing, a portable dance floor can be used. Portable dance floors typically come in 3-by-3-foot sections that are locked in place by set screws. The size of the dance floor will depend upon the number of people that will be dancing and the type of dancing that will take place. Most full-service rental stores stock portable dance floors.

Many fine restaurants, hotels, resorts, and clubs that host catered events have a piano available for guest entertainment. When a piano is to be used for an event, the caterer should make certain well in advance that it will be in tune. It may also be necessary to check that the piano is indeed in tune closer to the day of the event.

**Piano**

Costume rental stores can supply appropriate costumes for guests or solely for the people who are filling special functions, such as the doorman, the greeter, the bartender, and so on. When a costume is appropriately matched to a party theme, the party often begins to take on a life of its own. Some affairs encourage the guests to develop their own individual costumes. The most natural time for a costume is at a Halloween party.

**Costumes**

Balloons are available in numerous colors and sizes and can be decoratively placed on tables, chairs, arches, and throughout the room. Balloons are an inexpensive way to decorate and can be included in just about any party theme. The caterer must allow enough time to fill the balloons with helium, tie, and place them, but not prepare them too far in advance of the event. Under normal temperature conditions, latex and mylar balloons will keep helium for several hours, although extreme heat will quickly shorten the time.

**Balloons**

The caterer should be informed as to the photography and/or videography plans, objectives, and time schedules during an event, such as a wedding, bar mitzvah, award or recognition dinner, and party where clowns, magicians, or other entertainers may be performing. The serving of food and beverages and clearing of dishes must be well coordinated so as not to distract from or be in the way of the activities being photographed or recorded.

**Photography and Videography**

Some events include the use of a tent, for example, when a large party or wedding reception is to take place at a private home that is not large enough to accommodate the number of guests. A tent may be setup in the backyard of the home, accommodating the guests and protecting them and the food from the sun or possible rain.

Most cities have companies that specialize in tent rental and setup and are knowledgeable as to whether or not a tent permit is required by the city or county. A rental company will be able to recommend the most appropriate tent or canopy to use for the function.

**Tents**

A comfortable room temperature is essential. If the room is either too hot or too cold, the guests will not be able to relax and enjoy the occasion, and they will be looking for an opportunity to leave early. It is important to remember that the room temperature will rise when the room becomes full, so adjust for comfort by having the room a bit cooler prior to the guests' arrival. The temperature may need to be adjusted for any entertainment activities during the

**Room Temperature**

event. For example, dancing may require that the temperature be a bit cooler than normal, depending on the pace of the dance steps.

**Special Instructions**

There are certain events that require the caterer to focus on a specific detail or to be attentive to a specific situation, such as a guest who may be receiving special recognition. Whatever the circumstances may be, the caterer should clearly note the customer's request in the special instructions section of the catering contract. An example might be providing 90-year-old Uncle Henry with his favorite dessert—a large strawberry shortcake—while the other guests are served the chocolate mousse.

**Agreement of Charges**

When the guaranteed guest count has been determined and the price per guest established based upon the menu details, the total can be calculated. Accessory charges will vary according to the caterer's policy. Some equipment, such as a beverage fountain, dance floor, or tent, may need to be rented for the event. When having to arrange for floral decor, printing, entertainment, or other services, the caterer may charge a standard fee (cost plus markup) or a commission based upon a percentage, which may range from 5 to 25 percent, on top of the cost for those items or services.

**Pricing**

Catering pricing is based upon the following specific conditions:

—The demand for the types of service being offered, such as:
**Upscale:** where the food and beverage selections are among the finest and the service and accessory details are exquisite.
**Midscale:** which represents most catered events, where the food, beverage, service, and accessory details are carefully chosen and professionally presented.
**Budget:** when customers have only a limited amount to spend, and the food, beverage, and service choices are restricted to what those dollar amounts can support.
—The level of competition among caterers within each type of service. The greater the number of caterers that offer similar service, the greater the need to be more price-competitive in attracting business.
—The reputation of the caterer. The caterer who consistently delivers superb quality and service in a manner that appeals to customers will have a performance-based reputation that can command a higher price. That caterer will not have to be price-driven in order to be competitive. Simply stated, the caterer's reputation earns the price.

The right price is one that produces a profit for the caterer and a good value for the customer. When effective pricing is coupled with doing a great job, the result will be a positive reputation leading to repeat and new business.

## Cancellations

Occasionally circumstances will force a customer to cancel a catered event. The caterer should have a cancellation policy in place that details a procedure that effectively deals with cancellations. Often, the customer will have to forfeit the entire deposit. The determining factors would be to what extent food and beverage products had been ordered and prepared and to what extent accessory items had been ordered and delivered. Once these costs are identified, along with a service charge for the caterer's professional services time, the balance of the deposit may be returned to the customer. The caterer should provide the customer with a written copy of the cancellation policy at the time the catering contract is signed.

## Gratuities

A percentage range of 15 to 25 percent of the total food and beverage charge is normally assigned for the service staff. This percentage will vary according to the type of service performed and the going rate within the local hospitality community.

## Deposits

The deposit amount will typically range from 10 to 50 percent of the total estimated cost of the catered event and is normally due at the time the contract is signed. Some caterers require an initial deposit amount of 25 percent, followed by a second deposit of an additional 25 percent just before the event, and the balance due at the conclusion of the event. The financial arrangements can vary according to the extent of the catering services, the dollar amount involved, and any previous experience the caterer may have had with the customer.

## Event Management and Financial Control

The caterer must be able to quickly organize the details, project a profit, control the preparation functions, account for last-minute changes, and maintain financial balance throughout the catering process. To accomplish these tasks, the caterer should identify a catering software program that will best meet the needs of his or her operation—a program that generates appropriate financial reports and specific management control information. The selected software supplier should be committed to customer service and support for application and use assistance and be timely with updates and new advancements.

The examples in this section are taken from EventMaster™ Windows program, by CaterMate™ Software, a company recognized for the ongoing development of software for the catering professional.

Customer correspondence printed on the caterer's stationery may include a confirmation letter, cover letter that accompanies the catering contract, deposit letter (as shown in Figure 2–13), and a follow-up letter of thanks after the event (as shown in Figure 2–14).

The deposit letter can be sent with the catering contract in lieu of a standard cover letter. This letter would also include all the pertinent customer and event information along with a schedule for the return of the deposit. A follow-up letter creates a final contact with the customer after the event to further express thanks and request the opportunity to be of service in the future.

Oct 22,2002

Jack Sullivan
Grosse Pointe Yacht Club
788 Lake Shore Drive
Grosse Pointe Shores MI 48236

Dear Jack:

Thank you for choosing CaterMate for your upcoming
Whitehouse/Barnes Reception on Dec 20, 2002. Enclosed
please find your catering contract.

Please sign and return a copy to me, and keep the original
for your records. Please include a deposit in the amount of
$4,355.69 no later than Nov 01, 2002. The check should
be made payable to CaterMate and sent to my attention.
In addition, I will need you to contact me no later than 1:00
pm on Dec 13, 2002 to confirm your final number of
guests. Otherwise, the number of guests listed on the contract will be used as your guarantee number.

We look forward to hosting your event. Feel free to contact
me with any questions you may have.

Sincerely,


Abby Bridgeman
Catering and Sales Manager

Figure 2–13 **DEPOSIT LETTER**
*Courtesy of CaterMate™ Software*

Dec 27, 2002


Jack Sullivan
Grosse Pointe Yacht Club
788 Lake Shore Drive
Grosse Pointe Shores MI 48236


Dear Jack:


Thank you again for choosing CaterMate for your recent event! I am pleased that everything was to your satisfaction and hope that your Whitehouse/Barnes Reception was a huge success!

It was a pleasure working with you and I look forward to the opportunity of doing so again.

Please contact me if I may be of any further service to you.

Sincerely,


Abby Bridgeman
Sales and Catering Manager

Figure 2–14 **FOLLOW-UP LETTER**
*Courtesy of CaterMate™ Software*

Event reports will help the caterer organize and prioritize his or her activities with a focused attention to all of the details. Reports, such as the Master Event Schedule shown in Figure 2–15, will provide a list of customers, event descriptions, event locations, times, number of guests, contract number, event status, and other important information over a range of days.

## Master Event Schedule

### for 12/18/2002 to 12/20/2002

**12/18/02**

| Event: | **Monthly Sales Meeting** | | | | |
|---|---|---|---|---|---|
| Room: | Annex Room 2 | | | | |
| Date: | 12/18/02 | # Guests: | 35 | Contract #: | 97000149 |
| Time: | 09:00 am To 12:00 pm | # Guaranteed: | N/A | Status: | DC *(Definite Contract)* |
| Contact: | Jo Bates | Setup Time: | 08:00 am | Last Change: | 00/00/00 |
| Phone: | 517-437-3311 | Event Type: | Conference | Sales Per: | KS |
| Customer: | Jo Bates | | | | |
| Company: | Dow Leadership Center | | | | |
| Address: | 22 East Galloway | | | | |
| Address: | Suite 3000 | | | | |
| City,St Zp: | Hillsdale MI 49242 | | | | |

| Event: | **Dance** | | | | |
|---|---|---|---|---|---|
| Room: | Sapphire Ball Room | | | | |
| Date: | 12/18/02 | # Guests: | 150 | Contract #: | 970000146 |
| Time: | 08:00 pm To 01:00 am | # Guaranteed: | N/A | Status: | DC |
| Contact: | Ms. Jane Smith | Setup Time: | 05:00 pm | Last Change: | 00/00/00 |
| Phone: | 201-729-6161 | Event Type: | Dance | Sales Per: | KS |
| Customer: | Mark Avondoglio | | | | |
| Company: | Perona Farms | | | | |
| Address: | 350 Andover Sparta Road | | | | |
| City, St Zp: | Andover NJ 07821 | | | | |
| Account #: | 76689 | | | | |

| Event: | **Holiday Breakfast Buffet** | | | | |
|---|---|---|---|---|---|
| Room: | Annex Room 1 | | | | |
| Date: | 12/18/02 | # Guests: | 45 | Contract #: | 97000147 |
| Time: | 08:30 am To 10:30 pm | # Guaranteed: | N/A | Status: | DC |
| Contact: | Joe Lenoch | Setup Time: | 08:00 am | Last Change: | 00/00/00 |
| Phone: | 708-354-4200 | Event Type: | Breakfast Buffet | Sales Per: | AB |
| Customer: | Joe Lenoch | | | | |
| Company: | Holiday Inn | | | | |
| Address: | 6201 Joliet Road | | | | |
| Address: | Countryside | | | | |
| City, St Zp: | La Grange IL 60525 | | | | |

**12/19/02**

| Event: | **Dinner Dance** | | | | |
|---|---|---|---|---|---|
| Room: | Onyx Ball Room | | | | |
| Date: | 12/19/02 | # Guests: | 75 | Contract #: | 97000145 |
| Time: | 06:00 pm To 09:30 pm | # Guaranteed: | N/A | Status: | DC |
| Contact: | Gary Arhendt | Setup Time: | 05:00 pm | Last Change: | 00/00/00 |
| Company: | Crystal Food Service | | | | |
| Address: | 9800 Crosspoint Blvd | | | | |
| Address: | Suite 4400 | | | | |
| City, St Zp: | Indianapolis, IN 46256 | | | | |
| Account #: | 123-456-789 | | | | |

Figure 2–15 **MASTER EVENT SCHEDULE**
*Courtesy of CaterMate™ Software*

Today's Schedule, shown in Figure 2–16, will create event listings for a specific date.

---

## Today's Schedule
### Dec. 20, 2002

**Monthly Sales Meeting**
09:00 am  To  12:00 pm
Dow Leadership
Annex Room 2

**Private Holiday Brunch**
10:00 am  To  12:00 pm
USACFSC-MIS
Anniex Room 1

**Guest Lecture Seminar**
10:00 am  To  04:00 pm
University of Nebraska
Sapphire Ball Room

**Baker Birthday Party**
02:00 pm  To  06:00 pm
Truffles
Annex Room 1

**Charity Holiday Dinner**
06:00 pm  To  11:00 pm
U.S. Senate Restaurant
Gold Ball Room

**Whitehouse/Barnes Reception**
06:00 pm  To  01:00 am
Grosse Pointe Yacht Club
Silver Ball Room

**Holiday Dinner**
07:00 pm  To  10:00 pm
Lake Michigan College
Sapphire Ball Room

---

Figure 2–16 **TODAY'S SCHEDULE**
*Courtesy of CaterMate™ Software*

The Event Order, shown in Figure 2–17, will present the most current information about any event. Every detail important to an event will appear on the event order.

---

**Event Order**                                    **Whitehouse/Barnes Reception**

| | | | |
|---|---|---|---|
| Customer: | Jack Sullivan | | |
| Date: | 12/20/02 | Contact: | Jack Sullivan |
| Time: | 06:00 pm To 01:00 am | Phone: | 313-884-2500 |
| # Guests: | 125 | Company: | Grosse Pointe Yacht Club |
| # Guarantee: | 120 | Addr 1: | 788 Lake Shore Drive |
| Setup Time: | 04:00 pm | Addr 2: | Suite 2000 |
| Event Type: | Reception Dinner | City, St: | Grosse Pointe Shores MI 48236 |
| Room: | Silver Ball Room | | |

_____Schedule_____

| | |
|---|---|
| 04:00 pm | Employees arrive at store |
| 06:00 pm | Bar Opens |
| 07:00 pm | Meal starts |
| 08:45 pm | Meal ends |
| 09:00 pm | Entertainment starts |
| 01:00 am | Entertainment ends |
| 12:00 am | Bar closes |

_____Orders_____                _____Staff_____

| Order | Qty | Staff |
|---|---|---|
| Soup Du Jour | 125 | Russ Nelson - Setup Helper |
| Mixed Green Salad w/Crouton | 125 | Joseph Paulson - Setup Helper |
| Raspberry Vinaigrette | 250 Ozs | Jessica Payton - Setup Helper |
| Snow Flake Rolls & Butter | 16 Dozens | Jessica Payton - Bartender |
| Sliced Top Round of Beef Bordelaise | 125 8 Ounces | Russ Neslon - Bartender |
| Franconia Roasted Potatoes | 125 Ea | Joseph Paulson - Bartender |
| Whole Green Beans w/ Toasted Almonds | 125 Portion | Erika Mann - Wait Staff |
| Cheesecake w/ Raspberry Sauce | 125 | Marie Denaston - Wait Staff |
| * Beer, Soda & Wine * | 125 Package | James Seward - Wait Staff |
| Soda, Juice & Bottled Water | 75 | Vaclav Sonorak - Wait Staff |
| Draft Beer | 22 Pitchers | Margaret Ann Pepperney - Wait staff |
| Bottles of White Wine | 25 750ml Btl | Ellie Lourd - Wait Staff |
| Bottles of Red Wine | 25 750ml Btl | Erika Mann - Manager |
| Coffee by the Gallon | 4 Gallons | George Haverford - Chef |
| DeCaf by the Gallon | 3 Gallons | Bob Carpenter - Cook |
| | | Anna Kowalski - Cook Helper |
| Table Centerpieces | 15 | Starlight Productions |

Set up head table with sound system and microphone.
Press tableskirts immediately before event.
Floral designer will set up 2 hours before event starts

---

FIGURE 2–17 **EVENT ORDER**
*Courtesy of CaterMate™ Software*

A Room Sheet, as shown in Figure 2–18, will detail each room's capacity, including minimum and maximum occupancy counts, the room's height, length, width, total square footage, and shape, along with any other pertinent information.

# Room Sheet

## Gold Ball Room

**Room Number:** 1

| | | | |
|---|---|---|---|
| **Room Code:** | Gold | Min Occ: | 300 |
| Floor: | 1 | Max Occ: | 600 |
| Building: | MC | Height: | 12 |
| Address: | 1234 Rodeo Way | Length: | 120 |
| | Diggstown IN 46200 | Width: | 50 |
| Phone: | (317) 555-1212 | Area: | 6,000 |
| | | Shape: | R |

**Usage Rules:**
May Book Room
Handicap Accessible

Phone Access

**Setup Information**

| Code | Abbrev | Minimum | Maximum |
|------|--------|---------|---------|
| AV | AV & Podium | 200 | 450 |
| CR | Clear Room | 300 | 600 |
| CT | Circle Table | 200 | 350 |
| RE | Reception | 300 | 500 |

**Associated Rooms**
3
6

FIGURE 2–18 **ROOM SHEET**
*Courtesy of CaterMate™ Software*

A Staffing Requirement Schedule, shown in Figure 2–19, will prepare a list of scheduled employees by name, skill (position), and reporting-to-work time. A separate schedule is prepared for each event over a range of dates.

## Staffing Requirements for Whitehouse/Barnes Reception on 12/20/2002

Customer:      GROSSE POINTE
Room:          SILVER
Contact:       Jack Sullivan
Guest Count:   125
Room Setup:    CT  *(Circle Tables)*
Event Status:  B   *(Booked)*

| Name | Skill | Rpt Time | In | Out | Net Hour |
|------|-------|----------|----|----|-----|
| Bob Carpenter | Cook | 06:00 pm | _____ | _____ | _____ |
| Marie Denaston | Wait Staff | 06:00 pm | _____ | _____ | _____ |
| George Haverford | Chef | 06:00 pm | _____ | _____ | _____ |
| Anna Kowalski | Cook Helper | 06:00 pm | _____ | _____ | _____ |
| Ellie Lourd | Wait Staff | 06:00 pm | _____ | _____ | _____ |
| Erika Mann | Manager | 05:00 pm | _____ | _____ | _____ |
| Erika Mann | Wait Staff | 06:00 pm | _____ | _____ | _____ |
| Russ Nelson | Setup Helper | 04:00 pm | _____ | _____ | _____ |
| Russ Nelson | Bartender | 06:00 pm | _____ | _____ | _____ |
| Joseph Paulson | Setup Helper | 04:00 pm | _____ | _____ | _____ |
| Joseph Paulson | Bartender | 06:00 pm | _____ | _____ | _____ |
| Margaret Ann Pepperney | Wait Staff | 06:00 pm | _____ | _____ | _____ |
| Jessica Payton | Setup Helper | 04:00 pm | _____ | _____ | _____ |
| Jessica Payton | Bartender | 06:00pm | _____ | _____ | _____ |
| James Seward | Wait Staff | 06:00 pm | _____ | _____ | _____ |
| Vaclav Sonorak | Wait Staff | 06:00 pm | _____ | _____ | _____ |

Figure 2–19 **STAFFING REQUIREMENT SCHEDULE**
*Courtesy of CaterMate™ Software*

An Items Required Report, shown in Figure 2-20, can sort all the items needed for upcoming events. This information can be cross-referenced with current inventories. If in-stock items are not in adequate supply, additional quantities can be ordered. If new items are required, sources of supply and competitive pricing would need to be identified.

**Items Required : Summary from Dec 15, 2002 To Dec 20, 2002 All Item Categories**

| Code | Category / Description | Quantity | Guests | Events |
|------|------------------------|----------|--------|--------|
| | **Appetizer** | | | |
| AP108 | Soup Du Jour | 125 | 125 | 1 |
| | **Breads** | | | |
| BR001 | Assorted Dinner Rolls & Butter | 425 Dozens | 425 | 2 |
| BR006 | Bakery Fresh Rolls & Butter | 6 Dozens | 35 | 1 |
| BR005 | Snow Flake Rolls & Butter | 136 Dozens | 245 | 2 |
| | **Buffet/Lunch/Dinner** | | | |
| BU015 | Carved Boneless Prime Rib | 35 Portions | 35 | 1 |
| BU017 | Carved Pork Tenderloin w/Mushroom Sauce | 35 Portions | 35 | 1 |
| BU021 | Fresh Salmon Filet | 35 Portions | 35 | 1 |
| BU010 | Ricotta Stuffed Pasta Shells/Marinara Sauce | 35 Portions | 35 | 1 |
| | **Beverages** | | | |
| BV102 | Coffee by the Gallon | 4 Gallons | 125 | 1 |
| BV100 | Coffee by the Pot | 12 Pots | 70 | 2 |
| BV104 | DeCaf by the Gallon | 3 Gallons | 125 | 1 |
| BV103 | DeCaf by the Pot | 6 Pots | 70 | 2 |
| BV001 | Hot & Cold Beverages | 545 | 545 | 3 |
| BV002 | Hot Beverages | 35 | 35 | 1 |
| BV106 | Hot Water by the Pot | 6 Pots | 70 | 2 |
| BV003 | Soda, Juice & Bottled Water | 75 | 125 | 1 |
| | **Condiments** | | | |
| CO003 | Creamers | 70 Each | 70 | 2 |
| CO001 | Sugar Paks | 42 Paks | 70 | 2 |

Figure 2-20 **ITEMS REQUIRED REPORT**
*Courtesy of CaterMate™ Software*

A Package Sheet, shown in Figure 2–21, serves to identify individual costs and the caterer's desired selling price, along with the quantity per package and the amount of that package delivered to the catered event.

## Package Sheet

| Code | Description | Item-Serves | Cost | Price | Qty | Del-UOM |
|------|-------------|-------------|------|-------|-----|---------|
| AM01P | * Afternoon Break * | | | | | |
| DS009 | Brownies | 1.0000 | $.28 | $1.25 | 16 | Each |
| DS010 | Assorted Cookie | 1.0000 | $.17 | $ .75 | 12 | Mixed |
| FR002 | Whole Fruit | 1.0000 | $.35 | $ .95 | 18 | Each |
| BV111 | Assorted Regular & Diet Sodas | 1.0000 | $.27 | $1.25 | 22 | Mixed |
| BS006 | Water, Avalon Each | 1.0000 | $.50 | $ .75 | 8 | Each |
| PP008 | Cup, Plastic Cold | 1.0000 | $.04 | | 30 | Each |
| PP011 | Napkins, Dinner | 1.0000 | $.02 | | 36 | Each |
| PP009 | Plate, 6" | 1.0000 | $.03 | | 28 | Each |

Figure 2–21 **PACKAGE SHEET**
*Courtesy of CaterMate™ Software*

The Total Costing Analysis shown in Figure 2–22 identifies cost categories, cost, price, cost percentage, and profit margin. The software program can adjust to the caterer's desired ratio of cost to customer price for an event or for a number of events over a date range, along with the caterer's desired percentages for surcharges (such as markups for services or on rental items). A percentage charge for gratuities and a percentage for any customer-given discounts, such as a discount off the normal room charge, can be quickly implemented.

# TOTAL COSTING ANALYSIS

Grosse Pointe Yacht Club
Jack Sullivan
Whitehouse/Barnes Reception
Dec/20/2002 At 06:00 pm      Contract #:        97000152
# Guests:      125            Salesperson:       AB

| Tax Category | Cost | Price | Percent | Margin |
|---|---|---|---|---|
| Food Items | $0.00 | $0.00 | 0.00% | $0.00 |
| Items for All Lists | $0.00 | $0.00 | 0.00% | $0.00 |
| Bar/Liquor Items | $0.00 | $0.00 | 0.00% | $0.00 |
| Flowers/Decorations | $0.00 | $0.00 | 0.00% | $0.00 |
| Food Items | $2,609.65 | $5,487.50 | 47.55% | $2,877.85 |
| Equipment Items | $0.00 | $0.00 | 0.00% | $0.00 |
| Other Items | $0.00 | $0.00 | 0.00% | $0.00 |
| Audio/Visual Items | $0.00 | $0.00 | 0.00% | $0.00 |
| Beverage | $0.00 | $0.00 | 0.00% | $0.00 |
| Purchased Materials | $225.00 | $675.00 | 33.33% | $450.00 |
| Staffing | $611.50 | $766.00 | 79.83% | $154.50 |
| Outside Services | $400.00 | $500.00 | 80.00% | $100.00 |
| Room Charge | $350.00 | $350.00 | 100.00% | $0.00 |
| Additional Charges | $0.00 | $0.00 | 0.00% | $0.00 |
| Surcharge | $0.00 | $0.00 | 0.00% | $0.00 |
| Gratuity | $0.00 | $0.00 | 0.00% | $0.00 |
| | | | | |
| **Subtotal Whole Proposal**: | $4,196.15 | $7,778.50 | 53.94% | $3,582.35 |
| **Subtotal Per Person**: | $33.56 | $62.22 | 53.94% | $28.65 |
| | | | | |
| Tax 1 | $274.38 | $274.38 | | |
| Tax 2 | $329.25 | $329.25 | | |
| Surcharge | | $384.13 | | |
| Gratuity | $439.00 | $439.00 | | |
| Discount | | $493.88– | | |
| | | | | |
| **Total Whole Proposal:** | $5,238.78 | $8,711.38 | 60.13% | $3,472.60 |

Figure 2–22 **TOTAL COSTING ANALYSIS**
*Courtesy of CaterMate™ Software*

A Tax Table Report shown in Figure 2–23 will print tax titles and percentage amounts for tax categories, such as state and city sales taxes.

**Tax Table:**    **Indiana Standard Taxes**

| | Tax 1 | Tax 2 | Surcharge | Gratuity | Discount |
|---|---|---|---|---|---|
| Food Items | 5.000 | 6.000 | 7.000 | 8.000 | 9.000 |
| Items for All Lists | 5.000 | 6.000 | 7.000 | 8.000 | 9.000 |
| Bar/Liquor Items | 5.000 | 6.000 | 7.000 | 8.000 | 9.000 |
| Flowers/Decorations | 5.000 | 6.000 | 7.000 | 8.000 | 9.000 |
| Food Items | 5.000 | 6.000 | 7.000 | 8.000 | 9.000 |
| Equipment Items | 5.000 | 6.000 | 7.000 | 8.000 | 9.000 |
| Other Items | 5.000 | 6.000 | 7.000 | 8.000 | 9.000 |
| Audio/Visual Items | 5.000 | 6.000 | 7.000 | 8.000 | 9.000 |
| Beverages | .000 | .000 | .000 | .000 | .000 |
| Purchased Materials | .000 | .000 | .000 | .000 | .000 |
| Staffing | .000 | .000 | .000 | .000 | .000 |
| Outside Services | .000 | .000 | .000 | .000 | .000 |
| Room Charges | .000 | .000 | .000 | .000 | .000 |
| Additional Charges | .000 | .000 | .000 | .000 | .000 |
| Surcharge | .000 | .000 | N/A | N/A | N/A |
| Gratuity | .000 | .000 | N/A | N/A | N/A |

**Tax Table:**    **Illinois Standard Taxes**

| | Tax 1 | Tax 2 | Surcharge | Gratuity | Discount |
|---|---|---|---|---|---|
| Food Items | .000 | .000 | .000 | .000 | .000 |
| Items for All Lists | .000 | .000 | .000 | .000 | .000 |
| Bar/Liquor | .000 | .000 | .000 | .000 | .000 |
| Flowers/Decorations | .000 | .000 | .000 | .000 | .000 |
| Food Items | .000 | .000 | .000 | .000 | .000 |
| Equipment Items | .000 | .000 | .000 | .000 | .000 |
| Other Items | .000 | .000 | .000 | .000 | .000 |
| Audio/Visual Items | .000 | .000 | .000 | .000 | .000 |
| Beverages | .000 | .000 | .000 | .000 | .000 |
| Purchased Materials | .000 | .000 | .000 | .000 | .000 |
| Staffing | .000 | .000 | .000 | .000 | .000 |
| Outside Services | .000 | .000 | .000 | .000 | .000 |
| Room Charge | .000 | .000 | .000 | .000 | .000 |
| Additional Charges | .000 | .000 | .000 | .000 | .000 |
| Surcharge | .000 | .000 | N/A | N/A | N/A |
| Gratuity | .000 | .000 | N/A | N/A | N/A |

Figure 2–23 **TAX TABLE REPORT**
*Courtesy of CaterMate™ Software*

An Invoice for an event, as shown in Figure 2–24, can be a recap of all the charges for the event including taxes, gratuities, and service charges.

```
┌─────────────────────────────────────────────────────────────────────────┐
│ Dec 22, 2002                    .              Contract #:  97000152      │
│                                                Invoice #:   00000038      │
│ Mr. Jack Sullivan                                                         │
│ Grosse Pointe Yacht Club                                                  │
│ 788 Lake Shore Drive                                                      │
│ Grosse Pointe Shores, MI 48236                                            │
│                                                                           │
│ Dear Mr. Jack Sullivan:                                                   │
│                                                                           │
│ It was a pleasure to serve your Whitehouse/Barnes Reception on Dec 20,    │
│ 2002. The invoice below represents your total charges. We appreciate      │
│ this opportunity to serve you.                                            │
└─────────────────────────────────────────────────────────────────────────┘
```

| | | | |
|---|---|---|---|
| Soup Du Jour | | | |
| Mixed Green Salad w/ Crouton | | | |
| Raspberry Vinaigrette | | | |
| Snow Flake Rolls & Butter | | | |
| Sliced Top Round of Beef Bordelaise | $35.95 | 125 | $4,493.75 |
| Franconia Roasted Potatoes | | | |
| Whole Green Beans w/ Toasted Almonds | | | |
| Cheesecake w/ Raspberry Sauce | | | |
| * Beer, Soda & Wine * | $ 7.95 | 125 | $993.75 |
| Soda, Juice & Bottled Water | | | |
| Draft Beer | | | |
| Bottles of White Wine | | | |
| Bottles of Red Wine | | | |
| Coffee by the Gallon | | | |
| DeCaf by the Gallon | | | |
| Table Centerpieces | $ 45.00 | 15 | $675.00 |
| Starlight Productions | $125.00 | 1 | $500.00 |
| Consolidated Staffing Charges | $  .00 | 16 | $766.00 |
| Room Charges | $350.00 | 1 | $350.00 |
| Subtotal for Invoice #00000038 | $7,778.50 | 1 | $7,778.50 |
| Discount applied to $5,487.50 | $493.88– | 1 | $493.88– |
| Surcharge applied to $5,487.50 | $384.13 | 1 | $384.13 |
| Gratuity applied to $5,487.50 | $439.00 | 1 | $439.00 |
| Tax 1 applied to $5,487.50 | $274.38 | 1 | $274.38 |
| Tax 2 applied to $5,487.50 | $329.25 | 1 | $329.25 |
| Total for Invoice #00000038 | $8,711.38 | 1 | $8,711.38 |

**Total Credits:** *(includes deposit and any other credits)*  $4,355.69
**Total Due:**  $4,355.69

Once again, thank you for using CaterMate. We look forward to serving you again.

Sincerely,

Banquet Sales

FIGURE 2–24 **INVOICE**
*Courtesy of CaterMate™ Software*

The caterer must have the knowledge and ability to be able to accurately project the total cost and profit for each catered event. Therefore, he or she should have a thorough understanding of food costing, inventory management, purchasing, and receiving and processing invoices, along with quality standards, specifications, yield analysis, plate cost, beverage cost, bar and inventory control, and payroll cost. The caterer's profit can range from 10 to 50 percent of the gross selling price of the catered event, depending upon the nature of the event, type of service performed, competitive market conditions, and reputation of the caterer. For more extensive information on cost controls, refer to *Foodservice Profitability: A Control Approach*, by Edward E. Sanders and Timothy H. Hill (Upper Saddle River, N.J.: Prentice Hall, 1998).

**Overview**

This chapter explains the many details that can be involved in any catered event. Although the caterer cannot be expected to be an expert in every aspect of the accessory details, he or she is expected at least to be knowledgeable as to what is required in these details. The caterer should also identify every item requested by the customer for the catered event. This can be accomplished through the use of a catering contract. The example shown in this chapter is very complete, and the authors recognize that not all catering operations would be able to provide all of the services and details listed. Therefore, the catering company should set forth a contract that identifies what can successfully be done. The contract, when referred to frequently, can reduce the likelihood of neglecting important details. Catering software can be the most effective tool for managing catered events and maintaining financial control.

***The details make the difference!***

### Discussion Questions and Exercises

1. Why is it important to have a complete list of catering options available to review with a customer?
2. What is the purpose of a catering contract?
3. Explain why the time schedule is a critical factor in allowing a catered event to function smoothly.
4. Define approximate guest count, guaranteed guest count, and confirmed guest count.
5. Explain how to calculate a room's capacity for seating.
6. Calculate the banquet seating capacity of a room that is 40 feet by 25 feet.
7. Calculate the traditional seating capacity of a room that is 80 feet by 90 feet. There will be 275 guests attending a buffet dinner. Show the room dimensions, table arrangements, and buffet table setup using graph paper.
8. What are the most popular table sizes?
9. Sketch four different banquet table arrangements.

10. Define the guidelines for seating arrangements.

11. Why is it important to inquire as to the profile of the average guest? What questions would be asked in determining that profile?

12. Why should the caterer be familiar with wines and other specialty beverages?

13. When fitting a tablecloth to a table or table arrangement where guests will be seated, how high should the tablecloth be draped above the chairs?

14. Describe how table skirting is used.

15. When would chair covers be used?

16. Describe the options that are available in floral decor. When might artificial silks be used?

17. When background music is requested, why is it important to know the menu theme?

18. Discuss some of the choices available when having to print menus or invitations.

19. Describe how ice sculptures are created from molds.

20. Explain how to use a beverage fountain.

21. How does the event's time schedule for valet parking affect the number of attendants to schedule?

22. Discuss the elements of an entertainment contract.

23. Where might computers be used at a catered event?

24. Explain how to set up a head table.

25. When would table numbers be used and where would they be placed?

26. What should be considered when using candles at a catered event?

27. Describe the procedure for coatroom checking with the use of double theater tickets.

28. When would a registration desk be used and how might it be set up?

29. How should a lectern be set up for a speaker at a business luncheon?

30. When using a stage, what part of the stage should be covered from guests' view and how would that be accomplished?

31. Explain how to position the United States flag when displayed with another flag; give the exception to that rule.

32. What type of occasion would require the caterer to set up an exhibit with tripods and easels?

33. Name a few types of audio and video equipment that could be used at a catered event.

34. When a piano is requested by the customer, what should be checked well in advance?

35. Give an example of when a tent would be used and what may be required before the tent is erected.

**36.** Why would the caterer initially set the room temperature to be on the cool side just before guests arrive?

**37.** How would the caterer charge for accessory details?

**38.** Discuss the specific conditions that affect pricing.

**39.** Explain how a deposit might be handled when a customer cancels an event.

**40.** What is the typical percentage range for service staff gratuities and how might this vary?

**41.** What are the factors to consider when arranging for deposits?

**42.** Explain the functions that catering software can perform in event management and financial control.

# 3

# Serving the Food

**Learning Objectives**

After reading this chapter and completing the discussion questions
and exercises, you should be able to

1. Recognize the value of recruiting people who are service and
   performance oriented.
2. Explain the five different methods of serving food for a catered
   event.
3. Know the basic rules for serving food and beverages.
4. Understand the importance of being prepared for emergencies.
5. Know how to do table settings.
6. Explain the three different ways that rolls and butter may be
   served.
7. Understand how to select the appropriate dinnerware and flatware.
8. Know when to use holloware items.
9. Demonstrate various napkin folds.
10. Explain the guidelines for preparing a buffet.

**Introduction**

The key component to a successful catered event can be defined
in one word: *service.* The caterer can ensure that a high level of service is delivered to the customer when the right formula is in place.
That formula begins with recruiting people who are service and performance oriented and who relate well to other people. Catering staff
must work independently and yet be team players able to perform in
an environment that often demands flexibility and quick solutions.
The catering business typically requires people who can work on a
part-time basis. People seeking weekend and evening employment

are often recruited from colleges, universities, culinary schools, and the local community.

The second part of the formula deals with employee training and development that results in a top-notch catering staff. Such a staff is always well groomed with crisply pressed uniforms, restrained hair, immaculate hands with neatly trimmed nails, and an overall professional appearance. They can pleasantly answer guests' questions about any of the food or beverages being served. They know what to do if an accident occurs, a guest becomes ill, or a tray of food spills. They understand that the details make the difference in accommodating guests in every way.

The formula is completed with a staff meeting prior to the catered event. Here the caterer assigns responsibilities, reviews the serving schedule and menu details, including the uniqueness of any recipes, and answers any questions from the staff. The staff should then be ready to deliver what is expected for a well-organized event that should flow smoothly.

## Types of Service

There are five distinctively different methods of serving food for a catered event: butler service, American service, Russian service, French service, and buffet. It is important to choose the type of service that is best suited for the event.

***Butler service.*** Hors d'oeuvres are placed on serving trays and served to guests during a cocktail or social hour prior to a dinner. This method may be used when only hors d'oeuvres and light refreshments are being served or for the cocktail portion of a catered event.

***American service (individual plate service).*** The food is plated in the kitchen and individually served to the guests. This service is ideal for maintaining portion control where exact amounts can be planned.

***Russian service (family style service).*** The food is served at the guests' tables on platters (sometimes with covers) and serving dishes. Guests can be served desired portions or are allowed to serve themselves. The obvious advantage is that guests are certain to get enough to eat in the family style setting.

***French service.*** This is the most formal way of serving food and requires the most space, time, and culinary skill. The food is served from a gueridon cart or a flambé trolley, as shown in Figure 3–1, which is a narrow cart equipped with a small gas stove for final cooking. The tables must be spaced farther apart to accommodate the carts. Since the food is individually cooked for each guest, a considerable amount of time is required, along with a certain culinary skill for the person preparing the food. This type of service is generally reserved for very formal restaurants, as the cost to serve food in this fashion is quite high. French service is not typically used for

FIGURE 3–1
**FLAMBÉ TROLLEY**
*Courtesy of Bon Chef*

catered events but can be incorporated for presenting and serving fancy desserts, such as cherries jubilee.

*Buffet.* Food is decoratively displayed, and guests are allowed to select the food and serve themselves. The buffet may be formal or informal and is appropriate with either a simple or an elaborate menu for breakfast, lunch, dinner, or hors d'oeuvres. This type of service is ideal for serving large groups with a limited serving staff.

**Service Rules**

Professional wait staff traditionally serve food and beverages according to the following rules:

1. Serve all dishes with the left hand, approaching the table to the left of the guest.
2. Serve all beverages and soups with the right hand and to the right of the guest.
3. Serve female guests before serving male guests at each table.
4. Remove dishes from the left with the left hand and beverages from the right with the right hand.
5. Remove dirty dishes, glasses, and flatware after each course.
6. Never stack dirty dishes in front of guests.
7. Constantly watch and refill water and beverage glasses/cups.
8. Completely clear all dishes, glasses not in use, and salt and pepper shakers before serving dessert.
9. Calmly and quickly clean up spills or broken dishes and resume service.
10. Properly load and balance trays before lifting; lift and carry according to the following procedure: The server drops into a squat position and firmly places one hand at the bottom center of the tray (which is on a tray stand), using the other hand to steady the tray, then stands upright. The person should never attempt to lift more than he or she is comfortable handling.

    *Cocktail trays* are used for serving cocktails, wine, beer, and other beverages. The trays should be carried with the left hand and beverages served with the right hand.

    **Note:** As a general rule, one person can comfortably serve twelve to fifteen guests.

**Being Prepared**

Knowing what to do when the unexpected occurs and maintaining a sense of calmness and order is essential for caterers. The staff should be trained and prepared to deal with any of the following situations: a guest slips or falls, a guest displays unacceptable behavior, a guest becomes ill or is choking on food, or a tray tips and plates and glasses are broken.

The caterer and staff should be trained in basic first aid, CPR, and first aid for the choking victim. A first-aid kit should be stocked and in place for quick access, and fire extinguishers should be available and regularly inspected and tested. When an emergency situation happens, the customer will expect the caterer to handle the situation in the most expedient and professional manner possible, so that the catered event can quickly return to its normal functioning.

**Table Settings**

The tables should be set up well in advance of the event, allowing enough time to be thorough and complete. Tablecloths should be placed on every table, keeping in mind that the ends of the tablecloths should be draped approximately 1 inch above each chair. The tables should be set with the appropriate plates, beverage glasses, cup, and flatware to accommodate the menu being served. For an example of table settings refer to Figure 3–2. The rule to follow is that flatware is placed in order of usage from the outside inward. The flatware and service plate (if one is used) should be 1 inch from the edge of the table. When a coffee cup is used, it should also be placed one inch from the edge of the table with the handle angled at four o'clock.

**Salt and Pepper, Sugar and Creamer**

Salt and pepper shakers should be preset according to the number of guests at each table, typically one set per four to six persons, depending upon the menu. As a general rule, they are removed after the main course and the same number of sugar bowls and creamers are placed just prior to coffee being served.

**Rolls and Butter**

Rolls and butter may be served in several different ways, according to the customer's preference. For example:

—A roll and slice of butter uniformly placed on a bread and butter plate for each guest.
—Rolls in a basket and butter slices or balls in a dish for guests to serve themselves. The rolls may be served warm.
—Rolls and butter served to each guest by the person serving the food. This is typically done so that the rolls are served hot.

Breakfast and Lunch                    Dinner

FIGURE 3–2 **TABLE SETTINGS**

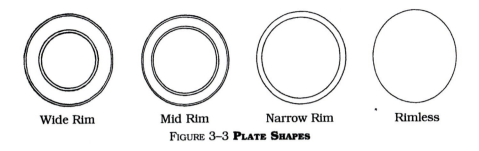

Wide Rim        Mid Rim        Narrow Rim        Rimless

FIGURE 3–3 PLATE SHAPES

Selecting the appropriate dinnerware for a catered event begins **Dinnerware** with an understanding of how to choose a shape, design, and color that will complement every aspect of the catering environment.

The shape of a plate is determined by rim size. The rim size can be wide, midrange, narrow, or rimless, as shown in Figure 3–3.

*Wide rims* allow smaller food portions to appear larger and create an open space presentation by separating food from other tabletop items.

*Mid rims* reduce the serving area, creating an appearance of larger portions while maintaining a balance between the rim and serving area.

*Narrow rims* allow for larger portions and/or additional foods, possibly reducing the need for additional plates or serving items.

*Rimless* plates allow a maximum serving area for food, with the total focus being on the food presentation.

The mid rim plate is the most popular for catering service, being versatile and appropriate for formal and casual dining. The wide rim would be used for customers who prefer smaller food portions or have several courses being served, which would require smaller portions. The narrow rim plates could be a choice for a buffet, allowing enough room for additional food items, such as salads or breads. The rimless is ideal for occasions that place the main focus on the meal presentation. Whatever the shape, it should always fit the need of the catered event.

Dinnerware design typically falls into five styles: lines and bands, florals, geometrics, themes, and embossed rims, as shown in Figure 3–4.

*Lines and bands* are clean, simple, and classic and naturally frame the food presentation.

*Florals* reflect an elegant look that is typically traditional in design, although they can be contemporary.

*Geometrics* can be bold and dramatic or subtle and understated with an emphasis toward an interesting look that captures attention.

*Themes* are inspired by the menu and/or the decor of the foodservice and catering environment.

*Embossed rims* decorate without color and add a certain flair and style to the meal presentation.

It is important to select a dinnerware pattern color that will complement the food being served, linen color, and interior decor.

Lines & Bands      Florals      Geometrics

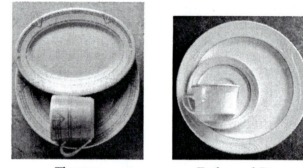

Themes      Embossed Rims

FIGURE 3–4 **DINNERWARE DESIGN**
*Courtesy of Oneida Foodservice*

Select one that will accent the softer rather than the dominant colors of the foodservice and catering environment. White is used most often and will work in almost every situation.

Any choice of dinnerware should be banquet weight, which is lighter than traditional dinnerware and thus more comfortable to handle. Along with being highly resistant to breakage from impact and thermal shock, the dinnerware should also be oven-safe for microwave, convection, and combination ovens. The edge should be rolled or corded to resist chipping and scratching during busing and washing. Figure 3–5 is an example of dinnerware that is ideal for catering service. The banquet weight provides ease of handling and durability. The edge combines the charactertistics of the rolled and corded edge in a patented "Roco" edge. The white color fits all decors, while the embossed rim distinguishes the shape with an upscale appearance. The service shown presents the options that are available in plate sizes, platters, bowls, cups, and mugs.

The right dinnerware can increase the perceived value of the meal. Therefore, the caterer should have several dinnerware choices available (from inventory or through rental services) that can match the menu, theme, decor, and type of service as well as the customer's preference and budget. Caterers will often have photos from previous events that show different dinnerware in service. This allows the customer to see what the food will actually look like when served on a given dinnerware.

FIGURE 3–5
**DINNERWARE FOR CATERING**
The Bel Tygere pattern from the Rego collection.
*Courtesy of Oneida Foodservice*

FIGURE 3–6 **FLATWARE AND HOLLOWARE**
*Courtesy of Oneida Foodservice*

*Flatware*

The selection of flatware should be from an established, successful, and enduring pattern. Choose a design that will add to and blend well with most decors and themes and that is well-crafted to project a professional quality image, as shown in Figure 3–6. Additional pieces in the pattern should be easily available when needed as replacements or for expansion. A very popular finish is 18/8 stainless, which contains 18 percent chrome and 8 percent nickel and has a lustrous finish.

Certain catered events may require a different or unique pattern that would complement the menu theme. There are also occasions when silverplate would be the service of choice. The caterer should be familiar with the pattern choices available at local full-service rental stores for those additional needs.

*Holloware*

Holloware creates an image of quality and establishes a positive impression when used in any foodservice or catered presentation. Holloware is available in both 18/8 stainless and silverplate finishes.

Figure 3–7 shows several holloware items that are typically used in catering: a punch bowl, wine coolers, ice bucket, and wine cooler stand. Figure 3–8 shows several different tray sizes that are often used in buffet service. Figure 3–9 shows two very popular service items, the coffee urn and chafing dish. The flexibility of using either electric or solid fuel adds to the versatility of these frequently

FIGURE 3–7
**Holloware** 5-gallon punch bowl, 1- and 2-bottle wine coolers, ice bucket, and wine cooler stand
*Courtesy of Oneida Foodservice*

FIGURE 3–8
**Holloware Serving Trays,** oval trays, round trays, square and oblong trays, serving bowl, and bread tray
*Courtesy of Oneida Foodservice*

FIGURE 3–9
**Electric Coffee Urn and Chafing Dish** The coffee urn and chafing dish can be used with electric heating element or with solid fuel
*Courtesy of Oneida Foodservice*

FIGURE 3–10
**Chaf-O-Matic™ Folding Chafing Dish**
*Courtesy of Oneida Foodservice*

used pieces of equipment. The Chaf-O-Matic™ folding chafing dish shown in Figure 3–10 is a lighter-weight chafing dish that is easily stored and conveniently transported with a faster setup time than the standard chafing dish. Also, the unit walls protect the heat source for additional safety during outdoor use.

Linen napkins folded in a distinct uniform pattern will further add to the professional look of the table settings. Napkin folds can range from the simple flat fold that is placed underneath the forks to any one of the more elaborate folds shown in Figure 3–11. The napkin can be placed in the center of a service plate; or if the first course, such as a salad, is to be present, the napkin would be placed above the first course. If a service plate is not used, the napkin can be in place of where the first course would be served.

**Napkin Presentation**

Fold the napkin in quarters with the four edges toward you.
Fold the edges up to form a triangle.

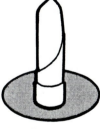

Bird of Paradise

Fold the left and right points of the triangle to the center, then fold the extended points under.

Lift the center and hold the base, then pull the four napkin edges out of the center to create the bloom.

Fold the napkin in half diagonally forming a triangle. Fold one-fourth of the base edge of the napkin up, forming a cuff.

Turn the napkin over. Carefully roll left to right. Tuck the remaining corner inside the cuff to hold the candle firm.

Position the candle with the highest point of the napkin facing you.

Candle

FIGURE 3–11 **NAPKIN FOLDS**
*Courtesy of Artex International*

*(Text continues on p. 75.)*

Opera Fan

Fold the napkin in half. Fold the width into accordion folds leaving the last 4 inches flat.

Fold the accordion in half with the folds on the outside; the 4-inch flat will protrude from the center.

Create a stand by folding the 4-inch flat diagonally in half from the open corner toward the folded edge. Stand the napkin on its edge letting the folds fan out.

Peak

Fold the napkin toward one end into quarters. Fold the right and left edge under and toward you, creating a triangle at the top of the napkin.

Roll the right and left edge up to the base edge of the triangle. Fold the right and left roll to the top point of the triangle.

Turn the fold over, standing the triangle point up with the open edge facing you.

Flame

Fold all corners of a flat napkin to the center.

Fold the bottom half under the top half.

Fold the right half over the left half.
Turn the napkin clockwise to create a diamond.

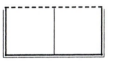 Roll the top layer toward the center, forming a band. Turn the second layer under to form a second band. Fold the left- and right-hand edges under.

 Fold the napkin in half with the edges at the bottom.

 Accordion pleat from right to left.

Goblet Fan

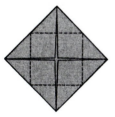 Fold the bottom third up.  Insert into goblet and spread pleat to form fan.

Fold all four corners of a flat napkin to the center; then fold four points again to the center.

Rose

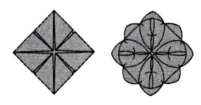 Turn the napkin over and fold four points again to the center pressing all folds tightly. Turn napkin to form a diamond. Use one hand to hold two points at the front center of the napkin and with the other hand reach under the napkin at that point and pull up flap. Repeat at the three other corners. Holding the center points, reach under the napkin between the petals and pull out the additional flaps.

Trifold

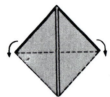

Fold the napkin in half diagonally forming a triangle with the folded edge away from you. Fold the far left- and right-hand corners of the triangle toward you to the bottom point.

Fold the napkin in half, bringing the bottom point under to meet the top point. Lift the napkin at the center to stand upright on the two side edges.

Cardinal Hat

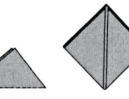

Fold the napkin in half diagonally, forming a triangle. Fold the left- and right-hand corners of the triangle to the top.

Turn the napkin over so that no folds are visible. Fold the bottom tip of the triangle partway up and fold the point down.

Fold the right side over the left, making a circle. Tuck one end of the triangle into the other. Place the cardinal hat in an upright position and flare out points slightly.

Crown

Fold the napkin in half diagonally, forming a triangle with the folded edge toward you. Fold the left- and right-hand corners of the triangle to the top, forming a diamond.

Fold the bottom point two-thirds of the way to the top point and fold the bottom point back again to the base line. Turn the far corners back, tucking them into one another to form a round base. Stand the napkin upright and flair out the two top corners to form the crown.

Fold the napkin in quarters forming a diamond with the open edges at the top. Roll the first layer of the napkin toward you to the center.

Tuxedo

Fold the second layer toward you and under the first—DO NOT ROLL. Leave the same width of napkin showing as the rolled edge.

Fold the next layer of napkin away from you and under the second, leaving the same width showing as the other two folds. Turn the napkin clockwise to form a square. Fold under the right and left edges to the center of the back.

---

## Buffet Setup

The following guidelines should be considered when setting up a buffet:

1. Arrange the buffet table(s) comfortably in the room. Guests should be able to move around easily. The table(s) should not be too large for the room. Always prepare a floor plan diagram with the room dimensions and table placements, as discussed in chapter 2.

2. Preparing a buffet table usually requires three tablecloths. One is draped over the front of the table reaching approximately 2 inches above the floor. The second is draped over the back of the table, again reaching approximately 2 inches above the floor. The tablecloths are best secured in place with masking tape. The third table cloth is draped in the usual manner, covering part of the first and second tablecloths. Also, table skirting can be used in different style and pattern selections, as discussed in chapter 2.

3. Layering the buffet table can create an exciting visual display and can be easily accomplished with the use of books, boxes, display steps, or step risers, as shown in Figure 3–12. Simply place these on the buffet table and then cover by neatly draping them with a tablecloth. Several varying heights can be created on one or more buffet tables and topped with decorative food platters. Round or oval mirror shapes in triple tiers can also be used for a more dramatic food presentation, such as with fancy desserts, as shown in Figure 3–13.

4. The buffet should be set up in the following order:
   a. serving plates
   b. bread basket and butter plate

FIGURE 3–12
**STEP RISERS**
*Courtesy of Carlisle Foodservice Products*

FIGURE 3–13
**MIRACRYL™ TRIPLE TIERS**
*Courtesy of Carlisle Foodservice Products*

c. salad bowl

d. vegetable bowl

e. potatoes

f. main item platter

This arrangement presents the food items in their natural order and allows the guests to fill their plates first with the items costing less, leaving just enough space for an adequate portion of the main item. A diagram (see Figure 3–16) should always be drawn when planning a buffet arrangement.

**5.** Keep the food safe. The food items should be kept at their recommended safe food temperatures. Keep hot food at 140°F or above and cold food at 41°F or below, as discussed in chapter 1. If foods are allowed to reach bacteria-incubating temperatures, they can cause foodborne illness.

**Hot foods:** Keep hot by using chafing dishes.

**Cold foods:** Keep cold by filling large pans, such as roasting pans, with crushed or small cubed ice; then place as many platters and bowls in the pans as will comfortably fit. The ice may be covered with fresh parsley or other greens. A round portable buffet bar, as shown in Figure 3–14, can also be used. The bottom of the bar, which is insulated, is filled with ice and maintains a long-lasting cold temperature.

FIGURE 3–14
**THE CAMBARREL™**
*Courtesy of Cambro Manufacturing Company*

FIGURE 3–15 **HOT OR COLD WELL BUFFET**
*Courtesy of Bon Chef*

Another option is to use a hot or cold well buffet table, as shown in Figure 3–15. The portable steam or cold buffet table adds safety and flexibility to any event. The buffet is also equipped with angled risers for easier serving and better display as the food is slanted toward guests.

6. The buffet should always have an appetizing appearance. This is accomplished by keeping the trays and bowls refilled. When the food item becomes three-quarters empty, replace or remove and place in a smaller tray or bowl, thus ensuring a fresh and full appearance.

The average single-line buffet can comfortably accommodate fifty to seventy-five guests within 15 to 20 minutes, with an average of three to four guests per minute going through the line. The speed at which the line moves will be determined by the variety of foods being served and how ornately they are presented. The greater the variety of foods and the more lavishly displayed, the more time needed for guests to make selections. A double-sided buffet, as shown in Figure 3–16, will obviously be able to accommodate twice the number of guests within the same time frame.

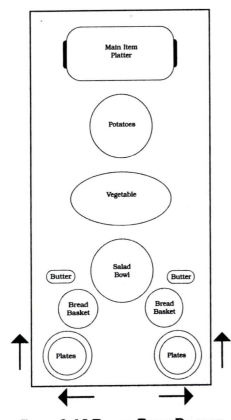

FIGURE 3–16 **BUFFET TABLE DIAGRAM**
(Utilizing both sides of the table)

**Overview**

This chapter explains all of the important functions that are critical to a catered event's success. It introduces what the caterer should look for when recruiting people to serve food and beverages, along with the importance of training and developing a competent and professional service staff. The methods of serving food for a catered event, which include butler service, American service, Russian service, French service, and buffet, are simply defined and explained. The traditional rules that are followed by professional waitstaff are listed, as is the correct procedure for handling trays.

The importance of being prepared when an unexpected emergency occurs is briefly focused upon with several examples. Specifics regarding table settings, salt and pepper shakers, and rolls and butter are defined. The value of selecting the dinnerware and flatware that best complement the menu is discussed, as are specifics on dinnerware shape, design, and color. Holloware used for catering and decorative napkin folds are explained and illustrated. Finally, the guidelines for setting up a buffet are presented, from arranging the buffet table to properly placing and displaying the food.

### Discussion Questions and Exercises

1. Describe the type of people that would need to be recruited for successfully serving food at a catered event.
2. What should be discussed with the service staff just prior to serving the food?
3. Discuss the five different methods of serving food for a catered event and explain when each one would be used.
4. List the ten rules for serving food and beverages.
5. Explain how to correctly lift a tray.
6. How many guests can one person comfortably serve?
7. Discuss some of the emergencies that can occur at a catered event and how the caterer should be prepared to handle them.
8. Set a table for dinner taken from a theme menu in chapter 6.
9. How many salt and pepper shakers should be put on a table?
10. What are three ways that rolls and butter can be served?
11. Explain how to choose dinnerware. Be specific about the different shapes and designs.
12. What should be considered when selecting flatware?
13. Define 18/8 stainless.
14. Give several examples of holloware and when it might be used.
15. Demonstrate six different napkin folds by using a linen napkin.
16. What is meant by layering a buffet table?
17. Explain the order in which a buffet should be set up.
18. How many guests per minute can go through the average single-line buffet?

# 4

# Kitchen Production

## Learning Objectives

After reading this chapter and completing the discussion questions and exercises, you should be able to

1. Understand recipe costing.
2. Prepare and use a food production and portion control chart.
3. Calculate an amount to prepare count.
4. Understand serving times and scheduling.
5. Understand how a dish-up serving line functions.
6. Know the procedures for maintaining portion control.
7. Set up a service table.
8. Know what to look for when inspecting an off-premise catering site.
9. Understand how to test recipes and convert the number of servings.
10. Determine what to order by comparing a current inventory with what is needed.

**Introduction**

Successful food preparation requires a complete understanding of the recipes, preparation, and cooking times. A production and dish-up procedure should be established and made easy to follow for every function. A critical factor to the success of any catered event is the ability to correctly forecast the amount of time that it will take to get the whole job done. The caterer must also know what will be required in terms of facilities, equipment, and kitchen and service staff skill levels. As the caterer's experience grows, so will his or her knowledge of preparation and cooking times, a kitchen's capacity, and the competency and speed at which the staff can perform.

Through the effective use of controls, the caterer will be able to maintain food production with a minimal amount of waste, eliminate the possibility of overproduction, and ensure that enough food will be prepared. Menu and portion costs will be able to be quickly identified through the use of an appropriate software application tied to current inventory and suppliers' pricing.

## The Menu Cost

A catering menu price is based upon standardized recipe costs. These costs are established by determining specific portion sizes. The cost of all the ingredients needed for each recipe within the menu and the number of portions that each recipe can produce will then determine individual portion costs. This enables the caterer to identify a given profit margin. It also allows for flexibility in dealing with a customer who may have a limited budget or is competitively comparing prices from other caterers. That flexibility can be demonstrated by changing a portion size to lower the cost. For example, a potential customer may have initially wanted a 12-ounce portion of prime rib, but may find an 8-ounce portion served au jus over a slice of French bread acceptable at a lower price. Another possibility might be to pair items in smaller portions, such as a 4-ounce steak with a 4-ounce breast of chicken. There are many possibilities once the portion costs are identified and the options are clearly explained to the customer.

The caterer should be able to quickly access current food pricing from his or her suppliers and be able to promptly identify menu and recipe costs. This can be accomplished through the use of any one of a number of computer software programs designed for recipe costing. (Refer to Appendix A, *ChefTec Software*.)

## Food Production

A food production and portion control chart, shown in Figure 4–1, should be prepared once the menu is determined and the date and time that the food is to be served are scheduled. Identifying whether the event will be full-service or buffet will allow the caterer to schedule the appropriate number of serving and kitchen staff. When preparing for a buffet, the food will be served in bowls and on trays instead of being individually plated and served to guests.

The food production and portion control chart functions as follows:

**Menu Items**—as planned with the customer.

**Quantity Prepared**—determined by the amount to prepare count. When the items are preplated, such as the cucumber shrimp boats and the hearts of romaine in the Figure 4–1 example, then the exact number can be prepared. For items such as sweet potatoes and buttered asparagus, the portion sizes must initially be determined. The yield will be determined by the recipe ingredients, preparation, and cooking procedures. Institutional foodservice packaging by weight, portion size, and quantity may provide easy portion control. For example, the 5-ounce chicken breasts may be portion packed from the supplier, making portion control simple. According

| NAME OF FUNCTION _Sanders Anniversary Party_ | | | PAGE _1_ OF _1_ | | |
|---|---|---|---|---|---|

NAME OF FUNCTION _Sanders Anniversary Party_  
PREPARED BY _The Chef_  
GUARANTEED GUEST COUNT _65_  
AMOUNT TO PREPARE COUNT _72_

☑ FULL SERVICE ☐ BUFFET  
CONFIRMED COUNT _70_

PAGE _1_ OF _1_  
DATE _August 2, XXXX_  
DAY _Sunday_  
FOOD SERVED TIME _7:00 pm_

| MENU ITEMS | QUANTITY PREPARED | PORTION SIZE | POSSIBLE NUMBER | AMOUNT LEFT | AMOUNT USED |
|---|---|---|---|---|---|
| Cucumber Shrimp Boats | _72_ / | 1 each | 72 | Weight ___ / 2 Portions | 70 |
| Hearts of Romaine w/Dates & Roasted Walnuts | _72_ / | 1 each | 72 | 2 | 70 |
| Chicken Kiev | 22½ lbs / 360 ozs | 5 oz. | 72 | 10 ozs / 2 | 70 |
| Sweet Potatoes on a Pineapple Ring | 18 lbs / 288 ozs | 3½ oz. | 82 | 21 ozs / 6 | 76 |
| Buttered Asparagus | 18 lbs / 288 ozs | 3 oz. | 80 | 13 ozs / 4 | 76 |
| Three Layer Strawberry & Cream Sheetcake | 1 / Sheet Cake | 2 x 2 cut | 96 | 14 | 82 |
| | ___ / | | | | |
| | ___ / | | | | |
| | ___ / | | | | |
| | ___ / | | | | |
| | ___ / | | | | |
| | ___ / | | | | |
| | ___ / | | | | |
| | ___ / | | | | |
| | ___ / | | | | |
| | ___ / | | | | |
| | ___ / | | | | |
| | ___ / | | | | |
| | ___ / | | | | |
| | ___ / | | | | |
| | ___ / | | | | |

FIGURE 4–1 **FOOD PRODUCTION AND PORTION CONTROL CHART**

to the recipe, the sweet potatoes will be portioned by using a pastry bag. A portion scale can be used to determine the correct amount for the sample plate, but it cannot guarantee the exact amount for every plate. Therefore, preparing a bit extra to cover any small degree of variance would be appropriate. The same is true for the buttered asparagus. The three-layer sheet cake would typically be ordered through a bakery with the customer being charged for the whole cake. When a special occasion cake is the dessert, some guests will request a second piece, and the customer may appreciate having some cake to take home.

**Portion Size**—is normally identified within a given recipe. A customer may request a larger or smaller size, depending upon the nature of the guests' appetites and the customer's budget. The portion size is shown as an individual serving, such as 1 each, 5 ounces, or 2-inch by 2-inch cut. When ounces are used, the quantity prepared will be converted to ounces, as shown with the sweet potatoes and buttered asparagus (converted from 18 pounds to 288 ounces).

**Possible Number**—will be determined by dividing the quantity prepared by the portion size. The example of sweet potatoes would be 288 ounces divided by 3 1/2 ounces (288 ÷ 3.5 = 82.3 rounded to 82).

**Amount Left**—is calculated by weighing the food that has not been used, then dividing that amount by the portion size. Again, in the example of the sweet potatoes, 21 ounces or 6 portions were left (21 ÷ 3.5 = 6).

**Amount Used**—is determined by subtracting the amount left from the possible number. The amount used for the entrée would be the number to use for the confirmed count.

*Amount to Prepare*

The amount to prepare count is derived by multiplying the guaranteed guest count by the percentage over that count that the caterer has agreed to prepare, then adding that number to the guaranteed guest count in anticipation of more people attending the event. If the guaranteed guest count were 65, as shown in Figure 4–1, with a 10 percent over, then the amount to prepare would be 72 (65 × 10% = 6.5 rounded to 7, 65 + 7 = 72).

The caterer would list all the menu items and determine the quantities to prepare based upon the amount to prepare count and the portion sizes. This enables the caterer to identify the correct quantities of food to order and purchase. Use of the chart ensures that enough food is prepared, with a minimal amount of waste during the production and serving process, and that each guest will receive the same amount of food. When the amount of food left is weighed, converted to portions, and subtracted from the possible number of servings, a final confirmed count can be determined. Of course, there may be some variances for the occasional accident when a plate gets dumped or a guest asks for an additional dessert or skips part of the meal.

When a full-service catered event is planned, the caterer should carefully review the scheduled serving times with the customer. Catered events can include a wide range of activities from speakers and presentations to entertainment and dancing. Therefore, the customer should determine the order of activities and the time for each meal course to be served. As a general rule, guests like to have enough time to comfortably eat and visit with other guests at their tables. It takes an average of 10 to 20 minutes to serve, eat, and remove each course, depending upon the nature of the course. Obviously a small salad will be consumed faster than a bowl of hot soup.

To help coordinate times and keep everything on schedule, the caterer may want to use a two-way radio, as shown in Figure 4–2. For large events as well as off-premise catering, a two-way radio provides instant communication at the push of a button. Either a headset with swivel boom microphone or an earphone and clip-on push-to-talk microphone allows staff to communicate without disturbing guests. Multiple channels and channel scan capability enables the caterer to monitor two different areas, such as the service staff and valet parking attendants, or communicate simultaneously with both the kitchen and service staff.

## Serving Times

FIGURE 4–2
**TWO-WAY RADIO, SPIRIT M. SERIES**
*Courtesy of Motorola*

## Dish-Up

When cold foods are served, such as the cucumber shrimp boats in the Figure 4–1 example, it is appropriate to prepare, plate, and refrigerate them until ready to serve. When hot foods are served, such as the entrée and main course, a dish-up serving line should be used, as shown in Figure 4–3. This allows the food to be quickly plated and placed on serving trays for the service staff to serve guests. The dish-up serving line is often a single- or double-sided steam table. For large events, several lines would be used. For off-premise catering, chafing dishes could be set up on one or more banquet tables, which would become a dish-up serving line.

The number of guests attending the catered event and the complexity of the entrée and main course will determine the number of

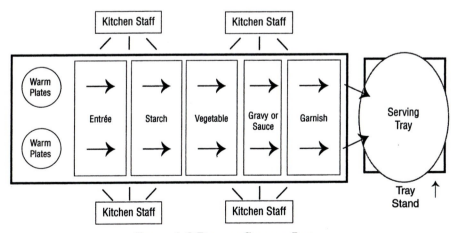

FIGURE 4–3 **DISH-UP SERVING LINE**

lines as well as the number of kitchen staff to schedule. An experienced kitchen staff of three can dish up 100 plates in 10 to 15 minutes on a single-sided line.

**Portion Control**

To ensure that the correct amount of food is served in the correct way during the dish-up process, the following procedures should be followed:

FIGURE 4–4
**PORTION CONTROL SCALE**
*Courtesy of Pelouze*

—For items such as prime rib and roasts that are portioned by the ounce, a portion scale (Figure 4–4) should be used. After the item is cut and weighed to the correct portion size, a meat slicer may be used to regulate the size of the cut into the exact number of ounces required.
—For other meats, poultry, or fish, purchase pre-portioned items when possible, such as 10-ounce steaks, 5-ounce boneless-skinless chicken breasts, or 8-ounce halibut steaks.
—For items such as mashed potatoes, dressing mix, or ice cream, use a scoop with the correct capacity size (Figure 4–5).
—For food in small pieces (e.g., peas, cut carrots, or corn), use a slotted spoon or spoodle (Figure 4–6) for the correct portion size.
—For gravies and sauces, use a ladle with the exact ounce capacity (Figure 4–7).

Food portion and production control is easy once a procedure is followed.

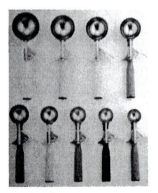

FIGURE 4–5
**SCOOP SIZES**
*Courtesy of the Vollrath Company*

### Scoop Sizes

| Capacity | Measure | Size | Color |
|----------|---------|------|-------|
| 5 1/3 oz. | 2/3 cup | 6 | White |
| 4 oz. | 1/2 cup | 8 | Gray |
| 3 1/4 oz. | 1/3 cup | 10 | Ivory |
| 2 2/3 oz. | 5 tbsp. | 12 | Green |
| 2 oz. | 4 tbsp. | 16 | Dark Blue |
| 1 5/8 oz. | 3 tbsp. | 20 | Yellow |
| 1 1/3 oz. | 2 2/3 tbsp. | 24 | Red |
| 1 oz. | 2 tbsp. | 30 | Black |
| 3/4 oz. | 1 tbsp. | 40 | Orchid |

FIGURE 4–6
**SPOODLE SIZES**
*Courtesy of the Vollrath Company*

### Spoodle sizes

| Capacity | Color |
|----------|-------|
| 2 oz. | Blue |
| 3 oz. | Ivory |
| 4 oz. | Gray |
| 6 oz. | Teal |
| 8 oz. | Orange |

**Ladle Sizes**

| Capacity | Color |
|----------|--------|
| 1 oz. | Black |
| 2 oz. | Blue |
| 3 oz. | Ivory |
| 4 oz. | Gray |
| 5 oz. | Teal |
| 6 oz. | Orange |

FIGURE 4–7
**LADLE SIZES**
*Courtesy of the Vollrath Company*

**Service Table**

A service table is typically used for beverages and other miscellaneous items, as shown in Figure 4–8. For off-premise or large catered events, it would be set up on one or more banquet tables in the kitchen or to one side of the dining area. When used in the dining area, the table would be conveniently accessible but placed near a wall, covered with a tablecloth, and skirted. Additional chilled wines or other items can be stored underneath. Tray stands covered with liners may also be used, as shown in Figure 4–9.

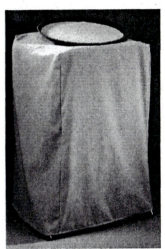

FIGURE 4–9
**TRAY STAND LINER**
*Courtesy of Artex International*

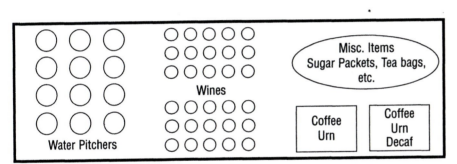

FIGURE 4–8 **SERVICE TABLE**

**Off-Premise Catering**

Off-premise catering involves the added challenge of a new and different working environment. Therefore, the caterer must be prepared to thoroughly inspect the catering site to ensure that the event will flow smoothly, noting the following areas of concern:

—The location of the kitchen (if one is to be used) and the serving area.
—The kitchen layout and capacity: refrigeration, ovens, work space, and dish-up arrangement.
—The layout and access of the serving area.
—The convenience of loading and unloading off-premise catering equipment, and access for delivery vehicles.
—The availability of parking for staff.
—The arrangements for clean-up and trash removal.

—The capability to adequately meet the needs for electricity, heating, ventilating and air conditioning, drinking water, and toilet facilities.

Off-premise catering could include such sites as private homes, offices, parks, museums, historical places, a beach, or any of a countless number of unusual and unique locations. Therefore, a site inspection by the caterer along with the customer is the first step in planning off-premise catering.

**Recipe Testing**

Successful food preparation can be simple and easy, but it requires a complete understanding of the recipes and preparation and cooking times. The caterer should test new recipes before the catered event by preparing small amounts. He or she may also want to have the customer taste the food and see a sample presentation for final approval. This reduces the possibility of any unpleasant surprises on the day of the catered event.

**Recipe Scaling**

The recipes in chapter 6 are designed to yield six servings, except the wedding menu, which is designed for twenty-five servings. The number of servings required will vary with every catered event. Therefore, it is necessary to know how to scale the recipes to the needed amounts in order to accommodate the number to be served. The following example, using a recipe from the "Lovers' Night" theme in chapter 6, will demonstrate just how easy it is to scale a recipe:

### Chicken Kiev, serves 6 as per recipe

| | |
|---|---|
| 6 (5-ounce) | chicken breasts, boneless, skinless |
| 1/2 cup | flour |
| 1 teaspoon | salt |
| 1 teaspoon | ground white pepper |
| 2 tablespoons | garlic, minced |
| 1/3 cup | parsley, chopped (approximately 1/4 bunch) |
| 1/2 cup (1 stick) | unsalted butter |
| 4 | eggs |
| 1/2 cup | bread crumbs, dry prepared |
| 3/4 cup | vegetable oil |

The food production and portion control chart in Figure 4–1 shows an amount to prepare of 72. This recipe would be increased by multiplying by 12 (6 x 12 = 72). So, a mathematic conversion would translate into the following:

### Chicken Kiev, serves 72

| | |
|---|---|
| 72 (5-ounce) | chicken breasts, boneless, skinless |
| 6 cups | flour |
| 1/4 cup | salt |

| 1/4 cup | ground white pepper |
| 1 1/2 cups | garlic, minced |
| 4 cups | parsley, chopped (approximately 3 bunches) |
| 6 cups (12 sticks) | unsalted butter |
| 4 dozen | eggs |
| 6 cups | bread crumbs, dry prepared |
| 4 1/2 pints | vegetable oil |

The professional chef will recognize that when certain recipes are significantly increased in size, the quantity of spices and seasonings may have to be adjusted downward so as not to be too overpowering. Every recipe component, such as marinating, cooking, or simmering, would need to be reviewed and taste-tested.

The preparation may need to be done in batches, especially when cooking (frying) in oil. Also, the quantity of eggs for the egg wash and the vegetable oil used in cooking would need to be adjusted downward, as less would be needed.

If the amount to prepare was a number that was not easily multiplied, then the simplest method to use would be as follows:

1. Convert the cups, pints, or pounds to ounces (refer to Figure 4–10).
2. Divide by 6 (the number of servings the recipe yields) in order to determine the quantity (number of ounces) for one serving.
3. Multiply by the number of guests.
4. Convert ounces back to cups, pints, or pounds.

The appropriate software application can handle the process of scaling recipe quantities, recipe and menu costing, and recipe nutritional analysis with speed and accuracy. Refer to Appendix A for an introduction to *ChefTec Software*.

## Determining What to Order

When the recipe amounts are finalized, it is time to prepare an order sheet. Some of the items to be used may already be in the caterer's existing inventory. Once the caterer compares the current

| | | | | | |
|---|---|---|---|---|---|
| 3 teaspoons (tsp) | = | 1 tablespoon (tbsp) | 1 pint | = | 16 ounces |
| 1 tablespoon | = | 1/2 ounce | 16 ounces | = | 1 pound (lb) |
| 2 tablespoons | = | 1 ounce | 2 pints | = | 1 quart (qt) |
| 16 tablespoons | = | 1 cup | 1 quart | = | 1/4 gallon, 32 ounces |
| 1 cup | = | 8 ounces | 1 gallon | = | 128 ounces |
| 2 cups | = | 1 pint | 16 cups | = | 1 gallon |

FIGURE 4–10 **WEIGHTS AND MEASURES**
This chart can be referenced when scaling recipe amounts

inventory with what is needed for each recipe, an order sheet can be prepared, as shown in Figure 4–11. The actual purchasing function can range from a simple telephone order to a several-step process that involves a bidding procedure from suppliers, so it is important to allow enough time to process the order. Every foodservice/catering business should have a set procedure for all purchasing, along with a software application that identifies inventory items, quantities, and current pricing.

## Order Sheet

**Grocery Items**

_____
_____
_____
_____
_____
_____
_____
_____

**Meat/Fish/Poultry**

_____
_____
_____
_____
_____
_____
_____
_____

**Spices & Seasonings**

_____
_____
_____
_____
_____
_____

**Produce**

_____
_____
_____
_____
_____
_____

**Bakery**

_____
_____
_____
_____
_____
_____

**Dairy**

_____
_____
_____
_____
_____
_____

**Beverage**

_____
_____
_____
_____
_____
_____

**Frozen**

_____
_____
_____
_____
_____
_____

**Miscellaneous**

_____
_____
_____

FIGURE 4–11 **ORDER SHEET**

The kitchen is at the center of the catering function. It is where raw and prepared products are cooked and assembled into finished items that are served to guests. The caterer must be able to manage the kitchen operation, which begins with an understanding of what is actually needed in terms of preparation, cooking, holding, and serving equipment. The caterer must also be able to set forth and work with an established procedure for timely food production and portion control.

Portion control must be consistent so that every guest receives the identical amount of food and the projected profit margin is realized. This can be accomplished with the use of a food production and portion control chart.

Recipe knowledge is accumulated through experience, and every new recipe should be tested before its actual use. When scaling recipes, there are many excellent software programs that will convert recipes upward or downward as needed along with identifying yields and, when tied to inventory pricing, portion costs. The caterer should always have the most up-to-date pricing from his or her suppliers.

Off-premise catering will require the caterer to be extremely attentive to all of the additional requirements needed to successfully service the event, from the legal issues of permits discussed in chapter 1 to the operational complexities that may exist in an out-of-the-ordinary location. The caterer must be able to deal with every challenge that off-premise catering presents.

## Discussion Questions and Exercises

1. Explain how a menu is priced.
2. Why is it important to be able to quickly determine a menu's portion costs?
3. What is the function of a food production and portion control chart?
4. Create a food production and portion control chart for a menu selected from chapter 6, with a guaranteed guest count of 120 and a 10 percent over amount. Refer to Appendix B for a blank chart.
5. What procedure should be followed when determining serving times?
6. Explain how a dish-up serving line works by using the menu selected in question 4.
7. How might a dish-up serving line be different for off-premise catering?
8. How many plates can an experienced kitchen staff of three dish up in 10 to 15 minutes on a single-sided dish-up serving line?
9. List and explain the procedures for dishing up five different types of food that will ensure that a correct amount of food is served.
10. What is the purpose of a service table?

**11.** List five different off-premise catering locations.

**12.** When evaluating an off-premise catering site, what areas must be looked at and adequately addressed?

**13.** Why is it important to test new recipes?

**14.** Explain the procedure for converting a recipe from 6 servings to 136 servings.

**15.** What is the procedure for determining the correct quantities of supplies to order?

# 5

# *Beverages*

**Learning Objectives**

After reading this chapter and completing the discussion questions and exercises, you should be able to

1. Understand pairing beverages with food.
2. Know the types of beverage functions that a caterer would be asked to service.
3. Recognize the importance of knowing the laws that govern alcoholic beverage service.
4. Understand the fundamentals of winemaking.
5. Know the grapes that dominate the great wine lists of the world.
6. Understand the process of beer making.
7. Recognize the different types of beer.
8. Understand how distilled spirits are made.
9. Identify the most common distilled spirits.
10. Recognize the characteristics of different coffees.
11. Understand the process of making espresso.
12. Know the difference between regular tea and herbal tea.
13. Identify the items to stock for a basic beverage bar.
14. Identify the appropriate glassware to use when serving beverages.
15. Know the best temperatures at which to serve wine, beer, distilled spirits, coffee, and tea.

**Introduction**

There are many situations when beverages help to mark the events of our lives, such as the traditional toasting of the bride and groom with a glass of champagne, and the hot eggnogs served after a Christmas feast. Although there are a few rules that govern the beverage choice for such events, a caterer should be thoughtful and imaginative when creating a beverage menu. The modern rule of service is that the beverage should reflect the event and the people who are present as well as the customer's preference.

In the past decade, a change in social consciousness has produced a dramatic shift away from cocktails and high-alcohol libations to beverages with little or no alcohol. In fact, imported mineral waters and specialty coffees have become very significant alternatives for a more health-conscious and socially aware consumer. Moderate, responsible alcohol consumption is definitely in vogue, especially in light of today's tough drinking and driving laws. Concern for guests' safety, and laws regarding hosts' accountability have established the obligation of hosts to be responsible alcohol servers. Consequently, more attention is necessary in beverage selection. Quality is certainly more important than quantity! More than ever before, spirits and wines are carefully selected to accompany and enhance elegant dinners. Offering nonalcoholic beverage options, as well as traditional wines and spirits, is both smart and fashionable. A few ideas include pairing specialty coffees or espresso with dessert, serving a variety of flavored mineral waters or iced teas with hors d'oeuvres, and presenting sparkling cider in lieu of champagne for that celebratory toast.

The caterer is often asked for professional advice on selecting the proper beverages. Therefore, he or she should have a certain degree of expertise that will allow the customer to feel comfortable with suggestions. As the caterer's experience grows, so will his or her knowledge of beverage choices.

## Types of Beverage Functions

The beverage functions that the caterer will be asked to service will typically fall into the following categories:

—Cocktail reception that precedes a dinner being served. The reception time will usually be about 45 minutes to 1 hour, and hors d'oeuvres may also be served during that time.

—Hospitality suite during a convention. This operates as an "open house" for guests to come and go during a designated period of time, such as from 6:00 P.M. until midnight. These are hosted by businesses that want to have people attend a social gathering for networking and goodwill. Hospitality suites are set up in smaller private rooms within a hotel or resort or any other convenient location that will be within the legal licensing requirements.

—Wine and cheese tasting event to introduce new wines or to serve as a modified hospitality suite with a more limited time frame, such as between 4:00 P.M. and 6:00 P.M.

—Dinner wine service whereby one or more wines may be served with various courses during the dinner. The wine is poured by the waitstaff or by cocktail servers. The alternative would be to have the wine opened and preset on the tables for guests to serve themselves.

The bartenders and cocktail servers at these functions should be well trained, knowledgeable about the beverages they are serving, and able to relate well to guests.

The laws regarding serving alcoholic beverages may vary slightly from state to state. Therefore, the caterer should be totally familiar with the laws that govern alcoholic beverage service within the state in which he or she is doing business (as set forth in the requirements for an alcoholic beverage license). Figure 5–1 is an example of an application and authority to operate form, and Figure 5–2 is an example of what a caterer's license allows and requires.

**Alcoholic Beverage License**

OREGON LIQUOR CONTROL COMMISSION
APPLICATION AND AUTHORITY TO OPERATE

APPLICATION IS MADE FOR:

| | | |
|---|---|---|
| ____ Special Retail Beer | $10.00 per day ____ | |
| ____ Special Retail Wine | $10.00 per day ____ | |
| ____ Special Wine Auction | $10.00 per day ____ | |

| | | |
|---|---|---|
| ____ Community Event Dispenser | $25.00 per day ____ |
| ____ Special Dispenser | $25.00 per day ____ |
| ____ Special Event Winery | $10.00 per day ____ |
| ____ Special Event Grower | $10.00 per day ____ |
| ____ Special Wine Raffle | $10.00 per day ____ |

**APPLY AT LEAST 10 DAYS PRIOR TO EVENT**
Make Payment by Check or Money Order

1. Applicant _____ Phone _____

2. (For Licensees Only) Trade Name _____ License Type _____

3. Person responsible at the event _____ Phone _____

4. Mailing Address _____ City _____ Zip _____

5. Type of Event _____

6. Date(s) of event(s) _____ Hours of event(s) _____

7. Event address _____ City _____ Zip _____

8. Above Location is _____ within city limits _____ outside city limits

9. Boundaries of the area to be licensed: Inside Building _____ Outside Event _____

10. Expected attendance per day _____ Will minors attend? _____

11. Method of Supervision _____

12. I certify all information submitted is complete and correct to the best of my knowledge. I understand a false answer may be reason to deny this application.

Signature _____ Date _____

13. Authorization by property owner/operator. I own/control the property where this event will be held. I approve of the event, including service of alcoholic beverages as requested above.

Name (Please print) _____ Phone _____

Signature _____ Date _____

14. Recommendation of City Police Dept./County Sheriff's Office/Local Governing Body

_____ Grant _____ Acknowledge _____ Deny (Attach letter indicating grounds for denial.)

Approving Agency _____

Authorized Signature _____ Date _____

15. This authority valid when signed by an OLCC Representative.

License is _____ Granted _____ Refused

By _____ Title _____

Conditions/Restrictions: _____ Date _____

_____ Fee Paid _____

_____ Receipt # _____

Form 84545-478 (4/96)          SEE BACK FOR INSTRUCTIONS          APPLICANT'S COPY

FIGURE 5–1 LIQUOR LICENSE APPLICATION
*Courtesy of Oregon Liquor Control Commission*

## Caterer's License

**Caterer's License ...** A Caterer's Dispenser License allows a caterer to sell and serve distilled spirits, malt beverages, and wine at events where the caterer is serving food. A "caterer" must operate and clearly promote a catering business and contract with clients to provide food service at a variety of places other than a licensed business location. A caterer must have adequate kitchen facilities to prepare and cook regular meals. Typically, the kitchen and office comprise the licensed business location. A person may have a caterer's license without having any other liquor license or liquor business. The caterer may operate a permanent banquet location. However, at least 25 percent of the events the caterer serves must be at a variety of locations other than the banquet site. The cost of a caterer's license is $300.00 a year. It must be renewed annually.

**Food Service Requirements ...** The caterer must serve food at all events where alcoholic beverages are sold. When hard liquor is served at an event, either a regular meal or a variety of foods must be offered. A regular meal is defined as a complete meal requiring the use of dining implements for eating. Sandwiches and snack food do not qualify as a regular meal. A variety of foods includes desserts, casseroles, salads, and hors d'oeuvres. Some of the foods must be prepared and cooked by the caterer. If only beer and wine are served, the caterer must provide food items such as sandwiches and snack food at a minimum. The licensee must reasonably project and maintain at least a 25 percent ratio of food sales to total gross sales at all catered events where alcohol is served during the year. This annual ratio may not include food sales at events where no alcohol is served.

**Records ...** The caterer must keep a detailed record of the date, time, and location of each event where alcohol is served. The records must include food and alcoholic beverage sales amounts at the events. These records must be on file for two years. The licensee is also required to keep separate records of food sales at catered events where no alcohol is served.

**Servers/Bartenders ...** All servers of alcoholic beverages must be at least 21 years old. Servers must have valid OLCC service permits in order to sell and serve alcohol.

**Checking Identification—Minors ...** No one may provide alcoholic beverages to anyone under 21 years of age. If a person appears to be under 26 years old, servers must ask to see either a valid photo driver's license, an Oregon Division of Motor Vehicles I.D. Card or a valid passport. If one of these is not available, the customer must provide two pieces of identification: a descriptive piece of identification indicating the name, address, date of birth, physical description, and a signature, and a backup piece of identification with the person's name on it. They must also complete and sign an OLCC Statement of Age Card.

**Intoxicated Customers ...** No one is permitted to sell or serve alcoholic beverages to a person who is visibly intoxicated or under the influence of other drugs. The law also states that a server must make a good faith effort to remove the drink of a visibly intoxicated person. "Good faith effort" means placing your hand on the drink and trying to remove it. Or, if you have reason to believe that touching the patron's drink could cause a disturbance, you must make a verbal request for the drink. There are at least 50 signs of visible intoxication. For more information, please contact your local OLCC field office or call the OLCC Public Affairs Office.

**Civil Liability ...** Caterers with liquor licenses must maintain liquor liability insurance of $300,000 or a $300,000 bond with a corporate surety company.

**Hours of Sale ...** You may sell or serve alcoholic beverages from 7:00 A.M. to 2:30 A.M.

**Business Practices ...** When you will be catering a public event that will draw 300 or more people, contact the local OLCC office to discuss the event and your plans. As a licensee, you may not accept any financial aid, assistance, or gratuity from a wholesaler or manufacturer of alcoholic beverages. You must buy products at the same set prices paid by other licensed retailers. Wholesalers or manufacturers cannot offer you a price break, and you cannot ask for one. The wholesaler can buy back your unused alcoholic beverages only if you provide a "return of stock" letter from the Liquor Control Commission. Call you local OLCC office for details about the "return of stock" letter.

FIGURE 5–2 **CATERER'S LICENSE**
*Courtesy of Oregon Liquor Control Commission*

A little insight into the fundamentals of beverage making can help you select the appropriate beverage for any occasion. The flavors of various beverages will depend on the specific fruits and grains used, as well as the region of the world in which they were grown. Understanding the origins and ingredients of a given beverage will guide you when making your menu decisions.

*In the field.* Nature gives us the raw materials that make all beverages. Wine is made from grapes of the vinefera (fine wines) as well as other root stalks. Cereal grains are the basic requirement of most distilled alcohols, and from hardy green plants we derive coffee and tea. Most beverages include a high percentage of water. The source and quality of that water can also play a major role in the quality of the beverage.

*From grape to glass.* Grapes are harvested and crushed, creating juice. Fermentation is started by adding yeast to the natural sugar already in the juice. When the juice is fermented together in a vat with the skins and seeds, **red wine** results. This also imparts a quality known as tannin. Tannin comes from the seeds and skins. It makes red wine taste a little like dark tea, giving the taster an astringent sensation. Tannin creates the backbone that allows red wine to age more slowly than most white wines. Most red wines and some of the richer white wines (such as chardonnay) are aged in oak for a period of time, giving them a buttery, "oaky," rich quality. The kind of oak and the amount of barrel time can make a dramatic difference in the wine's taste. **White wine** is usually fermented without the skins and seeds. Typically, a white wine can (and should be) consumed at a younger age than a red. **Rosés** or **blush wines** are made by fermenting red grapes, skins, seeds, and juice, but only for a short time. This produces a light pink or salmon color and can yield a fruity, light wine. **Light whites** (such as Riesling) and rosés are aged for a short time in stainless steel to preserve their desired fruity, youthful qualities. **Sparkling wine** (technically called champagne only when it actually originates from the Champagne region of France) is frothy or "impetuous" due to a second fermentation process. This second fermentation is carefully initiated by the wine master and traps carbon dioxide bubbles in the bottle prior to corking. However, the actual winemaking process for sparkling wine is similar to that for the other wines and utilizes the same varieties of grapes.

**Note:** Keep in mind that there are no wine constants. In other words, the winemaking procedures presented are only guidelines. A knowledgeable winemaker may change a traditional technique to achieve a desired goal. Your goal as the professional caterer should be to expand your basic wine knowledge to accommodate a given situation. For example, what is a dessert wine and why is it so sweet?

There are thousands of different grape varieties in the world, and each has its own unique taste. By understanding the qualities of a few leading grape varieties, however, a caterer can command the necessary wine knowledge to impress even the most sophisticated wine drinkers. The following grape varieties dominate the great wine lists of the world, are found in all retail and grocery markets, and are on the lips of all good sommeliers:

### White Varieties

—**Chardonnay:** Dry (not sweet), big (rich, mouth-filling), oak (buttery).

—**Sauvignon Blanc:** Very dry, herbaceous (grassy), oak.

Generally, chardonnays and sauvignon blancs are more expensive and considered to be higher quality white wines.

—**Chenin Blanc:** Fruity, some residual sugar (aftertaste).

—**Gewürztraminer:** Somewhat dry, spicy (flavor).

—**Riesling:** Fruity, flowery, can be sweet.

These are more appropriately served during the day or to guests who want a light or sweeter wine.

### Red Varieties

—**Cabernet Sauvignon:** Dry, big, oak, long-lived.

—**Pinot Noir:** Dry, cherry (aftertaste), medium big, oak.

—**Gamay:** Dry, light (delicate), fruity.

—**Zinfandel:** Can produce excellent big wines, but we are most familiar with its light, fruity rosé wines.

Knowing the qualities of these grapes, the caterer makes an educated selection, based upon the customer's preferences and the catering menu. Most people have heard that white wine is served with seafood and chicken and red wine with meat. Generally, that is a good rule to follow. Ideally, the wine should complement the menu item, not dominate it. Consequently, dry wines are normally served directly with the entrée and sweeter wines are served with the dessert. Also, the time of day can certainly dictate one's choice. Even the most experienced wine drinker will prefer a light, fruity, or even blush wine during the lunch hour. If a wine is very big (rich, mouth-filling), it is perhaps best enjoyed on its own. Ultimately, if the caterer can describe the wine's qualities, the customer will appreciate both the caterer's expertise and the wine selection.

## Beers, Ales, and Lagers

***The process.*** Beer making begins with the malting process. First, barley is soaked in water for several days. This soft grain is then allowed to germinate and sprout during a three-week period. The germinated barley grain becomes malt, which contains an enzyme that has the ability to convert starch into sugars. The malt, mixed with cereal grains and more water, is then cooked. Hops are added for flavoring and texture. A pure yeast culture then starts the process of fermentation. It is now "beer" and goes through aging and filtering before the final bottling stage.

***The types.*** Most American beers are known as lagers. They are light-bodied, clear, and somewhat effervescent. Many brewers choose to call this light-style beer Pilsner, after the town of Pilsen in the former Czechoslovakia (known for its classical light beer). Bock beer is sweeter than lager and darker in color. Ale is made from malt with a slightly bitter quality and is more full-bodied and aromatic than beer. Stout is one of the "strongest" ales, dark in color, and high in alcohol. Porter ale is slightly less stout and has a bittersweet taste. Malt liquor is brewed like beer and usually has a higher alcohol content. It is often light in color. Sake is made from rice and is a specialized form of beer.

The caterer should be able to offer the customer a choice of bottled beer that includes premium domestic or imported, regular or light, local or regional microbrew, low-calorie, or nonalcoholic. Also, beer from the keg can be used for events that will cater to a larger number of people.

Distilled spirits are usually made from cereal grain or sugar. **Distilled Spirits** Mixed with water, the grain is made into a mash, then heated to release maltose, a form of sugar. Next, yeast is added to start the fermentation process, and it is distilled to increase its alcohol content.

Unique flavorings, colorings, and distinctive production methods generally finalize the diverse beverages that are tasted at cocktail hour. The following are the most common distilled spirits:

—**Bourbon:** American whiskey aged in charred-oak barrels.
—**Brandy:** Distilled from fruit.
—**Canadian Whiskey:** A blended whiskey imported from Canada.
—**Cognac:** Brandy from the Cognac region of France.
—**Cordials and Liqueurs:** These are made by adding flavorings from fruits, flowers, herbs, spices, roots, and seeds to a base of brandy or other spirits. They are sweetened with sugar and can be either low or high in alcohol content.
—**Gin:** A neutral grain spirit flavored with juniper berries and other aromatics. The name is derived from *genever*, the Dutch word for juniper.
—**Rum:** Distilled from sugar cane, sugar syrup, or molasses. Light rums are highly distilled to remove colors and increase alcohol content. Dark rums are distilled in pot stills and often aged in oak.
—**Rye:** Contains at least 51 percent rye grain.
—**Scotch:** Distilled from malted barley over open peat fires, giving it a distinctive "smokey" taste. Single-malt Scotch is very flavorful. Blended Scotch is lighter in style and more popular.
—**Vodka:** A clear, colorless, pure spirit usually made from grain (filtered through charcoal).
—**Whiskey:** Distilled from grain mash.

The coffee plant produces fruit called cherries. When the cher- **Coffee** ries turn dark red, they are ready to pick. Coffee beans are removed from inside the cherries and are then dried. **Arabica** and **robusta** are the two major classes of commercial coffee produced. Arabica is grown in high altitudes and is considered higher in quality, while being lower in caffeine. Robusta comes from hardier varieties of plants and is generally blended with arabicas to add body and flavor. The final step of roasting coffee beans brings out their inherent qualities such as aroma and flavor.

The types of roasts are as follows:

—**Light:** Light brown color, mild.
—**Medium:** Chestnut brown color, stronger flavor than light.
—**Full:** Rich, dark brown color with a touch of bitterness.
—**High:** Strong bittersweet aftertaste. Good for after-dinner coffees.
—**Italian:** The longest-roasted, strongest-flavored beans.

## *Espresso*

What started as a novelty in the 1950s is currently in vogue and continues to grow in popularity. *Espresso* is derived from an Italian verb meaning "to put under pressure"; the beverage name thus refers to the steam pressure utilized in the brewing method. Most small espresso machines cost under $200 and consist of a water reservoir, a receptacle to receive the extracted coffee, a metal filter basket for the coffee grounds, and a steam nozzle on the side or top for milk. Espresso machines require a finer grind and yield a smooth, yet strong, rich, heavy-bodied brew.

One can quickly become an expert in preparing caffe lattes (1/2 espresso and 1/2 steamed milk), cappuccinos (1/2 espresso, 1/4 steamed milk, and 1/4 foam), and mochas (1/3 espresso, 1/3 strong hot chocolate, and 1/3 steamed milk). By adding Italian syrups, a wide variety of flavors can be created, both hot and iced.

## *Tea*

Most people are aware of only a few different types of tea. Yet numerous varieties of tea can be found throughout the world. Many teas are named after the area they come from, such as Ceylon from Sri Lanka and Darjeeling from the Himalayas. Each tea has its own unique flavor, color, and aroma. Often, different teas are blended to create a new flavor. Earl Grey, English breakfast, and orange spice are examples of teas that are blends of different varieties. Regular tea tends to have less caffeine than coffee, and decaffeinated teas are also available. Herbal teas are 100 percent caffeine free. They are actually made from dried leaves and flowers that are steeped in boiling water.

## What to Stock

A busy caterer might want to keep a basic beverage stock at all times. When determining the inventory size and selection, the caterer should identify the type of customers, local and regional preferences, the type of catering, and the volume of business. The average customer's preference and budget will also be a guiding factor. Choices range from inexpensive brands referred to as well stock, medium-priced brands referred to as call brands, and expensive brands known as premium call. The following are some of the beverages and accessories that are recommended in chapter 6:

**Basic Beverage Bar**
—Angostura Bitters
—Beer (lager, light)
—Bourbon
—Brandy
—Coffee (regular and decaf)
—Gin
—Grenadine
—Juice (lime, orange, tomato)
—Lemons and limes (fresh)
—Liqueur (one or two of your favorites)
—Mineral water
—Rum
—Scotch
—Soda (club; regular, diet, and caffeine-free cola; ginger ale; lemon-lime)
—Sparkling water
—Stirrers
—Straws
—Sugar
—Tea (regular and decaf)
—Tequila
—Tonic water
—Vermouth (sweet and dry)
—Vodka
—Whiskey (blended and Irish)
—Wine (chardonnay, Riesling, cabernet sauvignon, sparkling wine)

If you really want to be prepared, add the following:

—Anejo Rum (aged)
—Beer (ale, porter, stout)
—Liqueurs (amaretto, Cointreau, crème de cacao, Crème de casis, crème de menthe, Grand Marnier, Kahlúa, Pernod)
—Port
—Sherry
—Wine (sauvignon blanc, Gewürztraminer, chenin blanc, late harvest Riesling or Sauternes (dessert wine), pinot noir, gamay or Beaujolais, rosé)
—Cinnamon sticks, nutmeg, cloves, cocktail olives and onions, maraschino cherries with stems.

**Note:** Most beverages lose either their color or quality when exposed to light, oxygen, or dramatic temperature changes. Therefore, it is best to keep your wine, spirits, tea bags, and coffee beans in a cool, dry, dark storage area.

**Glassware**

Most beverage glasses should be clear, as colored glassware may prevent a true investigation of the color of a particular beverage. Stems are a must for wineglasses, but are not appropriate for most cocktails, sodas, or water. When selecting a wineglass, make sure it

Wine          Champagne          Highball/Old Fashioned

Martini          Cordials          Beer

Nonalcoholic Beverages      Specialty Drinks      Frozen Drinks

FIGURE 5–3 **TYPES OF GLASSWARE**
*Courtesy of Oneida Foodservice*

has a bowl shape. This allows the wine to "breathe" and permits swirling the wine in the glass to test for "legs" (the rivulets of wine that slowly descend along the inside of the glass after swirling; sometimes regarded as an indication that the wine is full-bodied). Tall, narrow glassware called flutes are required for champagne and sparkling wine. This shape helps to capture the bubbles for a longer period of time. Refer to Figure 5–3 for an example of the various types of glassware.

## Temperature

Serving premium vodka at room temperature is like serving coffee lukewarm. It does not do the beverage justice. By knowing a few basic rules of beverage service temperatures, you can significantly enhance your guests' enjoyment.

**Wine.** White and sparkling wines should be served between 45°F and 50°F. Dessert wines should be served slightly cooler, at 40°F to 45°F. Figure 5–4 is an example of a wine cooler/bucket. Many experienced sommeliers recommend that a higher quality white wine (such as a notable chardonnay) be served at room temperature. This allows one to better experience the subtle flavors of these wines. Red wines are best enjoyed at a cool room temperature of between 60°F and 68°F. Again, there are exceptions, as some very light reds, like Beaujolais, should be served at 50°F to 55°F.

**Beer.** Surprisingly, the careful monitoring of beer temperature can be critical. Flat or cloudy beer is sometimes caused by serving it at too cool a temperature. If it is too warm, a beer will create foam and become what is known as "wild." Most beer should be served at 45°F, with ales and stouts served as high as 50°F to 55°F.

**Distilled spirits.** The key to finding the right service temperature for spirits is to ask the guest. If you know you have a vodka drinker, you may want to put a chill on the vodka bottle. Vodka and Dutch gin are best consumed after spending some time in the freezer.

**Coffee and tea.** The two main methods of making coffee are boiling (using boiling water to extract the flavor from the bean or ground coffee) and infusion (using water below the boiling point). The latter method is most often used today (through drip pots, percolators, and steeping). You should heat the brewing water to between 195°F and 205°F for the optimal extraction from the coffee grounds.

When preparing tea, it is best to pour boiling water over the tea and allow it to steep 3 to 5 minutes to develop its full flavor. Always serve your coffee and tea as hot as you or your guests can handle without danger of a burn. Figure 5–5 is an example of coffee and tea being served in clear cups.

FIGURE 5–4
**WINE COOLER/BUCKET**
*Courtesy of Cambro Manufacturing Company*

FIGURE 5–5
**COFFEE AND TEA CUPS**
*Courtesy of Oneida Foodservice*

**Open Up Your Senses**

Open up your senses and see what a wonderful experience a well-thought-out food and beverage presentation can be. First utilize your visual sense when approaching a beverage. Look for the signs that let you know it will be enjoyable. A glass of wine should be free of sediment and true to the color of its particular grape variety. A cup of coffee should be steaming and possess rich, dark characteristics. A full-bodied Jamaican rum should always be mahogany-colored. Beverages that look different from what you would expect may be objectionable.

Smell is the second critical step in assessing the quality of a beverage. Remember that your first smell will leave a lasting impression upon you. About wine, it is often said that "the nose is the price of admission." Take the time to reminisce about other experiences you have had with similar aromas. This will allow you to understand how a certain Riesling is described as having grapefruit or lemon tone or that a single-malt Scotch has a "peaty" quality.

Finally, the taste (and aftertaste) should reinforce the perceptions you received from sight and smell. Savor the beverage by swirling it around in your mouth. Remember that the tip of your tongue senses sweetness whereas the sides detect tartness or acid.

**Overview**

Many catering customers will naturally look to the caterer for a thorough understanding of beverages. They further expect the caterer to be able to offer suggestions for pairing wines with menu items. Along with traditional beverage choices, some customers will look for the innovative and creative. Therefore, the caterer should have a basic knowledge of the processes that are involved in producing beverages and the distinguishing qualities of the different varieties of each type of beverage. First and foremost is the winemaking process and the difference between red, white, rosé, and sparkling wines.

The choices in beers continue to expand with the ever-growing number of microbreweries, which offer many additional options to the catered event. Specialty coffees and teas continue to gain in popularity as do nonalcoholic beverages and specialty drinks.

The caterer should know his or her customer base when determining the type of beverage brands to stock. The caterer will also need to ensure that the bartenders and cocktail servers are well trained and knowledgeable about the beverages they are serving. Finally, the caterer should seek every opportunity to continually expand his or her knowledge of the growing choices of beverages and the many food pairing possibilities.

### Discussion Questions and Exercises

1. Give two examples of how beverages can successfully be paired with food items.
2. List and explain four beverage events that a caterer may have to service.

3. Why is it critically important for a caterer to thoroughly understand the laws regarding the service of alcoholic beverages?
4. Find out what is specifically required for a caterer to serve alcoholic beverages within your community.
5. List the steps that must be followed to apply for a license to serve alcoholic beverages within your community.

   **Note:** To answer questions 4 and 5, the student will need to check with the state liquor control agency along with city and county health departments for any rules and regulations that would apply.

6. What will affect the flavors of various beverages?
7. Explain the winemaking process.
8. What distinguishes red wine? white wine? rosés? sparkling wine?
9. Name the white varieties of grapes and define the qualities of each.
10. Name the red varieties of grapes and define the qualities of each.
11. Explain the beer-making process.
12. Name the different types of beer and define the qualities of each.
13. Explain the process for making distilled spirits.
14. List and define the eleven most common distilled spirits.
15. What are the two major classes of commercial coffee?
16. List the types of coffee roasts and define the qualities of each.
17. Explain the process for making espresso.
18. What are the ingredients for caffe lattes? cappuccinos? mochas?
19. What is the process for preparing tea?
20. How are herbal teas made?
21. What should the caterer consider when determining the inventory size and selection for a basic beverage stock?
22. List twenty items that might be included in a basic beverage stock.
23. Name the most popular types of glassware for beverage service.
24. Why should a wineglass have a bowl shape?
25. What are the best temperatures at which to serve wine? beer? distilled spirits? coffee and tea?

# 6

# Catering Menus and Recipes

**Learning Objectives**

After reading this chapter and being involved with the preparation, cooking, and serving of the menus, you should be able to

1. Identify all safe food temperature critical control points during the preparation, cooking, holding, and serving of food.

2. Make a preparation, cooking, and serving schedule based upon the time of the catering event, type of service, and quantity of food to be prepared.

3. Recognize that the type of service to be used will be an important factor when choosing foods that need to be quickly served or could be held for a period of time.

4. Assess a menu along with the quantity of food to be prepared in relation to the capability and capacity of the kitchen facility that is to be used.

5. Know how to develop menu ideas and themes from existing menus and recipes.

6. Recognize the importance of testing every new menu for food colors, tastes, textures, aromas, nutritional value, portion size, and beverage compatibility.

7. Create a menu that is pleasing to the catering customer, is cost efficient, and has a subtle uniqueness that sets it apart from the average menu.

**Introduction**

Each of the twenty-five catering menus presented in this chapter has been developed with a specific theme that could be adapted to a wide range of catered events. The beverage selections, which include wines as well as various alcoholic and nonalcoholic drinks, have all been appropriately paired with each menu.

The menus have been designed for color, taste, texture, aroma, nutritional value, and balanced portion sizes. The recipes were cooked individually and collectively within each menu theme. Preparation and cooking times are recorded for six servings throughout the chapter with the exception of the wedding menu, which serves twenty-five. Recipe quantities can be adjusted as explained in chapter 4 or by using the appropriate software application, such as *ChefTec Software* (see Appendix A). A designated serving schedule was picked for each menu and a preparation and cooking schedule set forth with service times, along with a few tips and details to enhance each menu. The recipes are written in easy-to-follow steps and are noted with a thermometer symbol for attention to safe food temperatures and a glove symbol for safe food handling.

The menu and recipe names can easily be changed to fit any given situation and to further personalize the service for the customer. The use of graphic designs, as shown with each menu theme, can economically be incorporated into the theme presentation through printed invitations, menus, and room decorations. The selection of graphics can range from the countless number of affordable design books and computer software programs to recruiting the talents of a graphic artist.

## Creating a Menu

When developing a catering menu and searching for creative ideas, it is important to consider the following:

—Catering themes can be simple but also unique with the right food combinations and serving presentations, along with the appropriate beverage choices. This often requires the joint effort of the catering manager, chef, and wine steward.

—Creative ideas often originate from existing menus that can be enhanced with a few slight changes to the recipes. Therefore, the caterer should constantly be looking for ways to improve a menu with something different as an added touch or an unusual accent to a recipe.

—A new menu should be tested in every detail by preparing and serving every item on the menu and checking for the compatibility of food colors, tastes, textures, aromas, nutritional value, and portion sizes, as well as beverage compatibility.

—Preparation and cooking times should be identified and further projected for the quantities to be prepared for the catering event.

—Type of service may become a factor when choosing foods that may need to be held for a period of time, such as buffets. The food must be able to retain a fresh appearance and quality taste.

—The capacity of the kitchen facility must be adequately assessed in terms of being able to accommodate the menu requirements. This is particularly critical for off-premise catering when another kitchen may be used for cooking, holding, and service. It is important to check for adequate refrigeration and freezer space and size and type of ovens, stovetops, grills, and any other kitchen equipment necessary to prepare, cook, hold, and serve the menu items.

# The Menus and Recipes

## Everyone Loves a Mystery

Consommé Royale

Fresh Fruit Salad with Raspberry Vinaigrette

Strawberry Sorbet

Roast Game Hen in Puff Pastry
with Pineapple Chutney

Classic Waldorf Salad

Chocolate Mousse

## Lovers' Night

Oysters Rockefeller*

Hearts of Romaine with Dates and Roasted Walnuts

Chicken Kiev

Sweet Potatoes on a Pineapple Ring

Buttered Asparagus

Trifle

* (alternative choice) Cucumber Shrimp Boats

# Rites of Spring

*Chilled Lemon Soup*

*Seasonal Greens with Mustard Poppy Seed Dressing*

*Grilled Salmon*

*Potatoes on the Half Shell*

*Carrots Vichy*

*Fresh Fruit Tarts*

# Mardi Gras

*Firecracker Salad*

*Shrimp Cocktail with Sauce Rémoulade*

*Chicken and Spicy Sausage Gumbo*

*Beignets with Powdered Sugar*

# People's Night In

*Consommé Spaghettini*

*Veal and Ham Florentine Pinwheels*

*Oven Roast Potatoes*

*Tomatoes Stuffed with Corn*

*Croissants and Butter*

*Broiled Pears*

# Olé

Nachos Grande

Gazpacho

Tamale Pie

Flan

# Concert in the Park

picnic

Assorted Fresh Fruit and Cheese

Finger Sandwiches and Chips

Four Bean Salad

Apricot Dessert Bars

# Boss's Night

What to prepare when you're entertaining the boss.

Crabmeat Cocktail with Savory Citrus Cocktail Sauce

Cream of Mushroom Soup

Tournedos Rossini

Baked Potato with Sour Cream and Chives

Green Beans Almondine

Baked Alaska

# Evening in Paris

*Pâté de Foie Gras with Fresh Fruit and Baguettes*

*Consommé Celestine*

*Raspberry Sorbet*

*Orange Spiced Roast Duck*

*Wild Rice Pilaf*

*Broccoli Florets with Sauce Hollandaise*

*Spinach Salad with Peanuts*

*Chocolate Truffle Cake*

# Meet Me at the Casbah

*Antipasto of Vegetables with Hummus,*

*Baba Ghanouj and Pita Bread*

*Tabbouleh*

*Lamb Brochette with Couscous*

*Baklava*

# School Is Out

*Stuffed Celery Sticks*

*Hot Smoked Turkey with Provolone*

*Snowballs*

# It's Your Birthday

*Caesar Salad*

*Baked Halibut Edward*

*Brabant Potatoes*

*Tomato Provençale*

*Birthday Cake (your favorite choice)*

# Irish Lullaby

*Dublin Potato Salad*

*Irish Stew*

*Raisin Bread Pudding and Irish Whiskey Accent*

*Soda Bread and Butter*

# A Touch of Venice

*Antipasto*

*Minestrone Soup*

*Italian Bread and Sweet Cream Butter*

*Sausage and Spinach Lasagna*

*Fried Creams*

# Backyard Barbecue

Roasted Corn and Red Pepper Salad

**Mixed Grill:**

Garlic and Fresh Mint Lamb Chops

Beer-Basted Flank Steak

Honey Dijon Chicken

Melon Surprise

# Wedding Bells

Wedding Reception serves 25

**Assortment of hors d'oeuvres buffet style**

Fresh Vegetables and Dip

Fresh Fruit Platters

Cheese Trays and Cracker Baskets

Pasta Salad

Swedish Meatballs

Quiche Lorraine

Teriyaki Chicken Wings

Shrimp Rumaki

Stuffed Mushrooms

Wedding Cake (your choice)

# Flower Drum Song

*Japanese*

*Sunomono*

*(Marinated Cucumber & Bay Shrimp Salad on a bed of glass)*

*Vegetable Sushi, Maki Style*

*Teriyaki Salmon with Steamed Rice and Snow Peas*

*Coconut Custard with Plum Sauce*

# Fall Harvest

*Cream of Pumpkin Soup*

*served in small hollowed-out pumpkins*

*Greens of Fall with Walnut Blue Cheese*

*Stuffed Green Peppers*

*Lyonnaise Potatoes*

*Baked Apples*

# New England Seafood Festival

*New England Clam Chowder*

*Parkerhouse Rolls and Butter*

*Shrimp and Crab Stuffed Avocado*

*Scallops and Tomatoes*

*Duchess Potatoes*

*Boston Cream Pie*

# For the Holidays

*Thanksgiving/Christmas*

*Sage Roasted Turkey with Apple-Walnut Stuffing*

*Brown Sugar Glazed Sweet Potatoes*

*Mashed Potatoes and Gravy*

*Honey Glazed Beets*

*Brandied Carrots*

*Pumpkin Raisin Pie*

# Superbowl Sunday

*Beer Sausage with Smoked Gouda*

*Meat Loaf with Walnut Stuffing*

*Sliced Baked Potatoes*

*Cloverleaf Rolls and Butter*

*Apple Cobbler with Ice Cream*

# Orient Express

*Chicken Spring Rolls*

*Oriental Barbecued Pork*

*Stir-Fried Bok Choy with Pork and Shrimp
over Steamed Rice*

*Peppermint Ice Cream and Fortune Cookies*

# Oktoberfest

Hot German Potato Salad

Grilled Bratwurst

Juniper Spiced Sauerkraut

Potato Pancakes

Fresh Applesauce

Fraulein Katherine's White Chocolate Cake

# Snows of Leningrad

Marinated Herring with Capers and Onions

Cold Borscht

Roast Pork with Potato Dumplings

Boiled Cabbage Wedges with Toasted Caraway

Mazourka (Walnut Cake)

# Breakfast at Tiffany's

*brunch*

Chocolate Waffles

Poached Eggs on Apple Rings

Peppered Bacon

Spanish Potatoes

Fresh Fruit Platter

Whole Wheat Toast and Bagels

**SUPERBOWL SUNDAY**
Beer Sausage with
Smoked Gouda
(Appetizer)

**FLOWER DRUM SONG**
Teriyaki Salmon
with Steamed Rice
and Snow Peas
(Main Course)

**BACKYARD BARBECUE**
Melon Surprise
(Dessert)

**OLÉ**
Nachos Grande
(Appetizer)

**MARDI GRAS**
Firecracker Salad

**FALL HARVEST**
Cream of Pumpkin
Soup

**RITES OF SPRING**
Fresh Fruit Tarts
(Dessert)

**117**

# Everyone Loves a Mystery

•

*Consommé Royale*
*Fresh Fruit Salad with Raspberry Vinaigrette*
*Strawberry Sorbet*
*Roast Game Hen in Puff Pastry with Pineapple Chutney*
*Classic Waldorf Salad*
*Chocolate Mousse*

•

# Beverage Selections

The theme of this evening conjures images of tradition, panache, and style. Although your guests will definitely be expecting some mystery, leave any guesswork for the game later. A classic beverage pairing is certainly in order.

For starters, select a **sparkling wine** that will be a bellwether for the entire evening. This drink of kings and queens heralds the start of a memorable event. Whether from the Champagne district in France or a local sparkler, this choice will be the perfect complement for the light consommé, fruit salad, and sorbet.

You can take several directions with the entrée. The game hen and pineapple chutney will allow for either a **medium-bodied red wine** or a **spicy white wine**. A domestic pinot noir or a red wine from Burgundy will stand up to this hearty dish. If you prefer to keep this course on the light side, choose an Alsatian Gewürztraminer by one of the better producers such as Trimbach.

Some guests will want to savor their mousse with pinot noir, whereas others will be ready for **espresso** to carry them through an evening of mystery clues.

## NONALCOHOLIC

If you prefer, **sparkling apple cider** from France or a quality domestic brand will also serve to set the mood for an elegant evening.

# When to Start Cooking

*When dinner is served at 7:00 P.M. . . . .*

| Cooking Preparation Schedule | | Cooking Times |
|---|---|---|
| 1:00 P.M. | Consommé Royale | 45 minutes |
| 1:45 | Fresh Fruit Salad | 30 minutes |
| 2:15 | Roast Game Hen in Puff Pastry | 1 hour 15 minutes |
| 3:30 | Chocolate Mousse | 15 minutes |
| 4:00 | Time to set the tables and arrange the room. | |
| 4:30 | Time to clean up, relax a bit, double-check everything, and dress for the occasion. | |

| Final Cooking and Preparation Schedule | | | Serving Times |
|---|---|---|---|
| 6:00 P.M. | Classic Waldorf Salad | 15 minutes | |
| 6:50 | Consommé Royale | 10 minutes | 7:00 P.M. |
| 7:00 | Roast Game Hen in Puff Pastry | 25 minutes | 7:30 |
| 7:05 | Fresh Fruit Salad | 5 minutes | 7:10 |
| 7:15 | Strawberry Sorbet | 5 minutes | 7:20 |
| 7:40 | Classic Waldorf Salad | 5 minutes | 7:45 |
| 7:50 | Chocolate Mousse | 3 minutes | 7:55 |
| | Final Beverage | | 8:00 |

## Tips and Details

Your local book or game store undoubtedly carries a variety of mystery theme games that will make this evening's fare complete. Many are designed around a dinner and will provide the perfect entertainment for the evening.

Serve the sparkling wines at about 45°F to 50°F. White wines are best at about 50°F to 55°F. Keep in mind that your refrigerator may be set at temperatures under 40°F, so bring your bottles out in advance of service.

Consommé is an elegant yet complicated item to make. If time demands are a concern, a canned beef consommé may be substituted.

## Consommé Royale

*serves 6 (serve in 6-ounce soup bowls)*

| | |
|---|---|
| 2 | carrots |
| 1 stalk | celery |
| 1 | yellow onion, jumbo |
| 1/2 pound | ground beef, minimum fat content |
| 4 | eggs |
| 1 leaf | bay leaf |
| 4 cups | beef stock (using a beef base with water) |
| 1/2 cup | half-and-half |
| 1/2 teaspoon | salt |
| 1/4 teaspoon | ground white pepper |
| 1/2 teaspoon | ground nutmeg |
| 1/8 cup | chives, cut (approximately 1/4 bunch) |

## Preparation

1. Wash and scrape the carrots, wash the celery, and peel onion; then mince the carrots, celery, and onion.

2. Combine the minced vegetables with the ground beef.

3. Take 2 eggs and separate the yolks and whites using plastic gloves or egg separator. Reserve the yolks for later use.

4. Combine the vegetables, meat, and the 2 egg whites along with the bay leaf; make a simple beef stock by mixing a beef base with water according to package directions; then add to the vegetable-beef mixture and place in a saucepan.

5. Slowly bring the beef stock mixture to a 180°F simmer without stirring; do not boil.

6. As the stock starts to simmer, gently make a small hole in the center of the vegetable-beef mix with a spoon so the stock can breathe.

7. While the stock is simmering, in a separate bowl combine the last 2 eggs with the 2 yolks, half-and-half, salt, ground white pepper, and nutmeg; thoroughly mix with a whip until smooth.

8. Put the egg mixture into a buttered pie tin and place into a 325°F preheated oven. Bake approximately 20 minutes until fully set and reaching 145°F or higher for at least 15 seconds. Refrigerate until ready to slice and serve as custard.

9. Slowly remove the clear stock from the saucepan with a ladle and pour through a coffee filter (or paper towel lying in a strainer); refrigerate the stock to an internal temperature of 40°F within 4 hours until ready to heat and serve. The vegetable-beef mixture is no longer needed.

10. Wash, drain, and cut the chives into 1-inch lengths and refrigerate.

## Ready to Serve

1. Bring the consommé to a quick boil for at least 15 seconds on stove top or in microwave.

2. Cut custard into small diced cubes or stars, approximately 1/2 inch.

3. If possible, warm soup bowls using the dishwasher dry cycle or oven; then evenly distribute the custard cubes and chives into each soup bowl; using a 5-ounce ladle, add hot consommé and serve.

**Note:** The consommé when served will be warm, not piping hot, as it is mixed with the cold custard.

**Preparation Time:** 45 minutes

**Final Cooking Time:** 10 minutes

# Fresh Fruit Salad
## with Raspberry Vinaigrette

*serves 6 (serve on sandwich plates or small dinner plates)*

| | |
|---|---|
| 2 tablespoons | raspberry vinegar |
| 1 | lemon |
| 2 | oranges |
| 1/4 cup | water |
| 2 tablespoons | sugar |
| 1/3 cup | salad oil |
| 1 | cantaloupe |
| 1 basket (12 ounces) | strawberries |
| 1 | d'anjou pear |
| 1/2 head | lettuce |
| 1/3 cup | raspberries (optional) |
| 6 sprigs | mint (approximately 1/4 bunch) |

**Preparation**

1. Combine the raspberry vinegar and the juice from the lemon in a mixing bowl and set aside.
2. Wash and carefully remove the peel of 1 orange by using a paring knife, then cut half of the peel into very fine strips (save the orange).
3. Place the orange strips into a small sauté pan over medium heat and cover with a mixture of the water and the sugar, which becomes a syrup.
4. Poach the orange strips in the syrup until tender, approximately 5 to 7 minutes; remove from the stove and allow to cool for about 5 minutes; then add all of it to the bowl with the raspberry vinegar and lemon juice.
5. Slowly add the salad oil to the ingredients in the bowl while mixing with a wire whip.
6. Place the dressing into the refrigerator to chill.
7. Cut the cantaloupe in half and remove the seeds; remove the cantaloupe from the rind by using a melon baller.
8. Remove the skin from the remaining orange; carefully section both oranges, removing any excess skin fragments.
9. Wash and remove the tops from the strawberries and cut the strawberries into quarters.

10. Wash and remove the stem from the top of the pear and cut the pear in half lengthwise; carefully cut out the core from both halves; lay each half flat side down on a cutting board and slice thin wedges, lengthwise.
11. Combine all of the fruit in a large bowl and pour the dressing over it; thoroughly mix, being careful not to bruise or break the fruit while mixing.
12. Refrigerate until ready to serve.

**Note:** Cover and refrigerate for no less than 1 hour.

### Ready to Serve

1. Wash, drain, and place a lettuce leaf on each plate. Start with fanning 2 or 3 pear wedges on the lettuce and then 2 or 3 orange sections, followed by the cantaloupe balls and sliced strawberry mix.
2. OPTIONAL . . . Wash fresh raspberries and drop 3 or 4 on each plate.
3. Wash and drain the mint; top off each plate with a mint sprig.

**Preparation Time:** 30 minutes

**Final Preparation Time:** 5 minutes

# Strawberry Sorbet

*serves 6 (serve in small fruit dishes)*

1 quart                    strawberry sorbet

### Preparation

1. Place a single 2-ounce scoop of sorbet in the center of a small fruit dish or stemmed glass and promptly serve.
2. OPTIONAL . . . Garnish with mint sprig.

**Note:** Remove sorbet from the freezer approximately 5 minutes before serving to allow for easier scooping.

**Final Preparation Time:** 5 minutes

# Roast Game Hen in Puff Pastry with Pineapple Chutney

*serves 6*

| | |
|---|---|
| 3 | Cornish game hens |
| 1 leaf | bay leaf |
| 2 tablespoons | rosemary |
| 2 tablespoons | thyme |
| 1 1/2 teaspoons | salt |
| 2 teaspoons | ground black pepper |
| 3/4 cup | mushrooms, fresh |
| 2 | shallots |
| 1 tablespoon | garlic |
| 1/4 cup (1/2 stick) | unsalted butter |
| 1/2 cup | chicken stock (using a chicken base with water) |
| 1/4 cup | sherry (optional) |
| 3 sheets | puff pastry, frozen |
| 2 | eggs |
| 1 cup | pineapple chutney (condiment garnish) |

## Preparation

1. Remove the Cornish game hens from the bags and thoroughly wash.
2. Crush bay leaf and combine with rosemary, thyme, salt, and ground pepper; then rub an equal amount of the spice mix both inside and out on each hen.
3. Place the seasoned hens into a shallow roasting pan, and put the pan into a 350°F preheated oven for approximately 45 minutes. The internal temperature of the hens should reach a minimum of 165°F or higher for at least 15 seconds (use a thermometer to check temperature) with a nice golden brown skin.

## While the Hens Are Baking

4. Wash and finely chop mushrooms, shallots, and garlic (keep separate).
5. Melt the butter in a sauté pan over medium heat until it begins to bubble.
6. Add the finely chopped shallots and garlic and sauté for a few minutes until they become clear.
7. Add the finely chopped mushrooms and sauté until they soften.

8. Make the chicken stock by mixing a chicken base with water according to package directions; then add the stock to the mushrooms and simmer over a medium heat, occasionally stirring so as to avoid sticking. This becomes a "duxelles."

9. OPTIONAL . . . While the mushroom duxelles is simmering, drizzle some of the sherry over the hens, which will give them a sweet nutty flavor. After 15 minutes, repeat this step with the remaining sherry.

10. When the mushroom duxelles becomes almost dry, promptly remove from the pan and allow to cool.

11. Remove the hens from the oven upon completion of baking. When they have cooled enough to be able to handle, cut each one in half, making 6 servings, and gently remove the skin and bones from each hen by pulling them free from the meat, making sure that all the bones have been removed.

12. Thaw pastry at room temperature for about 20 minutes before gently unfolding. Place 3 sheets of puff pastry on a clean flat counter.

13. Cut each sheet in half making 6 sheets.

14. Divide the mushroom duxelles in half; place an equal amount of the first half of the duxelles in the center of each of the 6 sheets of puff pastry.

15. Place the boneless hen halves on top of each duxelles portion.

16. Divide the remaining half of the duxelles equally on top of each hen half.

17. Crack the eggs into a bowl, add 2 tablespoons of water, and thoroughly beat; then with the use of a pastry brush, brush the outer perimeter of each puff pastry with the egg wash.

18. Fold over the puff pastry and press the edges together.

19. Place the pastry packages onto a baking pan; cover with plastic wrap and refrigerate until ready to brown and serve. Also, cover and refrigerate the remaining egg wash.

### Ready to Serve

1. Brush each pastry package with the remaining egg wash and place on the middle rack of a 375°F preheated oven; bake approximately 25 minutes or until nicely browned and the internal temperature has reached a minimum of 165°F for at least 15 seconds.

2. Remove from the oven and cool for about 3 minutes; place each pastry package in the center of a dinner plate with a tablespoon of pineapple chutney to the side of the plate as condiment garnish; promptly serve.

**Preparation Time:** 1 hour 15 minutes

**Final Cooking Time:** 25 minutes

# Classic Waldorf Salad

*serves 6 (serve on salad or bread and butter plates)*

| | |
|---|---|
| *1 stalk* | *celery* |
| *2 tablespoons* | *walnuts* |
| *2* | *lemons* |
| *4* | *red delicious apples, medium* |
| *1/4 cup* | *whipping cream* |
| *2 tablespoons* | *mayonnaise* |

### Preparation

1. Wash, drain, and dice the celery, then set aside.
2. Dice the walnuts and set aside.
3. Squeeze the juice from the lemons into a small bowl.
4. Core the apples and dice into 1/2-inch cubes; pour the lemon juice over the apples, thoroughly mixing.
5. Whip the cream with an electric mixer until it forms soft foamy peaks.
6. Combine the apples, celery, and walnuts and fold the mixture into the whipped cream along with the mayonnaise.
7. Refrigerate until ready to serve.

**Note:** Apples tend to turn brown if left too long; so prepare no sooner than about 30 to 45 minutes before serving.

### Ready to Serve

1. Remove from the refrigerator and with a large serving spoon place an equal amount of salad on each plate.

**Preparation Time:** 15 minutes
**Final Preparation Time:** 5 minutes

# Chocolate Mousse

*serves 6 (2-ounce portions)*

*(serve in small dessert cups or stemmed glasses)*

| | |
|---|---|
| 3/4 cup | semisweet chocolate chips |
| 2 tablespoons | unsalted butter |
| 2 | eggs, pasteurized |
| 4 tablespoons | sugar |
| 3/4 cup | whipping cream |
| 2 tablespoons | rum (or 1 tablespoon rum extract, no alcohol) |
| 6 | pirouette (3-inch long, round, wrapped) cookies (optional) |

## Preparation

1. Melt chocolate in a saucepan over low heat.
2. Add butter, melt, and mix with chocolate.
3. Separate egg yolks and whites by using plastic gloves or egg separator.
4. Add 2 tablespoons of sugar to the egg yolks and beat until light and creamy.
5. Beat the egg whites until they double in volume and form light peaks; add the remainder of the sugar (2 tablespoons) while continually beating.
6. Fold the egg whites gently into the egg yolks, being careful not to deflate the foam.
7. Once the chocolate has slightly cooled, add it to the egg mixture and lightly mix.
8. Whip the cream until it has formed a slightly stiff foam peak.
9. Add the whipped cream to the chocolate egg mixture along with the rum (or rum extract) and thoroughly blend.
10. Pour into small dessert cups or stemmed glasses and refrigerate until ready to serve.

## Ready to Serve

1. OPTIONAL . . . Garnish with pirouette cookies.

**Note:** Alternative for those in a hurry . . . purchase a packaged dark chocolate mousse dessert mix and add rum or rum extract.

**Preparation Time:** 15 minutes

**Final Preparation Time:** 3 minutes

# Lovers' Night

•

*Oysters Rockefeller\**
*Hearts of Romaine with Dates and Roasted Walnuts*
*Chicken Kiev*
*Sweet Potatoes on a Pineapple Ring*
*Buttered Asparagus*
*Trifle*

*\* (alternative choice) Cucumber Shrimp Boats*

•

# Beverage Selections

Arouse the imagination of your sweethearts with festive and original drinks that will make for an exceptional evening. **Champagne** is the predominant choice of most lovers, therefore you need to be creative to make the moment special. Why not select a Perrier Jouet, Fleur de Champagne. This champagne is less expensive than Dom Perignon and comes in a hand-painted floral bottle. The exquisite taste is matched by the beautiful presentation.

A novel approach to the salad course might be **ginseng tea.** This will certainly stand up to the balsamic vinaigrette and, if tradition is to be believed, will put the partners in the mood for love.

**Pouilly Fuisse,** a French chardonnay, is not only fun to pronounce, but also very well suited to pair with chicken Kiev.

Why not complete the meal with some **créme de menthe?** This popular liqueur is infused with peppermint for its distinctive flavor. The refreshing spirit will not overwhelm the senses and should rejuvenate your guest for the long evening ahead.

## NONALCOHOLIC

Those who choose an alcohol-free evening might brew up a potpourri of teas to accompany each one of the courses. **Ruby mist** to begin, **ginseng** with the salad and entree, and a rich **Earl Grey** to savor with the trifle.

# When to Start Cooking

*When dinner is served at 7:00 P.M. . . .*

| Cooking Preparation Schedule | | Cooking Times |
|---|---|---|
| 12:30 P.M. | Balsamic Vinaigrette (refrigerate 2 hours) | 10 minutes |
| 2:00 | Oysters Rockefeller* | 45 minutes |
| | *(alternative) Cucumber Shrimp Boats | (20 minutes) |
| 2:45 | Hearts of Romaine | 15 minutes |
| 3:00 | Sweet Potatoes | 40 minutes |
| 3:05 | Chicken Kiev | 30 minutes |
| 3:45 | Time to set the tables and arrange the room. | |
| 4:30 | Time to clean up, relax a bit, double-check everything, and dress for the occasion. | |

| Final Cooking and Preparation Schedule | | | Serving Times |
|---|---|---|---|
| 6:15 P.M. | Trifle | 15 minutes | |
| 6:45 | Oysters Rockefeller | 15 minutes | 7:00 P.M. |
| 7:05 | Hearts of Romaine | 10 minutes | 7:15 |
| 7:10 | Chicken Kiev | 20 minutes | 7:30 |
| 7:15 | Sweet Potatoes | 15 minutes | 7:30 |
| 7:15 | Buttered Asparagus | 15 minutes | 7:30 |
| 7:45 | Trifle | 5 minutes | 7:50 |
| | Final Beverage | | 7:55 |

# Tips and Details

Fresh flowers are a **must** for most romantic occasions, so pick a colorful selection for the centerpiece.

Vinegar-based salad dressings are about the only food item that is not agreeable with wine. Therefore, offer guests a substitute beverage with the salad course.

Although some people may balk at oysters, this item is one that most people will appreciate due to its subtle flavors and delicate consistency.

Trifle is a classic English dessert that is best displayed in a clear crystal or glass bowl to showcase the beautiful layers of cake, pastry cream, and fruit.

# Oysters Rockefeller

*serves 6 (4 half shells each)*

| | |
|---|---|
| 24 | oysters in the shell |
| 2 | shallots |
| 2 tablespoons | garlic, minced |
| 1 package (10 ounces) | chopped spinach, frozen |
| 1/4 cup (1/2 stick) | unsalted butter |
| 1/4 teaspoon | salt |
| 1/4 teaspoon | pepper |
| 4 | lemons |
| 1/4 cup | white wine (optional) |
| 3/4 cup | Parmesan cheese, grated |

## Preparation

1. Thoroughly wash oysters in cold water using a brush to remove any dirt from the outside.
2. Peel and mince shallots and garlic.
3. Thaw frozen spinach in a microwave oven and drain.
4. Place the butter into a sauté pan and melt over a medium heat; then quickly add the minced shallots and garlic and sauté for about 1 minute; add spinach and continue to sauté for about 2 minutes.
5. Add salt, pepper, and the juice of 1 lemon to the spinach mixture and continue to sauté for about another 2 minutes.
6. OPTIONAL . . . Add the white wine and reduce the heat to low.
7. Simmer this mixture until it becomes almost dry (liquid evaporating) and then remove and allow to cool.
8. Carefully open the oysters with an oyster knife or a large wide screwdriver; save as much of the oyster juice as possible.
9. Separate the oysters from both sides of the shell; place the flatter of the two shell halves in a shallow oven pan; throw away the other half.
10. Place the oyster in the half shell; continue to follow this procedure with the remaining oysters.
11. Cover each oyster in the half shell with an equal amount of the spinach mixture.
12. Cover the oysters in the pan with plastic wrap and refrigerate until ready to bake.
13. Zigzag cut the remaining 3 lemons into crown-shaped halves; remove the large seeds, cover, and refrigerate.

## Ready to Serve

1. Remove the plastic wrap and sprinkle the grated Parmesan cheese over the top of each oyster-spinach mixture.
2. Place the pan into a 325°F preheated oven and bake until the cheese has turned to a nice golden brown, approximately 12 to 15 minutes, being careful not to overbake. The oyster-spinach mixture should reach 165°F or higher for at least 15 seconds.
3. Remove from the oven and place 4 oyster shells on each plate; garnish with the crown-shaped lemon halves.

**Preparation Time:** 45 minutes

**Final Cooking Time:** 12 to 15 minutes

# Cucumber Shrimp Boats

*serves 6*

| | |
|---|---|
| *1 quart* | *spinach, chopped (approximately 1/2 bunch)* |
| *6* | *small cucumbers* |
| *1 cup* | *Thousand Island dressing* |
| *12 ounces* | *bay shrimp, precooked, frozen* |
| *1* | *lemon* |

## Preparation

1. Wash the spinach and chop leaves into bite-size pieces and place equal amounts onto salad plates; separate in the center to create a space for the cucumber halves to be placed.
2. Peel the cucumbers and cut lengthwise into halves; then scrape out the seeds with a spoon to form a cavity.
3. Slice cucumber halves into 1/4-inch cuts. **Do not separate.** Carefully pick up the sliced cucumber halves, holding each half together, and place into the open space in the center of the chopped spinach.
4. Ladle 1 ounce of Thousand Island dressing into the cucumber cavities.
5. Remove shrimp from the bag and place in a colander; put the colander in a sink and run cold water over the shrimp until thawed, approximately 3 or 4 minutes. Then drop 2 ounces of shrimp on top of the Thousand Island dressing in the cavity of each cucumber.
6. Slice the lemon into 6 wedges and remove the large seeds; garnish each plate with a lemon wedge and refrigerate until ready to serve.

**Preparation Time:** 20 minutes

# Hearts of Romaine
# with Dates and Roasted Walnuts

*serves 6*

| | |
|---|---|
| 2 heads | romaine |
| 3/4 cup | dates, pitted |
| 3/4 cup | walnuts |
| 1 cup | balsamic vinaigrette (according to recipe) |

## Preparation

1. Prepare the balsamic vinaigrette according to the recipe that follows and refrigerate. Prepare 2 hours ahead of time.
2. Remove the large leaves from the romaine heads; wash, drain, and put these in the refrigerator for another use.
3. Select the small inner leaves of the romaine; wash, drain, and cut into pieces approximately the size of a silver dollar; refrigerate until ready to serve.
4. Coarsely chop the dates and set aside.
5. Coarsely chop the walnuts, being careful not to chop them too fine, and set aside.

## Ready to Serve

1. Place the nuts in a sauté pan over a medium heat and toss them in the pan until they become light brown and crisp, approximately 5 to 7 minutes.
2. Place the romaine on the salad plates; sprinkle the chopped dates over the romaine along with the roasted walnuts.
3. Ladle 1 ounce of the balsamic vinaigrette over each salad and promptly serve.

**Preparation Time:** 15 minutes
**Final Preparation Time:** 10 minutes

# Balsamic Vinaigrette

*serves 6*

| | |
|---|---|
| 2 | shallots |
| 1 tablespoon | garlic, minced |
| 3/4 cup | salad oil |
| 1/4 cup | balsamic vinegar |
| 1 tablespoon | sugar |
| 1 1/2 teaspoons | salt |
| 1 teaspoon | ground black pepper |

## Preparation

1. Peel and mince the shallots and garlic.
2. Combine all of the ingredients together in a bowl and mix; cover and refrigerate for at least 2 hours.

**Note:** Most vinaigrettes are much better 1 to 2 days after they are made, as the time allows the flavors to mull together.

**Preparation Time:** 10 minutes

# Chicken Kiev

*serves 6*

| | |
|---|---|
| 1/2 cup | flour |
| 1 teaspoon | salt |
| 1 teaspoon | ground white pepper |
| 2 tablespoons | garlic, minced |
| 1/3 cup | parsley, chopped (approximately 1/4 bunch) |
| 1/2 cup (1 stick) | unsalted butter |
| 6 (5-ounce) | chicken breasts, boneless, skinless |
| 4 | eggs |
| 1/2 cup | bread crumbs, dry prepared |
| 3/4 cup | vegetable oil |

## Preparation

1. Combine the flour, salt, and ground white pepper in a bowl and set aside.
2. Peel and mince the garlic.
3. Wash, drain, and finely chop the parsley.
4. Cut the butter into small pieces so it can soften faster; combine softened butter, minced garlic, and chopped parsley in a bowl and thoroughly mix into a paste by using a fork.
5. Place the chicken breasts between 2 pieces of plastic wrap, smooth side down, and flatten with the back of a small sauté pan using a sliding motion while hitting. The chicken breasts should be reduced to 1/4-inch thickness.
6. Divide the butter paste into 6 portions and make an "egg" shape with each portion; place 1 on top of each chicken breast, smooth side down.
7. Roll the chicken breast firmly around the butter "egg."
8. Bread the chicken by first rolling in the flour mix, being careful not to allow the butter to become exposed.
9. Crack the eggs into a bowl and whip; then dip the floured chicken into the egg wash, again being careful not to expose the butter.
10. Immediately place the chicken into the bread crumbs and pack crumbs around the breast.
11. Place the breaded chicken on a plate, cover with plastic wrap, and put into the refrigerator for at least 15 minutes or until ready for final cooking.

## Ready to Serve

1. Pour the vegetable oil into a sauté pan over medium heat.
2. Place the chicken into the hot oil and cook on all sides until it is golden brown, approximately 4 or 5 minutes, being careful not to burn.
3. Remove the chicken from the pan and place onto paper towel to absorb oil.
4. Place the chicken onto a baking pan and place into a 325°F preheated oven for 10 minutes or until it has reached 165°F or higher for at least 15 seconds; remove and serve.

**Preparation Time:** 30 minutes

**Final Cooking Time:** 20 minutes

# Sweet Potatoes on a Pineapple Ring

*serves 6*

| | |
|---|---|
| 1 1/2 pounds | sweet potatoes |
| 1/2 cup (1 stick) | butter |
| 1/2 cup | brown sugar |
| 3/4 teaspoon | salt |
| 6 slices | pineapple rings, canned |

## Preparation

1. Peel, wash, slice, and boil sweet potatoes for approximately 20 to 30 minutes or until tender enough for mashing.
2. Mash potatoes; add butter, brown sugar, and salt and whip until fluffy.
3. Drain pineapple rings on a paper towel and then place onto a nonstick baking pan.
4. Place sweet potato mixture into a pastry bag with a large rose tip and squeeze a 3 1/2-ounce portion onto each pineapple ring; carefully cover with plastic wrap and refrigerate.

## Ready to Serve

1. Place into a 375°F preheated oven for 15 minutes, reaching 165°F or higher for at least 15 seconds.
2. Remove with a spatula and serve.

**Preparation Time:** 40 minutes

**Final Cooking Time:** 15 minutes

# Buttered Asparagus

*serves 6*

| | |
|---|---|
| *1 1/2 pounds* | *asparagus, fresh* |
| *1 teaspoon* | *salt* |
| *2 tablespoons* | *butter* |

**Preparation**

1. Wash and cut asparagus into 5-inch lengths (measure from the tip).
2. Place into a pot of water, adding 1 teaspoon of salt; bring to a boil and cook for approximately 8 to 10 minutes or until done. Carefully remove and place on paper towels to absorb excess water.
3. Melt the butter, pour over the asparagus, and serve.

**Preparation Time:** 15 minutes

# Trifle

*serves 6 (serve in a glass bowl)*

| | |
|---|---|
| 1 basket (12 ounces) | strawberries |
| 2 | bananas |
| 1 can (16 ounces) | apricot halves in heavy syrup |
| 1 (16 ounces) | pound cake, prepared |
| 1 cup | whipping cream |
| 2 teaspoons | vanilla extract |
| 2 tablespoons | sugar |
| 1 ounce | brandy (optional) |
| 1 ounce | rum (optional) |

### Preparation

1. Wash the strawberries, remove tops, and slice.
2. Peel and slice the bananas into thin cuts.
3. Open the can of apricots, drain, and save the syrup; cut the apricot halves into 4 pieces.
4. Remove the pound cake from the container and slice into 1/2-inch cuts.
5. Place the whipping cream and vanilla extract into a mixing bowl and whip until it starts to thicken, then add sugar and continue to whip until a stiff peak has been reached.
6. Take a medium-sized glass bowl (punch bowls work very well) and line the bottom with 3 slices of pound cake.
7. OPTIONAL . . . Drizzle 2 teaspoons of brandy and rum over the pound cake.
8. Drizzle 1 tablespoon of apricot syrup over the pound cake.
9. Spread a layer of whipped cream over the pound cake.
10. Divide the strawberries, bananas, and apricots into 3 batches; randomly sprinkle the first batch over the layer of whipped cream.
11. Place 3 or 4 more slices of pound cake over the layer of fruit.
12. Repeat steps 7 through 10 two more times.
13. Top off the last layer with rosettes of whipped cream (by using a pastry bag) among the fruit. Refrigerate until ready to serve.

**Note:** Do not prepare more than 1 1/2 hours in advance.

### Ready to Serve

1. Place the glass bowl so that the guests can see the beauty of the layers of cake, whipped cream, and fruit.
2. Serve by using two large spoons, placing portions of the trifle onto dessert plates.

**Preparation Time:** 15 minutes

**Final Preparation Time:** 5 minutes

# Rites of Spring

•

*Chilled Lemon Soup*
*Seasonal Greens with Mustard Poppy Seed Dressing*
*Grilled Salmon*
*Potatoes on the Half Shell*
*Carrots Vichy*
*Fresh Fruit Tarts*

•

# Beverage Selections

Since this menu showcases many interesting seasonal products, you should be equally imaginative in your beverage selections. A classic **mint julep** (bourbon, mint, and sugar) adds an explosion of flavor to the soup course. Carefully blended, the strong flavors of the julep will enhance, rather than overwhelm, the delicate flavor of the lemon soup.

Spring is a reawakening of life and spirit after the long winter's night. Why not celebrate the season with something exuberant to accompany the greens and poppy seed dressing? A festive **Singapore sling** (sloe gin, orange juice, sweet-and-sour, and grenadine, with a float of brandy) is the perfect way to throw off the cold blanket.

Nothing quite brings out the flavor of fresh salmon like **pinot gris.** Many producers in the Pacific Northwest are matching the qualities found in Alsatian vintages. This will also pair well with the first two courses if wine is preferred.

This is the perfect occasion to bring out that old bottle of **berry wine** to serve with the fresh fruit tarts. If you are out of stock, pick up an Oak Knoll or Hood River raspberry wine from Oregon.

## NONALCOHOLIC

Both the **julep** and the **sling** can be prepared without alcohol and will still make great additions to the meal.

The julep: A lemonade julep (lemonade garnished with lime and mint) supplants the mint julep and pairs well with the lemon soup.

The sling: Add extra orange juice in place of the alcohol.

For dessert, **blueberry tea** or **tropical fruit iced tea** will also prove a good match for the tarts.

# When to Start Cooking

*When dinner is served at 5:00 P.M. . . .*

| Cooking Preparation Schedule | | Cooking Times |
|---|---|---|
| 2:00 P.M. | Potatoes on the Half Shell | 1 hour |
| 2:05 | Chilled Lemon Soup | 15 minutes |
| 2:20 | Seasonal Greens/Mustard Poppy Seed Dressing | 15 minutes |
| 2:35 | Grilled Salmon | 10 minutes |
| 2:45 | Carrots Vichy | 30 minutes |
| 3:00 | Fresh Fruit Tarts | 30 minutes |
| 3:30 | Time to set the tables and arrange the room. | |
| 4:00 | Time to clean up, relax a bit, double-check everything, and dress for the occasion. | |

| Final Cooking and Preparation Schedule | | | Serving Times |
|---|---|---|---|
| 4:55 P.M. | Chilled Lemon Soup | 5 minutes | 5:00 P.M. |
| 5:10 | Seasonal Greens | 5 minutes | 5:15 |
| 5:15 | Potatoes on the Half Shell | 15 minutes | 5:30 |
| 5:20 | Grilled Salmon | 10 minutes | 5:30 |
| 5:25 | Carrots Vichy | 5 minutes | 5:30 |
| 5:45 | Fresh Fruit Tarts | 3 minutes | 5:50 |
| | Final Beverage | | 5:55 |

# Tips and Details

If possible, serve the meal for lunch or early in the day. The theme is enhanced with the addition of sunshine and daylight. Check with your local produce manager to see what type of edible flowers are available and, if possible, integrate with each of your courses.

Be careful that you do not add too much alcohol to any drinks that you serve. You do not want to overpower the meal or intoxicate the guests.

Springtime lends itself to the service of chilled soups. The lemon soup is especially appropriate due to its cleansing and fresh finish. Removing grease and other deposits from tastebuds is one of the properties found in lemons.

# Chilled Lemon Soup

*serves 6 (serve in 6-ounce soup bowls)*

| | |
|---|---|
| 1 1/4 cups | sour cream |
| 1/4 cup | sugar |
| 1 1/2 teaspoons | salt |
| 1 cup | half-and-half |
| 2 cups | chicken stock (using a chicken base with water) |
| 1 tablespoon | Worcestershire sauce |
| 4 | lemons |
| 1/4 cup | water |

## Preparation

1. Combine 1 cup of sour cream, 2 tablespoons of sugar, and the salt in a bowl and thoroughly mix with a whip until smooth and creamy.
2. Slowly blend in the half-and-half, chicken stock (make the chicken stock by mixing a chicken base with water according to package directions), and Worcestershire sauce; cover the bowl with plastic wrap and refrigerate.
3. Wash and remove the rind from 1 lemon and cut the rind into very thin slices.
4. Cut the 4 lemons in half and squeeze out the juice into a bowl and set aside.
5. Combine the water with the remaining 2 tablespoons of sugar in a sauté pan over low heat; bring to a boil, which creates a simple syrup.
6. Add the thin slices of lemon rind to the simple syrup and simmer for 2 minutes; set aside to cool.
7. Remove the chilled soup from the refrigerator and fold in the fresh lemon juice; cover and refrigerate until ready to serve.

## Ready to Serve

1. Ladle (using a 5-ounce ladle) into soup bowls and place a teaspoon of sour cream into each bowl.
2. Top off with some of the poached lemon rind.

**Preparation Time:** 15 minutes

**Final Preparation Time:** 5 minutes

# Seasonal Greens
# with Mustard Poppy Seed Dressing

*serves 6*

| | |
|---|---|
| 1/2 head | red leaf lettuce |
| 2 stalks (heads) | Belgian endive |
| 1/2 head | romaine |
| 1 head | radicchio (small round red cabbage lettuce) |
| 1 cup | mayonnaise |
| 2 tablespoons | Dijon mustard |
| 1 tablespoon | poppy seeds |
| 1 tablespoon | sugar |
| 1 tablespoon | white wine vinegar |

## Preparation

1. Wash, drain, and cut the red leaf lettuce, Belgian endive, romaine, and radicchio into bite-size pieces; mix in a large salad bowl, cover with plastic wrap, and refrigerate.
2. Place the mayonnaise in a mixing bowl and stir to a smooth, even consistency.
3. Add the Dijon mustard and poppy seeds to the mayonnaise and mix.
4. In a separate bowl, mix the sugar and white wine vinegar together; slowly add to the mayonnaise mixture, tasting along the way until the desired flavor is achieved; cover with plastic wrap and refrigerate until ready to serve.

## Ready to Serve

1. Place an equal amount of the salad mix onto the salad plates.
2. Ladle 1 ounce of the mustard poppy seed dressing over each salad and serve.

**Preparation Time:** 15 minutes
**Final Preparation Time:** 5 minutes

# Grilled Salmon

*serves 6*

| | |
|---|---|
| 6 (8-ounce) | salmon fillets |
| 1/2 cup | mayonnaise |
| 1 tablespoon | lemon juice |
| 1 tablespoon | white wine |
| 1 teaspoon | salt |
| 1 teaspoon | Worcestershire sauce |

## Preparation

1. When purchasing the salmon fillets, ask to have as many of the bones removed as possible.
2. Combine the mayonnaise, lemon juice, white wine, salt, and Worcestershire sauce in a bowl and thoroughly mix.
3. Spread an equal amount of the mayonnaise mixture over both sides of the salmon fillets; cover with plastic wrap and refrigerate for at least 1 hour.

## Ready to Grill

**Barbecue Method** (the preferred way to cook salmon)

1. Preheat the barbecue grill on medium heat for about 15 minutes.
2. Place the salmon on the grill with the skin side up; grill for approximately 3 minutes and then with a spatula lift and quarter-turn each fillet; grill for another 2 minutes.
3. Turn the salmon fillets over onto the skin side and cover with a large piece of aluminum foil formed into a tent shape; grill for another 3 to 4 minutes while checking for doneness by flaking with a fork. When the fish begins to flake and has reached 145°F or higher for at least 15 seconds, it is done.

## Oven Method

1. Place an oiled baking pan into a 325°F preheated oven for approximately 5 minutes. (**Note:** Spread a thin layer of vegetable oil over the surface of the pan.)
2. Place the salmon fillets on top of the hot oiled baking pan with the skin side up and bake for approximately 4 minutes.
3. Turn the salmon fillets over and continue to bake for an additional 4 minutes. Check for doneness by flaking with a fork. When the fish begins to flake and has reached 145°F or higher for at least 15 seconds, it is done.

**Preparation Time:** 10 minutes

**Final Cooking Time:** 8 to 10 minutes

# Potatoes on the Half Shell

*serves 6*

| | |
|---|---|
| 6 | potatoes, medium |
| 1/4 cup (1/2 stick) | butter |
| 1 teaspoon | salt |
| 1/4 teaspoon | ground white pepper |
| 1/4 cup | milk |
| 2 tablespoons | Parmesan cheese, grated |

## Preparation

1. Thoroughly wash potatoes, dry, and place in a 375°F preheated oven for 45 minutes or until done.
2. Cut into halves lengthwise.
3. Scoop out the inside of the potatoes with a tablespoon, being careful not to break the shells.
4. Whip potatoes while adding butter, salt, ground white pepper, and milk; whip until the potatoes are a soft fluffy mixture.
5. Spoon the potatoes back into the half shells in a piled-up manner. Do not pat down and smooth.
6. Sprinkle with grated Parmesan cheese.
7. Place the half shells on a baking pan, cover with plastic wrap, and refrigerate.

## Ready to Serve

1. Remove plastic wrap and place the potatoes into a 375°F preheated oven for 10 to 12 minutes until the potatoes are lightly browned and reach 165°F or higher for at least 15 seconds.
2. Remove and promptly serve 2 half shells per plate.

**Preparation Time:** 1 hour
**Final Cooking Time:** 15 minutes

# Carrots Vichy

*serves 6*

| | |
|---|---|
| *2 pounds* | *carrots* |
| *1/4 cup (1/2 stick)* | *butter* |
| *1/4 cup* | *sugar* |
| *1/3 cup* | *parsley, chopped (approximately 1/4 bunch)* |

## Preparation

1. Thoroughly scrape and wash carrots; slice crosswise into very thin cuts and place into a sauté pan over medium heat.
2. Cover with cold water.
3. Add the butter and sugar; boil for approximately 20 minutes or until the water has almost evaporated and the carrots are tender.
4. Wash, drain, and chop parsley and sprinkle over the carrots.
5. Place in a bowl, cover with plastic wrap, and refrigerate.

## Ready to Serve

1. Microwave on high for 1 or 2 minutes until reaching 190°F for at least 15 seconds, then serve.

**Preparation Time:** 30 minutes
**Final Cooking Time:** 5 minutes

# Fresh Fruit Tarts

*serves 6*

| | |
|---|---|
| 6 | tartlet shells, frozen prepared |
| 2 | Hershey chocolate bars |
| 2 | bananas |
| 1 basket (12 ounces) | strawberries |
| 1 | cantaloupe |
| 6 | peaches |
| 3/4 cup | strawberry jelly |

## Preparation

1. Purchase the tartlet shells frozen prepared. If not available, then purchase puff pastry and follow the package directions for making tartlet shells.

2. Break the chocolate bars into small pieces and place in a bowl; put into the microwave for short bursts (10 to 15 seconds), frequently stirring, until the chocolate has melted evenly. **Caution:** Be careful not to overheat.

3. Brush a thin layer of melted chocolate into the tartlet shells.

4. Slice bananas and evenly place into the tartlet shells on top of the chocolate.

5. Wash and remove the tops from the strawberries, then cut strawberries into quarters.

6. Cut the cantaloupe in half and remove the seeds; remove the cantaloupe from the rind by using a melon baller.

7. Wash and remove the skin from the peaches and slice into bite-size pieces.

8. Mix the strawberries, cantaloupe balls, and sliced peaches and divide equally among the tartlet shells.

9. Place the strawberry jelly into a small saucepan over low heat. When the jelly becomes liquid, pour an equal amount over the top of the fruit; promptly refrigerate until ready to serve.

## Ready to Serve

1. Individually plate and serve.

**Note:** To further enhance the plate presentation, a small amount of chocolate syrup may be drizzled on each plate.

**Preparation Time:** 30 minutes

**Final Preparation Time:** 3 minutes

# Mardi Gras

•

*Firecracker Salad*
*Shrimp Cocktail with Sauce Rémoulade*
*Chicken and Spicy Sausage Gumbo*
*Beignets with Powdered Sugar*

•

# Beverage Selections

Americans have only recently grasped what Europeans have known for centuries. Good food and good wine together make the perfect marriage. Today, fine wine now takes its rightful place on the table in many American homes and restaurants.

That being said, it is time to declare, though it might be abhorrent to many wine stewards, that other beverages are often perfectly apropos for a theme party. Try a traditional southern libation to start this New Orleans night. A good strong **hurricane** (Bacardi rum; Meyer's rum; pineapple, orange, and cranberry juices; garnished with an orange slice and a cherry) will really whip your guests into a Mardi Gras mood.

Grgich Hills zinfandel or another California zin would pair nicely with both the shrimp appetizer and the gumbo entrée. Zinfandel is a spicy, rich red wine that is right at home with "nawlins"-style cooking. Make sure that you do not purchase a white zinfandel, which is light and fruity and bears no resemblance to the deep red wine that is essential for this dinner.

**Chicory coffee** is sublime with beignets and a favorite of anyone who has ever been to the "Big Easy." Chicory is a root that, when roasted and ground, blends beautifully with coffee. The resulting brew is a strong, dark beverage that provides the ideal finale for your festival.

### NONALCOHOLIC

Nondrinkers will appreciate a good **sparkling water** with this meal. It will do an excellent job of cleansing the palate after each spicy course. Serve the sparkler with fresh lemon or lime for a refreshing twist.

# When to Start Cooking

*When dinner is served at 8:00 P.M. . . .*

| Cooking Preparation Schedule | | Cooking Times |
|---|---|---|
| 4:15 P.M. | Beignets | 15 minutes |
| 4:30 | Firecracker Salad | 20 minutes |
| 4:50 | Rémoulade Sauce | 20 minutes |
| 5:10 | Shrimp Cocktail | 20 minutes |
| 5:30 | Time to set the tables and arrange the room. | |
| 6:00 | Time to clean up, relax a bit, double-check everything, and dress for the occasion. | |

| **Final Cooking and Preparation Schedule** | | | **Serving Times** |
|---|---|---|---|
| 6:45 P.M. | Chicken and Sausage Gumbo | 1 3/4 hours | 8:30 P.M. |
| 7:58 | Firecracker Salad | 2 minutes | 8:00 |
| | Shrimp Cocktail | | 8:15 |
| 8:45 | Beignets | 5 minutes | 8:50 |
| | Final Beverage | | 8:55 |

# Tips and Details

Decorate the table(s) and dining room with confetti and streamers to emulate an authentic Mardi Gras.

Incorporate background music such as jazz, Dixieland, or Creole to make the evening complete and to put the guests in the true spirit of Mardi Gras.

The recipe for chicken and spicy sausage gumbo is but one of many styles of gumbo. If you like, try adding crab, crayfish, or clams to the dish.

# Firecracker Salad

*serves 6*

| | |
|---|---|
| *3* | *eggs* |
| *1/2 head* | *red leaf lettuce* |
| *1/2 head* | *romaine* |
| *2 stalks (heads)* | *Belgian endive* |
| *1* | *carrot* |
| *1* | *red bell pepper* |
| *1* | *red onion* |
| *1/4 head* | *red cabbage* |
| *12* | *green onions (approximately 2 bunches)* |
| *2 ounces* | *alfalfa sprouts* |
| *1 cup* | *classical French dressing, bottle prepared* |

## Preparation

1. Hard cook the eggs, peel, and slice into quarters.
2. Wash, drain, and cut the red leaf lettuce, romaine, and Belgian endive into bite-size pieces.
3. Thoroughly scrape and wash carrot then place on a cutting board and cut thin slices at a 45-degree angle.
4. Cut the red pepper in half, remove the seeds, and wash; cut into thin strips.
5. Peel and slice the red onion into very thin slices; place the onion slices into a colander and blanch in hot water for a few seconds to remove some of the bitterness.
6. Wash, drain, and shred the red cabbage into thin slices.
7. Mix the lettuce, romaine, endive, carrot, red pepper, red onion, and red cabbage together in a large salad bowl. Then place an equal amount onto the salad plates.
8. Remove the green hollow parts of the green onions; wash the white parts and lay on a cutting board and fan cut (thin slices) about 1/4 of the way up the onions; spread apart so as to resemble a blown-up firecracker; place 2 on each salad at opposite sides of the plate.
9. Wash and drain alfalfa sprouts, then use to top off each salad.
10. Garnish with 2 hard-cooked egg quarters and refrigerate.

## Ready to Serve

1. Ladle 1 ounce of classical French dressing over each salad and serve.

**Preparation Time:** 20 minutes
**Final Preparation Time:** 5 minutes

# Shrimp Cocktail with Sauce Rémoulade

*serves 6*

*(serve on salad plates or in cocktail glasses)*

| | |
|---|---|
| 1 pound | bay shrimp, precooked, frozen |
| 1 head | lettuce |
| 2 cups | rémoulade sauce (recipe follows) |
| 6 sprigs | dill (approximately 1/4 bunch) |
| 1 | lemon |

### Preparation

1. Remove shrimp from the bag and place in a colander; put the colander in a sink and run cold water over the shrimp until thawed, approximately 3 or 4 minutes.
2. Wash and drain the lettuce, then slice into a very fine shred. This is referred to as "chiffonade."
3. Place equal amounts of chiffonade onto salad plates or in cocktail glasses.
4. Ladle 2 ounces of rémoulade sauce on top of the chiffonade.
5. Place 2 1/2 ounces of bay shrimp on top of the rémoulade sauce.
6. Slice the lemon into 6 wedges, remove any large seeds; place a lemon wedge on each plate.
7. Garnish with a sprig of fresh dill; refrigerate until ready to serve.

**Optional:** Larger shrimp may be used, such as the 13 to 15 per pound size. See recipe "Cooked Prawns" that follows.

**Preparation Time:** 20 minutes

# Cooked Prawns (Optional)

*serves 6 (3 or 4 each)*

| | |
|---|---|
| 1 1/2 quarts | water |
| 1/2 cup | white wine |
| 1 | lemon |
| 2 tablespoons | garlic, chopped |
| 1/4 | yellow onion, jumbo |
| 1 leaf | bay leaf |
| 1/4 bunch | parsley |
| 1 tablespoon | salt |
| 1/2 tablespoon | black peppercorns |
| 1 1/2 pounds | prawns, 13 to 15 per pound size |

## Preparation

1. Put the water and wine in a gallon pot over medium heat.
2. Slice the lemon, chop the garlic and the onion, and add to the water.
3. Add the bay leaf, parsley, salt, and black peppercorns to the water and simmer at about 180°F for 10 minutes.
4. Place the prawns with the shells still on into the simmering mix and simmer for 4 minutes. **Note:** Be careful not to overcook the prawns as they may become tough and rubbery.
5. Remove the prawns from the water mix and cool in the refrigerator for approximately 10 minutes.
6. Peel the shells off, clean, and wash the prawns under cold water; refrigerate until ready to serve.

**Note:** Serve the same way as the shrimp cocktail, using 3 or 4 large prawns instead of the bay shrimp on top of the rémoulade sauce.

**Preparation Time:** 35 minutes

# Rémoulade Sauce

*serves 6*

| | |
|---|---|
| 1 stalk | celery |
| 1/2 | yellow onion, jumbo |
| 1/4 cup | green onions (approximately 1/2 bunch) |
| 1 | cornichon (sour dill pickle) |
| 1 tablespoon | garlic, minced |
| 1 1/2 ounces | anchovies |
| 1 3/4 cups | mayonnaise |
| 1/3 cup | chili sauce |
| 1 tablespoon | horseradish, prepared |
| 1 tablespoon | tarragon |
| 1/4 teaspoon | thyme |
| 1 teaspoon | Worcestershire sauce |
| 1/4 cup | stone-ground mustard |
| 1 teaspoon | tabasco |
| 1/4 teaspoon | cayenne |

## Preparation

1. Wash and drain celery; dice celery, yellow onion, green onions, and cornichon.
2. Mince garlic and chop anchovies.
3. Combine the diced and minced ingredients with all of the remaining recipe ingredients together in a bowl, thoroughly mix, cover with plastic wrap, and refrigerate until ready to serve.

**Preparation Time:** 20 minutes

# Chicken and Spicy Sausage Gumbo

*serves 6 (serve in large soup bowls)*

| | |
|---|---|
| 5 (5-ounce) | chicken breasts, boneless, skinless |
| 2 cups | water |
| 1 tablespoon | salt |
| 1 tablespoon | ground black pepper |
| 2 tablespoons | gumbo filé (or) Creole seasoning |
| 1 | green bell pepper |
| 1 | yellow onion, jumbo |
| 1 cup | gumbo roux (recipe follows) |
| 1 1/2 pounds | pork sausage (regular, medium, or hot) |
| 4 cups | water |
| 1/2 cup | green onions (approximately 1 bunch) |

## Preparation

1. Place the chicken breasts in a pot with 2 cups of water.
2. Add the salt, ground black pepper, and gumbo filé or Creole seasoning and bring to a boil; reduce heat and simmer at 180°F for about 30 minutes or until chicken reaches 165°F or higher for at least 15 seconds.
3. Wash and drain green pepper; dice the green pepper and yellow onion.
4. Prepare the gumbo roux (according to the recipe that follows).
5. Add the diced onion and green pepper to the roux and heat until onion and pepper become tender and translucent.
6. Add the sausage to the roux-onion-pepper mixture and brown well, reaching 155°F or higher for at least 15 seconds. **Note:** Purchase sausage according to taste: regular, medium, or hot.
7. To the sausage and roux mixture add 4 cups cold water. **Caution:** Add the water very slowly so that spattering doesn't occur.
8. Remove the chicken from the water solution (save the water) and shred by hand into bite-size pieces.
9. Combine the sausage-roux mixture in a large pot with the reserved water solution and the shredded chicken; cover and cook over low heat for 1 hour, occasionally stirring.
10. Wash, drain, and chop green onions and add to the gumbo; cook for an additional 10 minutes.
11. Serve in large soup bowls using a 6-ounce ladle.
12. Place additional gumbo filé (or creole seasoning) on the table for those who wish to "spice it up."

**Preparation Time:** 1 hour 45 minutes

# Gumbo Roux

| 3/4 cup | peanut oil |
|---------|------------|
| 1 cup   | flour      |

### Preparation

1. Place the oil in a large sauté pan and heat over medium heat, approximately 3 or 4 minutes.
2. Sift the flour into the oil while constantly stirring, and cook until the roux has become a deep brown color.

**Preparation Time:** 5 minutes


# Beignets

*(pronounced: ben-yeh)*
*serves 6*

| 2 cups        | flour           |
|---------------|-----------------|
| 1 tablespoon  | sugar           |
| 1 teaspoon    | baking powder   |
| 1 cup         | milk            |
| 1             | egg             |
| 2 cups        | vegetable oil   |
| 3 tablespoons | powdered sugar  |

### Preparation

1. Mix the flour, sugar, and baking powder in a bowl.
2. Add the milk and egg and thoroughly mix into a batter; refrigerate until ready to use.
3. Heat the vegetable oil in a saucepan over medium heat, reaching 180°F.
4. Drop the batter by tablespoonfuls into the hot oil and cook until golden on all sides, approximately 3 to 5 minutes. **Caution:** Be very careful to avoid burns.
5. Remove from the hot oil with tongs and place on a paper towel to drain.

### Ready to Serve

1. Roll in powdered sugar.
2. Place in a bread basket that is lined with a napkin and serve, allowing guests to help themselves.

**Note:** Beignets are traditionally rolled in or sprinkled with powdered sugar but may be served plain with sweet butter or with syrup.

**Preparation Time:** 15 minutes

**Final Preparation Time:** 5 minutes

# People's Night In

*Consommé Spaghettini*
*Veal and Ham Florentine Pinwheels*
*Oven Roast Potatoes*
*Tomatoes Stuffed with Corn*
*Croissants and Butter*
*Broiled Pears*

# Beverage Selections

Consider setting up a beverage bar that can accommodate many different tastes.

On one end of the beverage table display the **white wine** in an ice bucket and the **red wine** in a wicker wine basket. Place the glasses next to these in a geometric pattern. Present the coffee service similarly on the opposite end of the table.

Save the heart of the table to display ingredients for a nonalcoholic drink. As the group gathers to mix, this is where most of the action and fun will occur.

Choose several different **chardonnays** and **pinot noirs** for the evening's fare. This will enhance the evening's conversation by giving friends the opportunity to discuss similarities and differences between each of the wines.

An anonymous eighteenth-century writer noted: "Coffee works a miracle for those of little wit . . . with every drop it sharpens the memory . . . the most barren of authors is thereby made fertile . . . every cup empowers us to gabble without pause. . . ." Accordingly, do not forget **fresh brewed coffee** with the dessert course.

## NONALCOHOLIC

A nonalcoholic drink such as a **flamingo** (equal parts cranberry juice, pineapple juice, and club soda, with a lime wedge) will be exciting for the nondrinkers and imbibers alike. Encourage participation and watch the fun begin.

# When to Start Cooking

*When dinner is served at 7:00 P.M. . . .*

| Cooking Preparation Schedule | | Cooking Times |
|---|---|---|
| 2:00 P.M. | Veal and Ham Florentine Pinwheels | 45 minutes |
| 2:45 | Tomatoes Stuffed with Corn | 25 minutes |
| 3:10 | Broiled Pears | 30 minutes |
| 3:40 | Butter Balls | 10 minutes |
| 3:50 | Time to set the tables and arrange the room. | |
| 4:30 | Time to clean up, relax a bit, double check everything, and dress for the occasion. | |

| **Final Cooking and Preparation Schedule** | | | **Serving Times** |
|---|---|---|---|
| 6:00 P.M. | Veal and Ham Pinwheels | 1 1/4 hours | 7:15 P.M. |
| 6:15 | Oven Roast Potatoes | 1 hour | 7:15 |
| 6:40 | Croissants and Butter | 5 minutes | 7:00 |
| 6:45 | Consommé Spaghettini | 15 minutes | 7:00 |
| 7:00 | Tomatoes Stuffed with Corn | 15 minutes | 7:15 |
| 7:30 | Broiled Pears | 5 minutes | 7:35 |
| | Final Beverage | | 7:40 |

## Tips and Details

Classic beverage or punch garnishes usually include lime wedges, lemon twists, and orange slices. Fresh berries may be added when in season.

Specialty potatoes, such as red, white, and purple, become available during the summer months. Try one of these variations, and leave the peel on for added color and vitamins.

## Consommé Spaghettini

*serves 6 (serve in 6-ounce soup bowls)*

| 4 cups | *beef consommé, canned* |
|---|---|
| 2 ounces | *spaghettini (very thin spaghetti)* |
| 1/4 teaspoon | *salt* |

### Preparation

1. Place consommé into a saucepan and bring to a boil.
2. Break the spaghettini into 1-inch pieces and drop into lightly salted boiling water; boil until slightly undercooked; rinse in cold water and place 1 tablespoon into each soup bowl.
3. Ladle the boiling consommé into each bowl and serve piping hot.

**Preparation Time:** 15 minutes

# Veal and Ham
# Florentine Pinwheels

*serves 6*

| | |
|---|---|
| 6 (6-ounce) | veal cutlets |
| 1 package (10 ounces) | chopped spinach, frozen |
| 6 (1-ounce) | cooked ham slices |
| 2 teaspoons | ground black pepper |
| 2 teaspoons | ground nutmeg |
| 3 tablespoons | vegetable oil |
| 1 | yellow onion, jumbo |
| 1/2 cup | flour |
| 1 1/2 cups | chicken stock (using a chicken base with water) |
| 3/4 cup | white wine |
| 3/4 cup | mushrooms, fresh |
| 1/3 cup | half-and-half |

## Preparation

1. Place the veal cutlets between two pieces of plastic wrap and flatten with the back of a small sauté pan using a sliding motion while hitting cutlets. The cutlets should be no more than 1/4 inch in thickness.

2. Thaw frozen spinach in a microwave oven, drain, and allow to cool; then divide into 6 portions.

3. Lay the veal cutlets flat and cover each with a slice of ham. Then sprinkle with ground pepper and nutmeg.

4. Place a portion of spinach in the center of each veal and ham cutlet; roll up tightly, using wooden picks to hold each one together.

5. Place the oil in a large sauté pan over medium heat; add the veal and ham pinwheels and sauté until nicely browned on all sides; remove and place in a shallow roasting pan, cover with plastic wrap, and refrigerate.

6. To make the sauce, chop the onion and sauté in the remaining oil for approximately 3 minutes; slowly sift in flour, add chicken stock (make the chicken stock by mixing a chicken base with water according to package directions) and white wine, and continue to mix while bringing to a boil.

7. Remove from the stove; wash and slice mushrooms then mix into the sauce; add the half-and-half and thoroughly mix; pour the sauce into a bowl, cover with plastic wrap, and refrigerate.

**Ready to Serve**

1. Pour the sauce over the veal and ham pinwheels; then cover the roasting pan with foil and bake in a 350°F preheated oven for 1 hour, reaching 165°F or higher for at least 15 seconds.
2. Remove from the oven and pull out the wooden picks; place a pinwheel on each plate and serve.

**Preparation Time:** 45 minutes

**Final Cooking Time:** 1 hour 10 minutes


# Oven Roast Potatoes

*serves 6*

| | |
|---|---|
| 12 to 18 | small potatoes (even in size) |
| 1/3 cup | vegetable oil |
| 2 teaspoons | garlic salt |
| 1 teaspoon | ground white pepper |
| 1 tablespoon | paprika |


**Preparation**

1. Peel and wash potatoes then dry on a paper towel.
2. Pour vegetable oil into a small bowl and dip each potato into the oil and place on a roasting pan (save vegetable oil).
3. Sprinkle the garlic salt, ground white pepper, and paprika over all sides of the potatoes (save some of the spices for step 5).
4. Place the potatoes in a 375°F preheated oven for approximately 45 to 55 minutes or until done.
5. Mix the remaining salt, ground white pepper, and paprika with the remaining vegetable oil, and baste the potatoes several times while baking.
6. Serve 2 or 3 per plate depending upon size.

**Note:** If you have only one oven, these potatoes may be cooked on the upper rack of a 350°F oven for 60 to 75 minutes or until done, while the Florentine pinwheels are baking on the lower rack. Remember to remove the pinwheels at the end of their 60-minute cooking time.


**Preparation Time:** 1 hour

# Tomatoes
# Stuffed with Corn

*serves 6*

| | |
|---|---|
| 6 | tomatoes, medium, firm |
| 2 cups | corn, frozen |
| 1/2 teaspoon | salt |
| 1/4 teaspoon | ground white pepper |
| 2 tablespoons | butter |
| 2 tablespoons | bacon bits, prepared |

## Preparation

1. Wash and drain the tomatoes; cut the top off each tomato with a paring knife, then carefully remove the centers of the tomatoes with a spoon.
2. Stand the tomatoes upright in a baking dish.
3. Cook corn, drain, and lightly mix with salt, ground white pepper, and butter.
4. Sprinkle bacon bits into the bottom of each tomato cup.
5. Spoon the corn into each tomato cup; cover with plastic wrap and refrigerate.

## Ready to Serve

1. Remove the plastic wrap and place into a 350°F preheated oven for 15 minutes, reaching 165°F or higher for at least 15 seconds.
2. Pick up each tomato cup with a spatula and serve.

**Preparation Time:** 25 minutes
**Final Cooking Time:** 15 minutes

# Croissants and Butter

*serves 6*

| | |
|---|---|
| 6 | French croissants |
| 1/2 cup (1 stick) | sweet cream butter |

## Preparation

1. Purchase fresh French croissants from your local bakery.
2. Soften butter and scoop into round balls by using a melon baller; place butter balls into the refrigerator to harden.

## Ready to Serve

1. Score the butter balls with the tines of a fork and place one on each plate next to the croissant.

**Preparation Time:** 10 minutes
**Final Preparation Time:** 5 minutes

# Broiled Pears

*serves 6 (serve in small fruit dishes)*

| | |
|---|---|
| 3 | ripe bosc, red bartlett, or bartlett pears |
| 2 tablespoons | lemon juice |
| 3 tablespoons | Neufchâtel cheese |
| 3 tablespoons | cottage cheese, drained (small curd) |
| 3 tablespoons | powdered sugar |
| 1/2 teaspoon | almond extract |
| 1 1/2 teaspoons | vanilla yogurt |
| 3 tablespoons | chopped pecans (or almonds or walnuts) |

### Preparation

1. Wash, drain, and slice pears in half lengthwise; remove the stem and core with a paring knife; clean out the core area with a melon baller, creating a small cavity.
2. Cut a small amount off the round side of the pear to prevent wobbling, allowing the pear half to sit flat.
3. Rub all surfaces with lemon juice and place on a baking pan. The lemon juice adds a flavor enhancement and will help to prevent the pear from turning brown prior to broiling.
4. Combine the Neufchâtel cheese, cottage cheese, powdered sugar, and almond extract; blend until smooth with an electric mixer or food processor.
5. Add vanilla yogurt and blend briefly.
6. Spoon the mixture into the cavity of each pear half.
7. Sprinkle with pecans (or almonds or walnuts).
8. Cover with plastic wrap and refrigerate.

### Ready to Serve

1. Remove plastic wrap and broil in a preheated oven, about 4 or 5 inches from the top of the oven, for approximately 2 or 3 minutes or until the nuts are lightly browned.
2. Promptly serve in small fruit dishes (with a lettuce liner if desired).

**Preparation Time:** 30 minutes
**Final Preparation Time:** 5 minutes

# Olé

•

*Nachos Grande*
*Gazpacho*
*Tamale Pie*
*Flan*

•

# Beverage Selections

It's fiesta time, and any south-of-the-border theme night should start with a **margarita.** This tequila-based drink is both traditional and excellent with spicy foods. (Add lime juice and an orange liqueur such as Cointreau, triple sec, or Grand Marnier.)

Tequila is made exclusively in Mexico from the distilled wine known as pulque. Aztecs were drinking this low-alcohol wine made from the mescal plant 1000 years before the superior distilled product we know as tequila became popular in California in the 1950s.

With the gazpacho, offer a shot of **tequila** served at the table. Better yet, for a classic presentation, serve each guest a 1-ounce bottle of tequila and encourage them to pour it into the chilled soup.

Many **Mexican beers** have become quite popular in the United States during the last decade and should be an option for the guests. You may want to display a variety of the brews on a bed of ice.

The final detail that is a must for any Olé night is a pitcher of **ice water.** Refill it often, depending on the temperature of your salsa.

## NONALCOHOLIC

**Nonalcohol beer** is generally not powerful enough to pair with a Mexican feast. When served with a wedge of lime, however, it becomes quite festive and can stand the heat.

An interesting coffee drink that is fun to make is **café de olla.** You can make this Mexican pot coffee by using a traditional boiling method. For a serving of eight, take 8 cups of water; 1 cup of Mexican coffee beans, coarsely ground; 4 sticks of cinnamon; 4 tablespoons of brown sugar; and 1 tablespoon of molasses; combine all ingredients and bring to a boil. Reduce the heat and simmer for a couple more minutes. The coffee will be a dessert in itself or will complement the flan perfectly.

# When to Start Cooking

*When dinner is served at 7:30 P.M. ....*

| Cooking Preparation Schedule | | Cooking Times |
|---|---|---|
| 2:00 P.M. | Nachos Grande | 30 minutes |
| 2:30 | Gazpacho | 20 minutes |
| 3:00 | Tamale Pie | 45 minutes |
| 3:45 | Flan | 45 minutes |
| 4:30 | Time to set the tables and arrange the room. | |
| 5:00 | Time to clean up, relax a bit, double-check everything, and dress for the occasion. | |

| Final Cooking and Preparation Schedule | | | Serving Times |
|---|---|---|---|
| 7:20 P.M. | Nachos Grande | 10 minutes | 7:30 P.M. |
| 7:35 | Gazpacho | 10 minutes | 7:45 |
| 7:45 | Tamale Pie | 15 minutes | 8:00 |
| 8:15 | Flan | 5 minutes | 8:20 |
| | Final Beverage | | 8:25 |

# Tips and Details

Use green, red, and white napkins and tablecloths (the colors of the Mexican flag) to underscore your commitment to a south-of-the-border theme.

This menu is written to accommodate most tastes. For the more adventurous guests, you might offer the traditional mescal (complete with an agave worm in the bottom of the bottle) and a small plate of jalapeños to spice up the meal.

This meal can be served buffet style for a more casual atmosphere and will lend itself very well to an outdoor garden party. Get the kids involved with a piñata that opens to small gifts and treats.

# Nachos Grande

*serves 6 (serve on a large platter)*

| | |
|---|---|
| 1 pound | chorizo sausage (omit for vegetarian dish) |
| 1/2 cup | green onions, chopped (approximately 1 bunch) |
| 1/2 cup | black olives |
| 1 | tomato, large |
| 1 can (16 ounces) | refried beans |
| 1 cup | cheddar cheese, grated |
| 10 ounces (1/2 bag) | tortilla chips |
| 3/4 cup | salsa |
| 1/2 cup | sour cream |

## Preparation

1. Break the chorizo sausage into crumbles and place in a sauté pan over a medium heat of at least 155°F until it is fully cooked and begins to brown; drain the grease on a paper towel and set aside.
2. Wash and finely chop the green onions; place in a bowl, cover, and refrigerate.
3. Chop or slice the black olives; place in a bowl, cover, and refrigerate.
4. Wash, drain, and dice the tomato; place in a bowl, cover, and refrigerate.
5. Place the refried beans into a saucepan over low heat, stirring until the beans become soft.
6. Grate the cheddar cheese or purchase pregrated cheese.
7. Evenly distribute the tortilla chips on a large oven-safe platter.
8. Spoon the hot refried beans over the tortilla chips.
9. Spoon the chorizo sausage over the refried beans.
10. Cover the chorizo sausage with the grated cheddar cheese; cover with plastic wrap and refrigerate until ready to heat and serve.

### Ready to Serve

1. Remove the plastic wrap and place the platter on the center rack of a 325°F preheated oven for approximately 7 minutes or until the temperature has reached 165°F or higher for at least 15 seconds and the cheese has melted.
2. **Carefully** remove the hot platter and cover the melted cheddar cheese with salsa, sour cream, chopped olives, diced tomatoes, and chopped green onions.
3. Serve family style in the center of the table.

**Preparation Time:** 30 minutes
**Final Cooking Time:** 10 minutes

# Gazpacho

*serves 6 ( serve in 6-ounce soup bowls)*

| | |
|---|---|
| *1/4 cup* | *green onions, chopped (approximately 1/2 bunch)* |
| *2 stalks* | *celery* |
| *1/2* | *yellow onion, jumbo* |
| *1/3 cup* | *cilantro, chopped (approximately 1/4 bunch)* |
| *1* | *tomato, large* |
| *1* | *lemon* |
| *1* | *lime* |
| *1 can (46 ounces)* | *V8 vegetable juice* |
| *1* | *avocado* |
| *3/4 cup* | *sour cream* |

## Preparation

1. Wash and finely chop green onions; place in a bowl, cover, and refrigerate.
2. Wash, drain, and dice the celery; place in a bowl, cover, and refrigerate.
3. Dice the yellow onion; place in a bowl, cover, and refrigerate.
4. Wash, drain, and cut the cilantro into a coarse chop; place in a bowl, cover, and refrigerate.
5. Wash, drain, and dice the tomato; place in a bowl, cover, and refrigerate.
6. Wash and drain the lemon and lime; cut a very thin layer of skin with a grater, creating a zest; place in a bowl, cover, and refrigerate.
7. Squeeze the juice from both the lemon and the lime, and mix with the V8 juice; refrigerate until ready to serve.

## Ready to Serve

1. Wash, drain, peel, and dice the avocado and set aside.
2. Fill each soup bowl with the V8 mixture; add equal amounts of celery, yellow onion, tomatoes, and avocados to each bowl.
3. Top each bowl with a scoop of sour cream, topped with a sprinkle of the lemon and lime zest, cilantro, and green onions.

**Note:** This can also be served family style in a large bowl with all of the ingredients in small cups or plates surrounding the bowl.

**Preparation Time:** 20 minutes

**Final Preparation Time:** 10 minutes

# Tamale Pie

*serves 6*

| | |
|---|---|
| 2 pounds | ground beef, lean |
| 1 1/2 cups | taco seasoning, package prepared |
| 1 | yellow onion, jumbo |
| 1 1/4 cups | corn, frozen |
| 2 cups | cornmeal |
| 2 | eggs |
| 1/2 cup | water |
| 1 cup | cheddar cheese, grated |

### Preparation

1. Place the ground beef in a large sauté pan over medium heat of at least 155°F; brown the ground beef until crumbly; drain grease; follow the directions on the package of taco seasoning to prepare, thoroughly mixing with ground beef.
2. Peel and dice the onion.
3. Defrost the corn.
4. Combine the taco meat, diced onions, and corn, then set aside.
5. Combine the cornmeal, eggs, and water and thoroughly mix.
6. Line the bottom and halfway up the sides (about 1 inch) of a 9-by-13-inch baking pan with 2/3 of the cornmeal mixture.
7. Carefully spoon the meat mixture into the pan on top of the cornmeal.
8. Spread the remaining cornmeal mixture over the top of the meat.
9. Grate the cheddar cheese or purchase pregrated cheese; cover the top layer of cornmeal with the grated cheese and cover with plastic wrap and refrigerate.

### Ready to Serve

1. Remove the plastic wrap and place the pan on the center rack of a 325°F preheated oven for approximately 10 minutes or until the temperature has reached 165°F or higher for at least 15 seconds and the cheese has melted and become light brown.
2. Remove from the oven and cool for about 5 minutes before serving.
3. Slice 6 even portions (approximately 4-by-4-inch cuts) and remove from the pan with a spatula to serve.

**Preparation Time:** 45 minutes

**Final Cooking Time:** 15 minutes

# Flan

*serves 6*

| | |
|---|---|
| 4 | *eggs* |
| 2 1/2 tablespoons | *sugar* |
| 1 teaspoon | *ground nutmeg* |
| 1 teaspoon | *cinnamon* |
| 2 teaspoons | *vanilla extract* |
| 3 cups | *half-and-half* |
| 2 tablespoons | *unsalted butter* |
| 6 sprigs | *mint (approximately 1/4 bunch)* |
| 4 ounces | *strawberries or peaches (optional)* |

## Preparation

1. Crack the eggs into a mixing bowl and beat until smooth; add the sugar, nutmeg, cinnamon, vanilla extract, and half-and-half to create the custard mixture; whip the custard mixture until smooth.
2. Use a paper towel with softened butter to grease the insides of 6 soup cups or coffee cups.
3. Pour an even amount of the custard mixture into the 6 cups.
4. Place the cups into a shallow roasting pan and add about 1 inch of water to the pan.
5. Place the pan in a 300°F preheated oven for approximately 40 minutes or until the custard has developed a light brown skin on top and has reached 145°F or higher for at least 15 seconds; remove from oven and refrigerate for at least 1 hour or until the custard is completely chilled to 40°F.

## Ready to Serve

1. Place a butter knife in a cup of hot water; remove the knife and slide it around the outside of the custard to loosen it from the cups; invert the cups onto small plates and remove the cups.
2. Sprinkle the top with some grated nutmeg and top off with a sprig of mint, which has been washed and drained.
3. OPTIONAL . . . Top off with fresh strawberries, raspberries, or diced peaches.

**Preparation Time:** 45 minutes

**Final Serving Time:** 5 minutes

# Concert in the Park

*picnic*

•

*Assorted Fresh Fruit and Cheese*
*Finger Sandwiches and Chips*
*Four Bean Salad*
*Apricot Dessert Bars*

•

# Beverage Selections

A picnic is the perfect occasion to bring out a bottle of well-chilled **rosé.** The light refreshing quality of this wine will match both the occasion and the food.

Rosés from the Loire Valley in France are considered the world's premium example of what Americans call blush wine. California's white zinfandels are sometimes a bit too sweet to pair successfully with many foods. If you prefer a domestic wine, choose a **white pinot noir** from the Pacific Northwest. The cool climate of this region helps retain the proper acidity, which will cleanse the palate and not overwhelm the food.

Although red and rosé wines are both made from red grapes, the differences between the two can be dramatic. Rosé is made by fermenting the grapes' juice, skins, and seeds for only a short time to prevent color and bitter tannin from entering into the equation. Unlike their full-bodied and oak-aged red cousins, rosé wines are then held for only a short period of time in stainless steel tanks before bottling. While the resulting young and fruity, pink-hued wine is inappropriate for most dinner parties, it is often the perfect choice for a picnic.

## NONALCOHOLIC

Don't forget to prepare some **tropical iced tea,** served in a large fruit jar with lemon wheels. (Cut the lemon wheels at the picnic site for freshness.) **Sparkling water** will also add zest to the occasion.

# When to Start Cooking

*When the picnic is at noon . . .*

| Cooking Preparation Schedule | | Cooking Times |
|---|---|---|
| 9:00 A.M. | Four Bean Salad | 10 minutes |
| 9:10 | Apricot Dessert Bars | 1 hour |
| 9:50 | Assorted Fruit and Cheese | 20 minutes |
| 10:10 | Finger Sandwiches | 15 minutes |
| 10:25 | Time to clean up, relax a bit, double-check everything, and get ready for the picnic. | |

| Final Cooking and Preparation Schedule | | Serving Times |
|---|---|---|
| 11:55 A.M. | Open the picnic basket(s) | 12:00 P.M. |

# Tips and Details

It is said that the Earl of Sandwich was an avid chess player. During one of his games he became hungry. Not wanting to take the time to eat, he instructed his servants to place a slab of roast between two pieces of bread, and thus, the sandwich was born.

If the picnic is planned near a stream, it is fun to hide a bottle(s) of wine in the water prior to the guests' arrival. At an opportune moment gallantly pull it from the cool water and surprise everyone with a properly chilled bottle of wine.

# Assorted Fresh Fruit and Cheese

*serves 6*

| | |
|---|---|
| 1 | Granny Smith apple |
| 2 | red delicious apples |
| 1 | lemon |
| 2 | oranges |
| 1 basket (12 ounces) | strawberries |
| 12 ounces | brie cheese |
| 12 ounces | mozzarella cheese |
| 12 ounces | Jarlsberg cheese |

### Preparation

1. Wash, drain, and cut the apples into 1/2-inch wedges by using a paring knife or apple cutter.
2. Squeeze the juice from the lemon and rub the juice onto the apple wedges. This reduces the browning and enhances the flavor.
3. Peel and section the oranges.
4. Wash the strawberries and remove the tops.
5. Slice the cheese into bite-size pieces.
6. Mound the strawberries in the center of a large platter and arrange the apples, oranges, and cheese around the platter; cover with plastic wrap and refrigerate until ready to serve.

**Preparation Time:** 20 minutes

# Finger Sandwiches and Chips

*serves 6*

| | |
|---|---|
| *18 slices* | *sourdough bread* |
| *1/4 cup* | *Dijon mustard* |
| *2 pounds* | *roast beef, deli sliced* |
| *1/2 pound* | *provolone cheese, deli sliced* |
| *18* | *black olives* |
| *1 bag (20 ounces)* | *potato chips* |

## Preparation

1. Stack 3 slices of sourdough bread; cut off the crusts.
2. Spread Dijon mustard on the top side of each slice.
3. Fold 2 slices of roast beef on top of one slice of sourdough bread; top with 1 slice of provolone cheese.
4. Top with a second slice of sourdough bread, and again top with 2 folded slices of roast beef and 1 slice of provolone cheese.
5. Top off with the third slice of sourdough bread.
6. Cut three evenly sliced finger sandwiches; insert a single wooden pick in each sandwich to hold it together.
7. Top off each wooden pick with a black olive. Repeat steps 1–7 five more times so each person will have three finger sandwiches.
8. Place sandwiches on a platter; cover with plastic wrap and refrigerate; serve with potato chips.

**Preparation Time:** 15 minutes

# Four Bean Salad

*serves 6*

| | |
|---|---|
| 1 cup | salad oil |
| 1/3 cup | red wine vinegar |
| 1 tablespoon | oregano flakes |
| 1 tablespoon | salt |
| 1 1/2 teaspoons | ground black pepper |
| 3 tablespoons | sugar |
| 2 tablespoons | garlic powder |
| 1 cup | cut green beans, canned |
| 1 cup | lima beans, canned |
| 1 cup | kidney beans, canned |
| 1 cup | fava beans, canned |
| 1 | yellow onion, jumbo |
| 1 | red bell pepper |
| 1/2 cup | mushrooms, fresh |

## Preparation

1. Combine the salad oil, red wine vinegar, oregano, salt, ground black pepper, sugar, and garlic powder in a mixing bowl; cover and refrigerate. This is the vinaigrette marinade.
2. Drain and combine the green beans, lima beans, kidney beans, and fava beans in a large salad bowl.
3. Peel and slice the onion into very thin slices; pull the slices apart and place over the beans.
4. Cut the red pepper in half, remove the seeds, and wash; cut into thin strips and place over the beans and onions.
5. Wash, drain, and slice the mushrooms into the salad.
6. Gently mix the beans, onions, red peppers, and mushrooms while adding the vinaigrette marinade; cover and refrigerate for at least 2 hours to develop flavor.

**Preparation Time:** 10 minutes

# Apricot Dessert Bars

*serves 6 to 10*

| | |
|---|---|
| 1 1/4 cups | apricots, dried and chopped |
| 3/4 cup | frozen lemonade concentrate, thawed |
| 1 cup | water |
| 1 cup | sugar |
| 2 cups | flour |
| 1 cup | pecans (or walnuts), chopped |
| 1 pound | butter, melted |
| 1 cup | light brown sugar |
| 1/2 teaspoon | salt |
| 1/2 teaspoon | baking soda |
| 1/2 teaspoon | nutmeg |
| 2 cups | oatmeal |
| 1 pint | lemon ice cream (optional) |

## Preparation

1. Combine apricots, lemonade concentrate (thawed), and water in a sauce pan; simmer over low heat for approximately 10 minutes or until apricots become tender.
2. Blend in the sugar and 1/4 cup of the flour, and stir until slightly thickened; add 1/2 cup of pecans; set aside to cool.
3. Combine butter and brown sugar; set aside.
4. Combine 1 3/4 cups of flour, salt, baking soda, and nutmeg; thoroughly mix.
5. Stir in the butter and brown sugar mixture until small crumbs are formed; then add the oatmeal and thoroughly mix.
6. Press 3/4 of the dough mixture over the bottom of a lightly buttered 9-by-13-inch baking pan.
7. Spread the apricot-pecan mixture over the dough.
8. Mix the remaining dough mixture with the remaining 1/2 cup of pecans; spoon the mixture over the top of the apricot mixture and gently pat down.
9. Place in a 400°F preheated oven for approximately 20 minutes or until lightly browned.
10. Cool on a wire rack and cut into the desired number of squares.
11. OPTIONAL . . . Can be served with lemon ice cream or cut into smaller bars and served as a cookie.

**Preparation Time:** 1 hour

# Boss's Night

*What to prepare when you're entertaining the boss.*

•

*Crabmeat Cocktail with Savory Citrus Cocktail Sauce*
*Cream of Mushroom Soup*
*Tournedos Rossini*
*Baked Potato with Sour Cream and Chives*
*Green Beans Almondine*
*Baked Alaska*

•

# Beverage Selections

**Sauvignon blancs** from California offer a beautiful blend of herbaceous fruit characteristics to match with the appetizer, soup, and salad courses.

A rich **cabernet sauvignon** is the perfect accompaniment for the tournedos. A skillfully made cabernet is well structured and complex and best drunk with some age in the bottle. This will give it time to mellow some of the tannins that yield bitterness when young. Cabernets from Bordeaux and California are truly outstanding due to their respective growing climates and the winemakers' attention to detail in making this regal wine.

Fortified wines are those enhanced with higher proof alcohol such as brandy. Hundreds of years ago this enabled wine to make long journeys overseas with the flavors still intact. Fortified wines last longer once open and pack a potent punch as closer for an elegant dinner. Therefore, a fortified wine, such as **port** or **sherry,** supplies the right flavors to enhance the dessert course.

## NONALCOHOLIC

The power of this menu makes it difficult to select a nonalcoholic accompaniment that would not be overwhelmed. So, the wisest choice would be a **well-chilled bottled water. Earl Grey** or **English breakfast tea,** loose brewed and served in an elegant teapot, would be a fine selection with dessert.

# When to Start Cooking

*When dinner is served at 7:00 P.M. ....*

| Cooking Preparation Schedule | | Cooking Times |
|---|---|---|
| 3:00 P.M. | Savory Citrus Cocktail Sauce | 10 minutes |
| 4:30 | Baked Alaska | 10 minutes |
| 4:40 | Green Beans Almondine | 20 minutes |
| 5:00 | Crabmeat Cocktail with Citrus Sauce | 25 minutes |
| 5:30 | Time to set the tables and arrange the room. | |
| 5:45 | Time to clean up, relax a bit, double-check everything, and dress for the occasion. | |

| Final Cooking and Preparation Schedule | | | Serving Times |
| --- | --- | --- | --- |
| 6:55 P.M. | Crabmeat Cocktail with Citrus Sauce | | 7:00 P.M. |
| 6:10 | Cream of Mushroom Soup | 1 hour | 7:10 |
| 6:20 | Baked Potato | 1 hour | 7:20 |
| 7:00 | Tournedos Rossini | 20 minutes | 7:20 |
| 7:10 | Green Beans Almondine | 10 minutes | 7:20 |
| 7:35 | Baked Alaska | 5 minutes | 7:40 |
| | Final Beverage | | 7:45 |

## Tips and Details

Since this meal is intended to impress, create an elegant and unusual napkin fold for the place setting.

To break the ice, put on some soft music and prominently display some hobby or art piece that you know would be of interest to the guests.

Many fumé blancs from California are made from sauvignon blanc grapes but simply have a different name (borrowed from France). Don't be afraid to select one of these from a good vintner, such as Robert Mondavi.

The zenith of the evening can be the baked Alaska course. Dim the lights during service to feature this classical flaming dessert. This will be a fitting climax to an elegant evening.

# Crabmeat Cocktail
# with Savory Citrus Cocktail Sauce

*serves 6*

| | |
|---|---|
| 2 stalks | celery |
| 1 | yellow onion, jumbo |
| 2 tablespoons | garlic, minced |
| 1 tablespoon | vegetable oil |
| 1 1/2 pounds | crabmeat (or imitation crabmeat) |
| 1/2 head | red leaf lettuce |
| 1 cup | savory citrus cocktail sauce (recipe follows) |
| 1 | lemon |
| 1/8 cup | chives, chopped (approximately 1/4 bunch) |

**Preparation** (prepare cocktail sauce first)

1. Wash, drain, and dice celery; set aside.
2. Peel the onion and cut in half; save half for another use and slice the remaining half very thin.
3. Peel and mince the garlic.
4. Place the vegetable oil in a sauté pan over medium heat; add the onions and garlic, and sauté until they become transparent.
5. Remove the onions and garlic and combine with the crabmeat, then refrigerate.
6. Wash, drain, and slice the red leaf lettuce into a very fine shred.
7. Drop some of the shredded lettuce into each cocktail glass; ladle 1 ounce of cocktail sauce on top of the lettuce; sprinkle some of the diced celery on top of the cocktail sauce; place the crabmeat on top of the diced celery.
8. Wash, drain, and cut the lemon into 6 wedges and place a wedge next to the crabmeat in each glass.
9. Wash, drain, and chop the chives into small bits; sprinkle on top of the crabmeat. Refrigerate the crab cocktails until ready to serve.

**Note:** Cocktail or salad forks may be placed in the refrigerator to chill so that the cocktails may be served with cold forks.

**Preparation Time:** 25 minutes

# Savory Citrus Cocktail Sauce

*serves 6*

| | |
|---|---|
| 1/2 | lemon |
| 1/2 | lime |
| 1/2 | orange |
| 1/4 cup | V8 vegetable juice |
| 1 teaspoon | Worcestershire sauce |
| 3/4 cup | sour cream |
| 2 tablespoons | horseradish |
| 1/2 teaspoon | salt |
| 1 teaspoon | sugar |

## Preparation

1. Squeeze the juice from the lemon, lime, and orange.
2. Combine all of the ingredients together in a bowl and thoroughly mix.
3. Cover the bowl and place the cocktail sauce in the refrigerator for at least 2 hours.

**Preparation Time:** 10 minutes

# Cream of Mushroom Soup

*serves 6*

| | |
|---|---|
| *1* | *yellow onion, jumbo* |
| *4 cups* | *milk* |
| *1 leaf* | *bay leaf* |
| *1 cup (2 sticks)* | *unsalted butter* |
| *1/3 cup* | *flour* |
| *1 pound* | *fresh mushrooms* |
| *1 cup* | *chicken stock (using a chicken base with water)* |
| *1 tablespoon* | *salt* |
| *1 tablespoon* | *ground black pepper* |
| *1/4 cup* | *sherry (optional)* |

## Preparation

1. Cut the onion in half and dry sauté one half over medium heat, placing the cut side down toward the pan. Sauté for approximately 5 minutes or until it becomes dark brown; set aside.
2. Combine the milk, bay leaf, and sautéed onion half in a saucepan over low heat. Do not boil.
3. Melt 3/4 cup of butter in a sauté pan over medium heat; add the flour and stir it in with a wooden spoon; continue to heat and stir until it becomes a light golden color. This is called a "roux." Set aside.
4. Wash and finely chop the mushrooms and the other half of the onion.

5. Melt 1/4 cup of butter in a clean sauté pan over medium heat; add the chopped mushrooms and chopped onions and sauté for 10 minutes.

6. Remove the onion half and bay leaf from the hot milk; combine the sautéed mushrooms and onions with the hot milk and bring to a boil.

7. As soon as the milk mixture reaches a boil, start adding some of the roux by blending a little bit at a time with a whip.

8. Lower the heat and add the chicken stock; simmer at 180°F for approximately 30 minutes, stirring occasionally.

9. Stir in the salt, ground black pepper, and sherry (optional); simmer for an additional 5 minutes and serve.

10. OPTIONAL . . . garnish with thinly sliced fresh mushrooms.

**Preparation Time:** 1 hour

# Tournedos Rossini

*serves 6*

| | |
|---|---|
| 12 (4-ounce) | beef tenderloins |
| 12 slices | white bread |
| 6 ounces | pâté de foie gras, canned (fresh where available) |
| 3/4 cup (1 1/2 sticks) | butter |
| 1 1/2 teaspoons | ground black pepper |
| 2 cups | brown gravy mix, package prepared |
| 1/2 cup | Madeira wine |

## Preparation

1. Remove the crusts and cut the bread to approximately the same size as the beef tenderloins; place the round bread slices onto a dry baking pan; put the pan into a 325°F pre-heated oven and toast bread until golden. The beef tenderloins will be placed on top of these croutons (round toasted bread slices).

2. Carefully remove pâté de foie gras by removing both ends from the can and gently pushing pâté onto a cutting board; with a sharp knife cut 12 equal slices; dip the knife into a cup of water between cuts so that the slices are smooth. Place the slices on a plate, cover with plastic wrap, and refrigerate.

3. Melt the butter in a large sauté pan (it may require 2 pans).

4. Sprinkle ground black pepper over the beef tenderloins and place into the sauté pan over medium heat for approximately 4 minutes.

5. Turn the tenderloins and sauté the other side for another 4 minutes or until the desired degree of doneness, reaching 145°F or higher for at least 15 seconds.

6. Remove from the pan, place on a plate, and put into a warm oven to hold until the sauce is prepared.

7. Prepare the brown gravy according to the package directions and set aside.

8. Pour the Madeira into the same sauté pan that was used to sauté the tenderloins; increase the heat to medium/high and, with a wooden spoon, rub the bottom and the sides of the pan to remove all of the flavor. This process is called "deglazing."

**9.** Add the brown gravy to the pan with the Madeira and the juices from the tenderloins and thoroughly blend with a whip.

### Ready to Serve

**1.** Place 2 toasted croutons on each plate; top the croutons with the tenderloins; top the tenderloins with the 1/2-ounce slices of pâté de foie gras.

**2.** Pour an equal amount of sauce over each tenderloin fillet.

**Preparation Time:** 15 minutes
**Final Preparation Time:** 5 minutes

# Baked Potato
# with Sour Cream and Chives

*serves 6*

| | |
|---|---|
| 6 | baking potatoes |
| 2 tablespoons | vegetable oil |
| 1/2 cup (1 stick) | butter |
| 1/2 cup | sour cream |
| 1/2 cup | chives, chopped (approximately 1 bunch) |

### Preparation

**1.** Thoroughly wash potatoes, dry, and completely rub with vegetable oil; wrap each potato in aluminum foil and place in a 375°F preheated oven for 45 minutes or until done.

**2.** Remove the foil, slice at the top, and squeeze open.

**3.** Wash, drain, and chop chives into 1/4-inch pieces.

**4.** Add an equal amount of butter to each potato and mix in; add the sour cream and top off with chopped chives.

**Preparation Time:** 1 hour

# Green Beans Almondine

*serves 6*

| | |
|---|---|
| *1 pound* | *green beans, fresh* |
| *1 tablespoon* | *salt* |
| *1/4 cup (1/2 stick)* | *butter* |
| *1/2 cup* | *almond slivers* |
| *1* | *lemon* |

## Preparation

1. Wash and remove the stems from the green beans; cut into 3-inch pieces. (Frozen green beans may be used.)
2. Add the salt to 2 quarts of water in a saucepan and bring to a boil.
3. Place the green beans into the water and boil for 3 minutes; drain the hot water and replace with cold water; cover and refrigerate.

## Ready to Serve

1. Melt the butter in a large sauté pan over medium heat; add the drained green beans and sauté for about 2 minutes.
2. Add the slivered almonds to the green beans and sauté for an additional 4 minutes.
3. Squeeze the juice from the lemon over the green beans and toss the green beans; remove and serve.

**Preparation Time:** 20 minutes
**Final Cooking Time:** 10 minutes

# Baked Alaska

*serves 6*

| | |
|---|---|
| 8 | *eggs, pasteurized* |
| 1/2 teaspoon | *cream of tartar* |
| 1 (16-ounce) | *pound cake, prepared* |
| 1 quart | *chocolate chip ice cream* |
| 1/3 cup | *brandy (optional)* |
| 6 | *sugar cubes (optional)* |

## Preparation

1. Separate the egg yolks from the egg whites using plastic gloves or egg separator; place the egg whites and cream of tartar in a mixing bowl and, with a mixer, whip the whites into a stiff peak.
2. Remove the pound cake from the container and slice into 6 equal pieces and place on dessert plates.
3. Top each slice of pound cake with a scoop of chocolate chip ice cream.
4. Evenly cover each scoop of ice cream and the pound cake with the whipped egg whites.
5. Place all the plates into the freezer.

## Ready to Serve

1. Place the plates in a preheated oven set for broiling for approximately 1 minute or until the whipped egg whites are lightly browned, reaching a temperature of at least 145°F.
2. Carefully remove the plates with a hot pad.
3. OPTIONAL . . . Soak the sugar cubes in brandy and place one on each dessert plate. Light the cubes with a match and serve.

**Note:** Choose dessert plates that are able to withstand extreme cold to hot temperature.

**Preparation Time:** 10 minutes
**Final Cooking Time:** 5 minutes

# Evening in Paris

•

*Pâté de Foie Gras with Fresh Fruit and Baguettes*
*Consommé Celestine*
*Raspberry Sorbet*
*Orange Spiced Roast Duck*
*Wild Rice Pilaf*
*Broccoli Florets with Sauce Hollandaise*
*Spinach Salad with Peanuts*
*Chocolate Truffle Cake*

•

# Beverage Selections

No "Evening in Paris" would be complete without French wine. The starter course of pâté can accommodate a wide range of wine pairings, and a well-made **Beaujolais** would certainly be an excellent choice. The wines of this region are made from the gamay grape and reflect different levels of quality. Consider one of the seven designated cru villages to ensure a superior wine. A perfect choice for this evening would be a Beaujolais from the village of St. Armour, which is easily recognized by the heart on its label.

While it's hard to go wrong with a safe bet, sometimes taking a risk can lead to a very memorable evening. Normally, a sweet **Sauternes** wine would be served with dessert, if not as dessert by itself. With this meal, however, selecting a Sauternes as a starter properly matches the rich, elegant quality of the foie gras. Since Sauternes are so well made, even a relatively inexpensive bottling would be sufficient for this course.

While a cabernet would overpower the duck and a gamay would not hold up, a **pinot noir** from Burgundy is perfectly suited for the entrée. Like Sauternes, red Burgundies are rather expensive, and a good choice would be a Village bottling that blends pinot noirs from several different locations. These are labeled as Bourgogne Village, or carry a place name from Burgundy along with the term *Villages*. Select one from a reliable negociant (bottler and shipper) like Joseph Drouhin, who will deliver excellent value.

**Framboise,** a raspberry liqueur, is unequaled when paired with a chocolate truffle cake.

### NONALCOHOLIC

**Evian bottled water** garnished with lemons is an invigorating alternative to alcoholic or heavy nonalcoholic beverages. A full bodied **French roast coffee** is also a nice finish with chocolate truffle cake. Sugar cubes and half-and-half complete the picture.

# When to Start Cooking

*When dinner is served at 7:30 P.M. . . .*

| Cooking Preparation Schedule | | Cooking Times |
|---|---|---|
| 3:00 P.M. | Chocolate Truffle Cake | 1 hour |
| 4:00 | Orange Spiced Roast Duck | 15 minutes |
| 4:15 | Broccoli Florets/Hollandaise | 15 minutes |
| 4:30 | Spinach Salad with Peanuts | 10 minutes |
| 4:45 | Pâté de Foie Gras with Fresh Fruit | 15 minutes |
| 5:00 | Time to set the tables and arrange the room. | |
| 5:30 | Time to clean up, relax a bit, double-check everything, and dress for the occasion. | |

| Final Cooking and Preparation Schedule | | | Serving Times |
|---|---|---|---|
| 5:45 P.M. | Orange Spiced Roast Duck | 2 1/4 hours | 8:05 P.M. |
| 6:55 | Wild Rice Pilaf | 1 hour | 8:05 |
| 7:00 | Consommé Celestine | 50 minutes | 7:50 |
| 7:25 | Pâté de Foie Gras/ Fresh Fruit | 5 minutes | 7:30 |
| 7:50 | Raspberry Sorbet | 5 minutes | 7:55 |
| 7:55 | Broccoli Florets/ Hollandaise | 10 minutes | 8:05 |
| 8:10 | Spinach Salad with Peanuts | 10 minutes | 8:20 |
| 8:25 | Chocolate Truffle Cake | 5 minutes | 8:30 |
| | Final Beverage | | 8:35 |

# Tips and Details

You will find that this intricate meal is very rich and should be enjoyed throughout the entire evening. Do not add other distractions such as games or entertainment. Make this the "event of the evening" so the guests can enjoy the full magnitude of culinary delights.

This meal is being served in a classical European style with the salad served after the entrée. In European cuisine an additional course called an intermezzo, in this case a sorbet, is served prior to the entrée to cleanse the palate.

# Pâté de Foie Gras
# with Fresh Fruit and Baguettes

*serves 6*

| | |
|---|---|
| 1 basket (12 ounces) | strawberries |
| 3/4 cup (1 1/2 sticks) | sweet cream butter |
| 2 | Granny Smith apples |
| 1 | lemon |
| 12 ounces | pâté de foie gras, canned (fresh where available) |
| 1/3 cup | capers |
| 6 | cornichons (small sour pickles) |
| 12 slices | sour baguettes (sour dough cocktail bread) |
| 6 sprigs | mint (approximately 1/4 bunch) |

## Preparation

1. Wash and remove the tops from the strawberries and set aside.
2. Soften the butter at room temperature to a consistency that can be spread or piped out of a pastry bag.
3. Wash, drain, and cut each apple into 12 wedges; squeeze the juice from the lemon and rub the apple wedges with the juice to enhance the flavor and reduce browning.
4. Carefully remove pâté de foie gras by removing both ends from the can and gently pushing pâté onto a cutting board; with a sharp knife cut 12 equal slices; dip the knife into a cup of water between cuts so that the slices are smooth.
5. Place the following on each of the plates: 2 slices of pâté, 4 slices of apple, 3 strawberries, 1 teaspoon of drained capers, 1 cornichon, 1 tablespoon of softened butter (this could be piped out of a pastry bag for added detail), and 1 sprig of mint (wash and drain the mint first). Refrigerate until ready to serve.

## Ready to Serve

1. Remove the plates from the refrigerator and set aside.
2. Place the baguettes in a 300°F preheated oven for approximately 5 minutes; remove, place in a bread basket, and serve on the table along with the pâté and fruit plates.

**Preparation Time:** 15 minutes

**Final Preparation Time:** 5 minutes

# Consommé Celestine

*serves 6 (serve in 6-ounce soup bowls)*

| | |
|---|---|
| 5 cups | chicken stock (using a chicken base with water) |
| 2 (5-ounce) | chicken breasts, boneless, skinless |
| 1/4 cup | tapioca pearls |
| 1/8 cup | chives, chopped (approximately 1/4 bunch) |

### Preparation

1. Prepare the chicken stock by mixing a chicken base with water according to package directions; place in a large saucepan and simmer at 180°F for 15 minutes.
2. Place the 2 chicken breasts into the pot with the stock and poach approximately 15 minutes or until chicken reaches 165°F or higher for at least 15 seconds; remove from the pot, cool, and dice into 1/2-inch pieces.
3. Slowly add the tapioca to the hot chicken stock, stirring constantly until the soup has reached a light sauce consistency like that of heavy cream. Set aside.
4. Wash, drain, and finely chop the chives and set aside.

### Ready to Serve

1. Evenly distribute the diced chicken to each bowl; pour in the soup.
2. Top off with the chopped chives.

**Preparation Time:** 45 minutes

**Final Preparation Time:** 5 minutes

# Raspberry Sorbet

*serves 6 (serve in small fruit dishes)*

| | |
|---|---|
| 1 quart | raspberry sorbet |

### Preparation

1. Place a single 2-ounce scoop of sorbet in the center of a small fruit dish and promptly serve.

**Note:** Remove sorbet from the freezer approximately 5 minutes before serving to allow for easier scooping.

**Final Preparation Time:** 5 minutes

# Orange Spiced Roast Duck

*serves 6*

| | |
|---|---|
| *2* | *ducks (whole)* |
| *2 tablespoons* | *garlic, minced* |
| *3 tablespoons* | *salt* |
| *1 tablespoon* | *allspice* |
| *1/4 cup* | *liquid smoke (prepare according to bottle directions)* |
| *1 cup* | *orange juice* |

## Preparation

1. When the ducks are frozen, allow 2 days for thawing in the refrigerator.
2. Peel and mince the garlic.
3. Rub the garlic, salt, and allspice over the ducks; pour liquid smoke over the ducks, cover, and place in the refrigerator to marinate for at least 1 hour.

## Ready to Serve

1. Put the ducks in a roasting pan and pour orange juice over the top of the ducks; place in a 375°F preheated oven for approximately 2 hours or until the ducks have reached an internal temperature of 165°F or higher for at least 15 seconds (using a thermometer), occasionally basting with the orange juice.
2. Remove from the oven and allow to cool; cut all the meat from the bones, slice, and evenly place on top of the wild rice on each plate.

**Preparation Time:** 15 minutes
**Final Cooking Time:** 2 1/4 hours

# Wild Rice Pilaf

*serves 6*

| | |
|---|---|
| *1* | *yellow onion, jumbo* |
| *6 cups* | *chicken stock (using a chicken base with water)* |
| *1/4 cup (1/2 stick)* | *unsalted butter* |
| *2 leaves* | *bay leaves* |
| *2 cups* | *wild rice* |

### Preparation

1. Peel and mince the onion.
2. Prepare the chicken stock by mixing a chicken base with water according to package directions.
3. Melt the butter in a large saucepan over medium heat; add the minced onions and bay leaves; sauté until the onions begin to turn clear; add the wild rice and continue to sauté for 1 minute.
4. Pour the chicken stock into the sauté mixture and bring to a boil for 1 minute; reduce the heat to low; place a lid on the pot and simmer at 180°F for 50 minutes; remove bay leaves and stir. Place an equal amount on each plate using a 3-ounce spoon.

**Note:** If there is still moisture left in the pan, remove the rice with a slotted spoon.

**Preparation Time:** 1 hour

# Broccoli Florets with Sauce Hollandaise

*serves 6*

| | |
|---|---|
| 2 quarts | broccoli, cut (approximately 2 bunches) |
| 1 tablespoon | salt |
| 2 cups | hollandaise sauce, prepared mix |

### Preparation

1. Cut the broccoli florets off so each is no larger than a quarter, and 1 1/2 inches long, and wash.
2. Place the broccoli florets into boiling water for 2 minutes.
3. Remove from the boiling water; drain the broccoli in a colander; rinse with cold water; drain, cover, and refrigerate.

### Ready to Serve

1. Prepare the hollandaise sauce as per package directions.
2. Place the broccoli florets into boiling water for approximately 45 seconds; remove and drain.
3. Place an equal amount of florets on each plate and pour the hollandaise sauce over the top.

**Preparation Time:** 15 minutes

**Final Preparation Time:** 10 minutes

# Spinach Salad with Peanuts

*serves 6*

| | |
|---|---|
| 2 quarts | spinach, chopped (approximately 1 bunch) |
| 2 tablespoons | lime juice |
| 1 1/2 tablespoons | soy sauce |
| 1/4 cup | peanut oil |
| 1 teaspoon | garlic, minced |
| 1 tablespoon | ginger, grated (fresh) |
| 2 tablespoons | brown sugar |
| 1/2 teaspoon | ground black pepper |
| 1/3 cup | peanuts, whole unsalted |
| 1/3 cup | croutons, package prepared |

## Preparation

1. Wash, drain, and chop the spinach leaves into bite size pieces and refrigerate.
2. Combine the lime juice, soy sauce, peanut oil, minced garlic, grated ginger, brown sugar, and ground black pepper in a bowl and refrigerate for at least 1 hour.

## Ready to Serve

1. Place the peanuts in a sauté pan over medium heat and toss them in the pan until they begin to turn golden brown, approximately 5 to 7 minutes.
2. Toss the fresh spinach with the dressing and croutons; place an equal amount on the salad plates.
3. Top off with the toasted peanuts and promptly serve.

**Preparation Time:** 10 minutes

**Final Preparation Time:** 10 minutes

# Chocolate Truffle Cake

*serves 6*

| | |
|---|---|
| 1 pound | semisweet chocolate |
| 1 cup (2 sticks) | unsalted butter |
| 6 | eggs |
| 1/4 cup | powdered sugar |

## Preparation

1. Break the chocolate into pieces and slice the butter and place in a metal bowl; set the bowl over a pan of hot water (140°F); when the chocolate and butter are fully melted, thoroughly mix.

2. Crack the eggs into a metal bowl; set the bowl over a pot of simmering water; heat the eggs, stirring constantly to keep them from cooking; remove from the water when the eggs are warm to the touch.

3. Beat the eggs with an electric mixer for about 5 minutes or until the eggs have tripled in volume and soft peaks have formed.

4. Fold half of the eggs into the chocolate and butter mixture until almost blended; fold the remaining half in and blend until thoroughly mixed.

5. Pour the mixture into an 8-inch springform pan. **Note:** If a springform pan is not available, a metal pie pan may be substituted.

6. Place the pan into a larger pan with about 1 inch of water in it to create a water bath.

7. Place in a 425°F preheated oven for 5 minutes; then cover the cake pan with a loosely fitted piece of buttered foil and bake for another 10 minutes; remove from the oven and cool on a rack for 45 minutes. **Note:** The cake will have a soft appearance.

8. Cover with plastic wrap and refrigerate for 4 hours or until very firm.

## Ready to Serve

1. Set the pan on a hot damp towel to help soften the chocolate.

2. Run a thin metal spatula (or knife) around the outside of the cake and remove the ring if using a springform pan or loosen the edge if using a pie pan.

3. Invert the cake onto a serving plate. If using a springform pan, remove the bottom of the pan; if a pie pan, remove the whole pan.

4. Sprinkle with powdered sugar, cut, and serve.

**Preparation Time:** 1 hour

**Final Preparation Time:** 5 minutes

# Meet Me at the Casbah

•

*Antipasto of Vegetables with Hummus,
Baba Ghanouj and Pita Bread
Tabbouleh
Lamb Brochette with Couscous
Baklava*

•

# Beverage Selections

**Arak,** an anise-flavored spirit similar to Greek ouzo, is traditionally served with the *mezza* (appetizer course). Pour one shot of Arak in an 8-ounce glass and fill with water, topping it off with a couple of ice cubes. The result is a refreshing, milky-colored drink with a slight licorice flavor.

Good, strong **Turkish coffee** is made by one of the oldest brewing methods in existence. The terms *Turkish, Arabic, Greek,* and *Armenian* are all virtually interchangeable in describing this technique. The coffee is traditionally prepared in an *ibrik*, which is a tall, long-handled copper or brass pot, conical in shape. These boilers come in different sizes, making from 1 to 8 servings, and have a pronounced lip for pouring.

If you happen to have an ibrik, you are in luck! If not, fill an old-fashioned coffee pot (or regular kitchen pot) half full with cold water. (Add sugar at this point if the guests have a sweet tooth.) Bring the solution to a boil. Remove from the heat, add 1 to 2 ounces of ground coffee, according to taste or preference, stir, and place over the flame. As soon as the coffee foams to the rim, remove from the heat. Repeat this boiling/foaming process two more times.

The final brew can then be poured into demitasse (small cups). A thin head of brown foam will cover the surface of this powerful drink. This foam is called the "face of the coffee." In the Middle East, a host who does not produce a good foam is disgraced and loses "face."

Unlike many other beverages, this concoction will stand up to the hearty foods on the evening's menu.

**Retsina,** a dry white Greek wine flavored with pine resin, is another interesting selection for this exotic evening. The tradition of making this wine with resin may be derived from the ancient custom of sealing wine amphorae (clay pots) with pitch. As with true Turkish coffee, one needs to acquire a taste for this pungent beverage. However, the rich oil-based cuisine of the Middle East and Greece is well suited to the wine.

## NONALCOHOLIC

**Sweetened pomegranate juice** can be found in any Middle Eastern specialty store. To create a traditional punch, dilute with water and add pine nuts or almonds and a mint leaf. The tangy drink will assure your dinner guests that you have done your homework. **Fresh-squeezed lemonade** is another nonalcoholic drink that is popular in the Middle East. Add orange blossom water (available at the same specialty stores) for character.

# When to Start Cooking

*When dinner is served at 8:00 P.M. . . .*

| Cooking Preparation Schedule | | Cooking Times |
|---|---|---|
| 2:25 P.M. | Greek Vinaigrette (refrigerate 2 hours) | 5 minutes |
| 4:30 | Antipasto of Vegetables (refrigerate 3 hours) | 20 minutes |
| 4:50 | Tabbouleh | 1 hour 10 minutes |
| 5:30 | Lamb Brochette (refrigerate 2 hours) | 5 minutes |
| 6:00 | Baklava | 45 minutes |
| 6:45 | Time to set the tables and arrange the room. | |
| 7:15 | Time to clean up, relax a bit, double-check everything, and dress for the occasion. | |

| Final Cooking and Preparation Schedule | | | Serving Times |
|---|---|---|---|
| 7:50 P.M. | Antipasto of Vegetables | 10 minutes | 8:00 P.M. |
| 8:05 | Lamb Brochette | 25 minutes | 8:30 |
| 8:10 | Tabbouleh | 5 minutes | 8:15 |
| 8:15 | Couscous | 15 minutes | 8:30 |
| | Baklava | | 8:50 |
| | Final Beverage | | 8:55 |

# Tips and Details

If the party is a large event, you might consider hiring a belly dancer. This traditional form of entertainment is quite tasteful and is available through local entertainment agencies.

You may not be familiar with some of the ingredients in this menu. Do not be afraid to venture down to your local health food store and ask for suggestions and advice. Many of these items are also carried in larger well-stocked grocery stores.

# Antipasto of Vegetables

*serves 6 (serve on sandwich plates or small dinner plates)*

| | |
|---|---|
| *1 cup* | *Greek vinaigrette (recipe follows)* |
| *1 quart* | *broccoli, cut (approximately 1 bunch)* |
| *3* | *carrots* |
| *1/2 pound* | *mushrooms, medium* |
| *3/4 teaspoon* | *salt* |
| *3/4 pound* | *jicama\** |
| *2* | *tomatoes, large (firm)* |

| 1 can | large pitted black olives (Greek olives) |
| 1 package (6 ounces) | hummus* |
| 1 package (6 ounces) | baba ghanouj (or melitzano)* |
| 1 teaspoon | paprika |
| 3 slices | pita bread |
| 1/3 cup | parsley, chopped (approximately 1/4 bunch) |
| 3/4 cup | olive oil |

*These items are typically available at health food stores or specialty markets.

### Preparation

1. Prepare the Greek vinaigrette according to the recipe that follows and refrigerate.

2. Cut the broccoli into florets about the size of a quarter and 1 1/2 inches long; blanch them in salted boiling water for 3 minutes or until tender; drain in a colander and shock with cold running water; drain and refrigerate. **Salted boiling water:** Place enough water in the pot to cover the vegetables and add 1/4 teaspoon of salt.

3. Scrape and wash carrots; slice into 1/4-inch rounds; blanch the carrots in salted boiling water for 5 minutes or until tender; drain in a colander and shock with cold running water; drain and refrigerate.

4. Slice the mushrooms in half; blanch in salted boiling water for 2 minutes or until tender; drain and refrigerate. **Note:** Do not shock with cold running water.

5. Peel the jicama and slice into 1/4-inch strips averaging 2 to 3 inches in length.

6. Wash, drain, and cut the tomatoes into 8 wedges each for a total of 16.

7. Drain the juice from the olives.

8. Combine the broccoli, carrots, mushrooms, jicama, tomatoes, and olives; thoroughly mix with the Greek vinaigrette; cover and refrigerate for at least 3 hours.

**Note:** This can be prepared the previous evening or first thing in the morning.

### Ready to Serve

1. Place an equal amount of vegetables on each plate; scoop 1 ounce of hummus and 1 ounce of baba ghanouj (or melitzano) and place on one side of the vegetables, top off with a sprinkle of paprika; slice the pita bread into triangle cuts (like small pizza slices) and place on the other side of the plate.

2. Wash, drain, and chop parsley and sprinkle over the plate.

3. Place even amounts of olive oil into 2 or 3 small fruit cups for dipping the pita bread.

**Preparation Time:** 20 minutes

**Final Preparation Time:** 10 minutes

# Greek Vinaigrette

*serves 6*

| | |
|---|---|
| 1 | lemon |
| 1/3 cup | olive oil |
| 1/4 cup | white wine vinegar |
| 1/3 cup | salad oil |
| 1 tablespoon | garlic, minced |
| 1 1/2 teaspoons | salt |
| 1 1/2 teaspoons | ground black pepper |
| 1 1/2 teaspoons | onion powder |
| 1 teaspoon | thyme, dried |
| 2 teaspoons | oregano, flakes |

## Preparation

1. Squeeze the juice from the lemon.
2. Combine all the ingredients together in a bowl and thoroughly mix; cover and refrigerate for at least 2 hours.

**Note:** Most vinaigrettes are much better 1 to 2 days after they are made, as the time allows the flavors to mull together.

**Preparation Time:** 5 minutes

# Tabbouleh

*serves 6*

| | |
|---|---|
| 1 1/4 cups | cracked wheat bulgur |
| 3 cups | boiling water |
| 2 | tomatoes, large (firm) |
| 1 | cucumber |
| 1 1/3 cups | parsley, chopped (approximately 1 bunch) |
| 1 | yellow onion, jumbo |
| 2 | lemons |
| 2 tablespoons | olive oil |
| 2 tablespoons | white wine vinegar |
| 1/3 cup | salad oil |
| 1 tablespoon | salt |
| 1 head | lettuce |

## Preparation

1. Place the bulgur into a large mixing bowl; pour in boiling water, stir, and set aside for 1 hour.
2. Wash, drain, and dice the tomatoes into 1/2-inch pieces and set aside.
3. Peel the cucumber, remove the seeds, and dice into 1/2-inch pieces and set aside.
4. Wash, drain, and coarsely chop the parsley and set aside.
5. Peel and cut the onion in half; save half for another use; cut the remaining half into a 1/4-inch dice; set aside.
6. Drain the bulgur in a colander and return to the bowl.
7. Squeeze the juice from the lemons and combine with the olive oil, white wine vinegar, salad oil, and salt.
8. Combine the bulgur with the diced tomatoes, onions, cucumbers, and chopped parsley; mix with the dressing mixture; cover and refrigerate.

## Ready to Serve

1. Wash and drain lettuce; place 1 or 2 leaves on each plate.
2. Place an equal amount of tabbouleh on top of the lettuce leaves and serve.

**Preparation Time:** 1 hour 10 minutes
**Final Preparation Time:** 5 minutes

# Lamb Brochette

*serves 6*

| | |
|---|---|
| 2 1/4 pounds | lamb cubes |
| 1 1/2 cups | milk |
| 1 1/2 cups | vegetable oil |
| 1 1/2 | yellow onions, jumbo |
| 18 | cherry tomatoes |
| 18 leaves | bay leaves |
| 18 | mushrooms |
| 3/4 cup | sour cream |
| 6 | 8-inch bamboo skewers |
| 1/2 cup | chives, chopped (approximately 1 bunch) |

## Preparation

1. Purchase leg of lamb cut into 1-inch cubes and place in a deep pan.
2. Mix the milk and oil, then pour over the lamb cubes; cover and refrigerate for 2 hours.

## Ready to Serve

1. Peel and cut the onions in half; lay the halves flat on a cutting board and slice each half into 6 wedges; set aside.
2. Wash and remove the stems from the cherry tomatoes; set aside.
3. Wash and remove the stems from the mushrooms; set aside.
4. Wash, drain, and chop chives into 1/4-inch pieces; set aside.
5. Drain the lamb cubes.
6. Soak the bamboo skewers in water for 1 hour prior to cooking. This will prevent them from splitting and will also allow them to slide through the meat easily. Arrange the skewers in the following order: 1 mushroom cap, 1 lamb cube, 1 onion wedge, 1 bay leaf, and 1 cherry tomato; repeat 2 more times.
7. Place the skewers in a roasting pan; put the pan in a preheated oven set for broiling; broil for approximately 5 minutes; reduce heat to 350°F and bake for an additional 5

minutes or until the desired degree of doneness and reaching 155°F or higher for at least 15 seconds.

**8.** Heat sour cream until it is warm enough to pour.

**9.** Place an equal amount of couscous (recipe follows) on each plate; set a brochette on top of the couscous, pour the warm sour cream on top of the brochette; sprinkle with chives and serve.

**Preparation Time:** 5 minutes

**Final Cooking Time:** 25 minutes

# Couscous

*serves 6*

| | |
|---|---|
| 1 | yellow onion, jumbo |
| 2 tablespoons | vegetable oil |
| 2 1/4 cups | water |
| 1/2 teaspoon | salt |
| 2 tablespoons | butter |
| 1 box (10 ounces) | couscous |

## Preparation

**1.** Peel and mince the onion.

**2.** Place the oil and minced onion in a sauté pan with a lid and sauté for about 3 minutes or until the onions become clear.

**3.** Add the water, salt, and butter and bring to a boil; slowly mix in couscous; cover, remove from the heat, and let stand for 5 minutes.

**4.** Fluff lightly with a fork; place an equal amount of couscous on each plate using a 3-ounce spoon. Serve as you would serve rice. Set a brochette on top of the couscous, as explained in Step 9 of the lamb brochette recipe.

**Note:** Brown rice may be substituted in place of couscous. Prepare according to package directions.

**Preparation Time:** 15 minutes

# Baklava

*serves 6*

| | |
|---|---|
| 2 | *lemons* |
| *3/4 cup (1 1/2 sticks)* | *unsalted butter* |
| *2 cups* | *sugar* |
| *1/2 teaspoon* | *cinnamon* |
| *1 1/2 teaspoons* | *cloves, ground* |
| *1 package (6 ounces)* | *sliced almonds* |
| *1/2 cup (1 stick)* | *unsalted butter* |
| *24 sheets* | *phyllo dough (if frozen, note package thawing time)* |

## Preparation

1. Squeeze the juice from the lemons and set aside.
2. Melt the 3/4 cup of butter in a saucepan over low heat; slowly mix in the sugar until evenly blended.
3. Add the cinnamon, ground cloves, sliced almonds, and lemon juice to the butter and sugar mixture and continue to cook for 5 minutes while stirring constantly; remove from the heat and set aside.
4. Melt the 1/2 cup of butter.
5. Spread an even amount of the butter with a pastry brush over the bottom of a 9-by-13-inch baking pan.
6. Start layering the phyllo sheets (leaves) and brush melted butter between each sheet; use 9 sheets for the bottom.
7. Spread 1/2 of the almond, sugar, and spice mixture on top of the phyllo.
8. Layer 6 phyllo sheets with brushed melted butter between each sheet on top of the mixture.
9. Spread the remaining half of the almond, sugar, and spice mixture on top of the 6 phyllo sheets.
10. Layer the top with 9 phyllo sheets with brushed melted butter between each sheet.
11. Place the pan into a 325°F preheated oven for 30 minutes or until the top layer of phyllo has become golden brown; **remove the pan from oven and allow to cool for 5 minutes, and then immediately cut into 6 square or diamond shapes with a very sharp knife.**
12. Remove from the pan with a flexible spatula and place on individual dessert plates; allow to cool at room temperature for at least 1 hour.

**Note:** When in a hurry, baklava can be purchased from many fine bakeries.

**Preparation Time:** 45 minutes

# School Is Out

•

*Stuffed Celery Sticks*
*Hot Smoked Turkey with Provolone*
*Snowballs*

•

# Beverage Selections

Plan the drinks for this party with as much imagination as you can muster. Cool, colorful concoctions with fun presentations will be favorites of both the girls and boys. Don't forget to keep a supply of **cold milk** on hand as well, especially for dessert.

**Kool-Aid**® is still a popular drink with kids and a perfect choice for this affair, but try serving it with a dramatic twist. Freeze some Kool-Aid® in a jello mold, using a different color than what you have chosen as the base drink. Then, prepare the actual Kool-Aid® punch with sparkling water. You may want to experiment with different combinations of flavors for some added pizazz. Place the frozen mold in a punch bowl and add the base drink. Float some orange slices in the bowl and have a cherry ready for each glass.

A festive and healthy alternative is the **fruit smoothie.** Suggested ingredients: frozen orange juice concentrate, milk, yogurt, sliced banana, strawberries, vanilla extract, and honey. Place chopped fruit and liquids into blender (add crushed ice if desired) and frappé. The smoothie should be about the consistency of a milkshake. Use your imagination and have fun.

# When to Start Cooking

*When lunch is served at noon . . .*

| **Cooking Preparation Schedule** | | **Cooking Times** |
|---|---|---|
| 11:00 A.M. | Hot Smoked Turkey with Provolone | 15 minutes |
| 11:15 | Stuffed Celery Sticks | 15 minutes |
| 11:30 | Time to set the tables and arrange the room. | |
| 11:45 | Time to clean up, relax a bit, and double-check everything. | |

| **Final Cooking and Preparation Schedule** | | | **Serving Times** |
|---|---|---|---|
| 11:55 A.M. | Stuffed Celery Sticks | 5 minutes | 12:00 P.M. |
| 12:00 P.M. | Hot Smoked Turkey | 10 minutes | 12:10 |
| 12:05 | Beverage | 5 minutes | 12:10 |
| 12:20 | Snowballs | 5 minutes | 12:25 |

# Tips and Details

Obviously, you will want to decorate the dining area with balloons and streamers for the youngsters. Children's attention spans are not as long as adults', so plan other events such as games and art projects before, during, and after the meal.

More young people seem to be drinking healthy these days. Substitute individual sparkling waters for soda and 1 or 2 percent milk for whole milk.

Set up a sundae bar so the children can create the desserts themselves. They may make a mess, so a plastic tablecloth is advisable.

# Stuffed Celery Sticks

*serves 6*

| | |
|---|---|
| 6 stalks | celery |
| 6 ounces | peanut butter, creamy |
| 1 | banana, firm, ripe |
| 1 | lemon |
| 1 tablespoon | chopped pecans |

## Preparation

1. Wash, drain, and cut celery stalks into 1 1/2-inch sticks.
2. Spread peanut butter into the center of each celery stick.
3. Slice banana into 1/8-inch cuts; slice cuts in half to form half circles.
4. Squeeze the juice from the lemon, dip the banana slices into the lemon juice, and drain. This reduces the browning and enhances the flavor.
5. Place a banana half circle firmly into the peanut butter in each celery stick, leaving the round side up.
6. Place a small chopped pecan into the peanut butter next to the banana.
7. Arrange on a serving dish, cover with plastic wrap, and refrigerate until ready to serve.

**Note:** Do not prepare more than 30 minutes in advance.

**Preparation Time:** 15 minutes

**Final Preparation Time:** 5 minutes

# Hot Smoked Turkey
# with Provolone

*serves 6*

| | |
|---|---|
| 6 | hero rolls |
| 2 tablespoons | butter |
| 6 ounces | cream cheese |
| 2 stalks | celery |
| 1 1/4 pounds | smoked turkey, deli sliced |
| 1/4 pound | provolone cheese, deli sliced |
| 2 tablespoons | Dijon mustard |
| 2 tablespoons | mayonnaise |
| 6 | whole purple plums, canned or fresh when in season |

**Preparation**

1. Cut hero rolls in half and spread butter on the cut sides of each roll; lightly grill, being careful not to burn.
2. Arrange the rolls on a baking pan with the top halves next to the bottom halves; spread cream cheese on the bottom halves of the rolls.
3. Wash, drain, and chop the celery into a small dice and sprinkle on top of the cream cheese.
4. Place 3 ounces (4 thin slices) of smoked turkey on top of the cream cheese and celery. **Note:** Drop each slice individually to create a stacked bunch effect versus a tight fold.
5. Place 1 slice of provolone cheese on top of the smoked turkey.
6. Mix the Dijon mustard and mayonnaise then spread on the top halves of each roll; cover with plastic wrap and refrigerate.

**Ready to Serve**

1. Remove the plastic wrap and place the baking pan in a 350°F preheated oven for 10 minutes or until the provolone cheese is melted, being attentive not to overbake.
2. Drain the liquid from the purple plums and place 1 plum on each plate next to the sandwich.

**Preparation Time:** 15 minutes
**Final Cooking Time:** 10 minutes

# Snowballs

*serves 6 (serve in dessert cups or fruit dishes)*

| | |
|---|---|
| *1/3 cup* | *chocolate syrup* |
| *1 half gallon* | *vanilla ice cream* |
| *1/3 cup* | *shredded coconut* |
| *6* | *maraschino cherry halves* |

## Preparation

1. Place 1 tablespoon of chocolate syrup into each dessert cup or fruit dish.
2. Place a 4-ounce scoop of vanilla ice cream on top of the chocolate syrup.
3. Sprinkle 1 tablespoon of shredded coconut over the top and sides of each scoop of ice cream.
4. Top off with a maraschino cherry half.

**Note:** Remove the ice cream from the freezer approximately 5 minutes before serving to allow for easier scooping.

**Preparation Time:** 5 minutes

# It's Your Birthday

•

*Caesar Salad*
*Baked Halibut Edward*
*Brabant Potatoes*
*Tomato Provençale*
*Birthday Cake (your favorite choice)*

•

# Beverage Selections

**Sparkling wine** makes any occasion more festive, especially a birthday. Make it a celebration. Bring out the long-stemmed tulip glasses and ice bucket. These are appropriate for the cider as well as the wine.

For those who prefer something less bubbly with their meal, serve a light **white wine** with the Caesar salad. Müller-Thurgau from Germany or the Pacific Northwest would be an ideal choice, but look for a drier style to pour during the main course. Either a chardonnay or sauvignon blanc from California will do nicely to bring out the subtle flavor of the halibut.

If the birthday dignitary is having a chocolate cake, serve a sumptuous cabernet sauvignon or red Bordeaux. If cheesecake, carrot cake, or white birthday cake is preferred, choose a late harvest Riesling or dessert wine from Sauternes. Many California vintners produce agreeable dessert wines made from the muscat grape, which would also do quite nicely on this menu.

A **cordial** (or liqueur) will finish the festivities on a high note. Some people prefer a coffee-flavored version such as Kahlúa or Tia Maria. (These can be added to a cup of coffee or enjoyed straight.) A snifter of **brandy** is also elegant and traditional for a birthday celebration.

## NONALCOHOLIC

**Sparkling cider** adds a touch of distinction and can be served throughout the meal. A **birthday punch** of white grape juice, pineapple juice, sparkling soda, and a touch of sherbet (in a color to accent your decorations) also makes for a great item.

# When to Start Cooking

*When dinner is at 6:00 P.M. . . .*

| Cooking Preparation Schedule | | Cooking Times |
|---|---|---|
| 4:00 P.M. | Caesar Salad | 10 minutes |
| 4:10 | Tomato Provençale | 15 minutes |
| 4:30 | Time to set the tables and arrange the room. | |
| 5:00 | Time to clean up, relax a bit, double-check everything, and dress for the birthday party. | |

| Final Cooking and Preparation Schedule | | | Serving Times |
|---|---|---|---|
| 5:40 P.M. | Brabant Potatoes | 30 minutes | 6:20 P.M. |
| 5:50 | Baked Halibut Edward | 30 minutes | 6:20 |
| 5:55 | Caesar Salad | 5 minutes | 6:00 |
| 6:10 | Tomato Provençale | 10 minutes | 6:20 |
| 6:35 | Birthday Cake | 5 minutes | 6:40 |
| | Final Beverage | | 6:45 |

**Postscript:** Order the birthday cake a couple of days in advance . . . and do not forget to pick it up!

## Tips and Details

An interesting note on that "classic" salad, known as a Caesar. It does not come from Rome. In 1924, a small cantina in Tijuana, Mexico, was the birthplace of Caesar salad. Many stories surround this time-honored dish.

One version of its inception is that a group of tourists, stranded during a storm, sought refuge in Caesar's Cantina. Romaine lettuce was the only foodstuff of substance available. All of the travelers each added what provisions they had brought with them. The resultant Caesar salad was made popular by word of mouth and reputation. Caesar's Cantina exists to this day.

All of the stories point to the undeniable fact that the Caesar salad was born out of necessity and utilization of available products (a good point for all aspiring chefs to remember).

# Caesar Salad

*serves 6*

| | |
|---|---|
| 1 head | romaine |
| 1 ounce | anchovies |
| 2 teaspoons | garlic, minced |
| 1 | egg, pasteurized |
| 2 tablespoons | balsamic vinegar |
| 2 tablespoons | olive oil |
| 2 tablespoons | Parmesan cheese |
| 1 1/2 cups | croutons, package prepared |

## Preparation

1. Wash, drain, and cut romaine into bite-size pieces; place in a bowl and refrigerate.
2. Peel and mince the garlic.
3. Mash the anchovies and garlic together to make a paste; set aside.
4. Crack the egg into a mixing bowl, add the balsamic vinegar, and beat with a whip until smooth; slowly add the olive oil while constantly beating; cover and refrigerate.

## Ready to Serve

1. Beat the dressing until blended and pour over the romaine until all the leaves are coated; sprinkle with the Parmesan cheese and toss in the croutons.
2. Place an equal amount on each plate and top off with an equally divided amount of the anchovy and garlic paste.

**Preparation Time:** 10 minutes
**Final Preparation Time:** 5 minutes

# Baked Halibut Edward

*serves 6*

| | |
|---|---|
| 6 (6-ounce) | halibut steaks, frozen |
| 2 tablespoons | butter |
| 1/4 teaspoon | salt |
| 1/4 teaspoon | ground black pepper |
| 1/3 cup | Thousand Island dressing, prepared |
| 1/3 cup | parsley, chopped (approximately 1/4 bunch) |
| 6 | black olives, pitted |

## Preparation

1. Refrigerate the halibut steaks long enough to thaw; dry both sides with a paper towel.
2. Spread butter over the entire bottom of a shallow roasting pan.
3. Salt and pepper both sides of the halibut steaks and place in the roasting pan.
4. Spread a tablespoon of Thousand Island dressing over the top of each halibut steak.
5. Place in a 350°F preheated oven for 20 minutes or until reaching 145°F or higher for at least 15 seconds, being careful not to overcook.
6. Wash, drain, and chop the parsley and set aside.
7. Remove the halibut steaks from the pan and serve with a spatula; top off with a sprinkle of parsley and 1 black olive placed in the center of each steak.

**Preparation Time:** 30 minutes

# Brabant Potatoes

*serves 6*

| | |
|---|---|
| *2 pounds* | *new potatoes, small* |
| *1/2 teaspoon* | *salt* |
| *1/3 cup* | *butter* |

## Preparation

1. Remove the skins and wash the potatoes.
2. Cover the potatoes with water and add the salt. Boil for 10 minutes.
3. Drain the potatoes and place in a shallow roasting pan.
4. Melt the butter and with a pastry brush spread over all sides of the potatoes.
5. Place the pan in a 350°F preheated oven for 10 minutes or until done, occasionally basting with (brushing on) the melted butter while baking. (May be placed on the top rack of the oven and baked with the halibut.)

**Preparation Time:** 30 minutes

# Tomato Provençale

*serves 6*

| | |
|---|---|
| 3 | tomatoes, medium (firm) |
| 1 tablespoon | garlic, minced |
| 1 1/2 tablespoons | chopped parsley |
| 1/2 cup | dry bread crumbs |
| 1/2 teaspoon | salt |
| 1/4 teaspoon | ground black pepper |
| 3 tablespoons | olive oil |

## Preparation

1. Cut the tomatoes in half and gently squeeze and shake out the juice and seeds; place the tomato halves in a shallow roasting pan with the cut side up; create a slight dip in each tomato half by lightly pressing down with the back side of a tablespoon, thus preparing a small cavity to hold the bread crumb mixture.
2. Peel and mince the garlic.
3. Wash, drain, and finely chop the parsley.
4. Mix the minced garlic, chopped parsley, dry bread crumbs, salt, and ground pepper; sprinkle an equal amount into the small cavity of each tomato half.
5. Pour the olive oil on top of each tomato half bread crumb mixture; cover with plastic wrap and refrigerate.

## Ready to Serve

1. Remove the plastic wrap and place in a 350°F preheated oven for 10 minutes or until the bread crumb mixture is nicely browned, being careful not to overcook (burn). (May be placed in the oven with the halibut beside the potatoes on the top rack.) Remove from the pan and serve with a spatula.

**Preparation Time:** 15 minutes
**Final Cooking Time:** 10 minutes

# Irish Lullaby

•

*Dublin Potato Salad*
*Irish Stew*
*Raisin Bread Pudding and Irish Whiskey Accent*
*Soda Bread and Butter*

•

# Beverage Selections

To duplicate the drink that is enormously popular in Belfast, **Cidona,** mix regular club soda with apple juice. This sets the perfect mood for an Irish menu. Another fashionable drink is **white lemonade** (7 Up mixed with a citrus juice such as orange or grapefruit juice). If you like, add some zing to each of these drinks by adding a shot of Irish whiskey.

Treat the guests to a true Irish pub tradition of **Guinness and stout beers.** For an authentic cocktail pour half a glass of Guinness (dark beer) into a clear pint glass. Add a half glass of light beer without mixing. You've created the Irish classic, black and tan.

**Irish coffee** (coffee with Irish whiskey), Baileys Irish Cream, regular strong coffee, and of course, tea are all excellent companions for the bread pudding.

### NONALCOHOLIC

**Ballygowen water** is the Irish equivalent of Perrier. You may be able to find it in an international deli. This or another sparkling water will serve to cleanse the guests palates between courses.

# When to Start Cooking

*When dinner is served at 7:00 P.M. . . .*

| Cooking Preparation Schedule | | Cooking Times |
|---|---|---|
| 2:45 P.M. | Dublin Potato Salad | 1 hour |
| 3:45 | Raisin Bread Pudding | 55 minutes |
| 4:30 | Time to set the tables and arrange the room. | |
| 5:00 | Time to clean up, relax a bit, double-check everything, and dress for the occasion. | |

| Final Cooking and Preparation Schedule | | | Serving Times |
|---|---|---|---|
| 5:45 P.M. | Irish Stew | 1 1/2 hours | 7:20 P.M. |
| 6:45 | Dublin Potato Salad | 15 minutes | 7:00 |
| 7:35 | Raisin Bread Pudding | 5 minutes | 7:40 |
| | Final Beverage | | 7:45 |

# Tips and Details

Invite the guests into a more casual setting for after-dinner coffee and drinks. Buy some gold foil and construct two "pots of gold." In the first pot place gold foil Godiva chocolates (or generic chocolates wrapped in gold foil). In the second pot wrap party gifts for each of the guests to select.

Irish whiskey is made only from malted barley and distilled three times. The resultant sweeter whiskey is somewhat different from its heavier cousins, bourbon and Scotch.

Although whiskey contains a high alcohol content, the recipe for the bread pudding with whiskey sauce has a negligible amount of alcohol in the sauce. When making the sauce, the alcohol content of the whiskey is mostly volatilized. During this process most of the alcohol evaporates, leaving primarily the flavor of the whiskey.

# Dublin Potato Salad

*serves 6*

| | |
|---|---|
| 3 (5-ounce) | chicken breasts, boneless, skinless |
| 1 teaspoon | salt |
| 2 teaspoons | ground black pepper |
| 2 pounds | red potatoes |
| 1 tablespoon | caraway seeds |
| 3/4 cup | mayonnaise |
| 1 teaspoon | ground white pepper |
| 1 teaspoon | salt |
| 1 tablespoon | Worcestershire sauce |
| 2 tablespoons | stone ground mustard |
| 1 | lemon |
| 1 head | lettuce |
| 2 | red delicious apples |
| 1 | lemon |

## Preparation

1. Season the chicken with 1 teaspoon of salt and the ground black pepper.
2. Put the chicken into a roasting pan and place in a 350°F preheated oven for 30 minutes or until it has reached 165°F or higher for at least 15 seconds; remove and place in the refrigerator to cool.
3. When the chicken if fully cooled, slice each breast into 6 slices, cutting lengthwise to create long strips.
4. Wash and boil the red potatoes whole for 15 minutes or until they are "fork tender" but not overcooked; remove from the water and cool at room temperature. (**Fork tender:** when a fork will slide into the potatoes with very little resistance.)
5. Toast the caraway seeds by placing them into a sauté pan over medium heat, moving them constantly by shaking the pan; remove and cool.
6. Prepare the sauce by combining the mayonnaise, ground white pepper, 1 teaspoon of salt, Worcestershire sauce, stone ground mustard, and the juice of 1 lemon; thoroughly mix, cover, and refrigerate.
7. Wash and drain the lettuce and separate the leaves.

## Ready to Serve

1. Slice the potatoes into 1/4-inch slices.
2. Wash, drain, and cut the apples into 1/2-inch wedges by using a paring knife or apple cutter.
3. Squeeze the juice from 1 lemon and rub the juice onto the apple wedges to reduce browning and enhance the flavor.
4. Place an equal amount of lettuce leaves on each plate.
5. Place an equal amount of sauce on top of the lettuce toward the bottom of the plate for dipping.
6. Arrange the sliced chicken, potato rounds, and apple wedges to create a fan pattern on the plate.
7. Top off with an equal sprinkle of the toasted caraway seeds.

**Preparation Time:** 1 hour
**Final Preparation Time:** 15 minutes

# Irish Stew

*serves 6 (serve in large soup bowls)*

| | |
|---|---|
| 2 1/4 pounds | lamb cubes |
| 2 tablespoons | vegetable oil |
| 1 | yellow onion, jumbo |
| 6 cups | chicken stock (using a chicken base with water) |
| 1 head | green cabbage |
| 1 pound | red potatoes |
| 1 leaf | bay leaf |
| 1 tablespoon | salt |
| 2 teaspoons | ground black pepper |
| 12 (1-inch) slices | soda bread or rye bread |
| 1/2 cup (1 stick) | butter |

## Preparation

1. Purchase leg of lamb cut into 1-inch cubes.
2. Place the oil in a sauté pan over medium heat; add the lamb cubes and sauté until nicely browned; drain off grease.
3. Dice the onion and sauté with the lamb for 2 minutes.
4. Prepare the chicken stock in a large stock pot by mixing a chicken base with water acording to package directions; over medium heat, add the lamb and onions.
5. Cut the head of cabbage into a 1 1/2- to 2-inch dice and add to the chicken stock.
6. Wash and cut the red potatoes into quarters and add to the stock.
7. Add the bay leaf, salt, and ground pepper; reduce the heat for the stew to a 180°F simmer; put the lid on the pot and simmer for 1 hour, checking for doneness of the lamb and reaching 155°F or higher for at least 15 seconds. Remove the bay leaf before serving.
8. Use a 6-ounce ladle to serve.
9. Put a loaf of soda bread or rye bread into a bread basket and place on the table.
10. Slice butter into 1/4-inch cuts; put on a small plate next to the bread.

**Preparation Time:** 1 1/2 hours

# Raisin Bread Pudding and Irish Whiskey Accent

*serves 6*

| | |
|---|---|
| 4 | eggs |
| 1 cup | half-and-half |
| 1/4 cup | sugar |
| 1 teaspoon | cinnamon |
| 1 teaspoon | cloves, ground |
| 1 teaspoon | allspice, ground |
| 1/4 cup | brown sugar |
| 12 slices | white bread |
| 1 cup | raisins |
| 1 teaspoon | butter |
| 3/4 cup | Irish whiskey (or maple syrup) |
| 1/3 cup | whipping cream |

## Preparation

1. Combine the eggs, half-and-half, 3 tablespoons of sugar, cinnamon, cloves, allspice, and 1 tablespoon of brown sugar in a mixing bowl and thoroughly blend.
2. Remove the crusts from the bread and slice bread into 1-inch cubes.
3. Mix the cut bread and raisins with the egg mixture.
4. Butter the inside of a 6-by-8-inch baking pan.
5. Pour the mixture into the pan; place the pan into a 325°F preheated oven for 45 minutes or until the pudding has set and is a nice golden brown color; remove and place on a wire rack to cool.
6. While the pudding is in the oven, place the whiskey in a saucepan over low heat for 3 to 5 minutes; just before it boils, add 3 tablespoons of brown sugar and continue to simmer until the sugar has completely dissolved. Be careful not to boil; set aside to cool. (If substituting maple syrup, use as is.)
7. Whip the cream with 1 tablespoon of sugar until it reaches a soft peak; cover and refrigerate.

## Ready to Serve

1. Cut the pudding into 6 equal pieces.
2. Place 1 tablespoon of the whiskey sauce (or maple syrup) on each plate.
3. Place the pudding on top of the sauce; top off with a spoonful of whipped cream.

**Preparation Time:** 55 minutes

**Final Preparation Time:** 5 minutes

# A Touch of Venice

•

*Antipasto*
*Minestrone Soup*
*Italian Bread and Sweet Cream Butter*
*Sausage and Spinach Lasagna*
*Fried Creams*

•

# Beverage Selections

When preparing a theme dinner, it is often fun to match the food with beverages from that particular region. Italians drink **wine,** so when in Rome . . .

Italian wines are often named for a particular area, and one of the most famous is Valpolicella. This northern Italian **red wine** is light, fruity, and perfect for openers. For those who prefer a **dry white wine,** the region is also well known for its Soave. Either, or both, would be well suited for the antipasto and salad courses.

A hearty **red wine** such as Barolo or Chianti will enhance the lasagna course. Barolo and most Chianti are richly textured, complex, and possess a distinctive bouquet reminiscent of raspberries, truffles, and roses.

### NONALCOHOLIC

**Sparkling cider** and **sparkling waters** can be served throughout the meal.

**Espresso** or **cappuccino** (espresso with steamed milk) are ideal with fried creams to complete the evening. These can also be enjoyed during dinner, in lieu of the wine.

# When to Start Cooking

*When dinner is served at 7:00 P.M. . . . .*

| Cooking Preparation Schedule | | Cooking Times |
|---|---|---|
| 12:45 P.M. | Italian vinaigrette (refrigerate 2 hours) | 5 minutes |
| 3:00 | Antipasto | 20 minutes |
| 3:20 | Sausage and Spinach Lasagna | 45 minutes |
| 4:05 | Fried Creams | 20 minutes |
| 4:30 | Time to set the tables and arrange the room. | |
| 5:00 | Time to clean up, relax a bit, double-check everything, and dress for the occasion. | |

**Final Cooking and Preparation Schedule**

| | | | Serving Times |
|---|---|---|---|
| 6:20 P.M. | Minestrone Soup | 1 hour | 7:20 P.M. |
| 6:40 | Sausage and Spinach Lasagna | 1 hour | 7:40 |
| 6:55 | Antipasto | 5 minutes | 7:00 |
| 7:50 | Fried Creams | 10 minutes | 8:00 |
| | Final Beverage | | 8:05 |

## Tips and Details

A traditional table condiment for Italian bread is extra virgin olive oil presented in a bowl. Not only does this oil taste good, but it is also healthy. Olive oil is high in monounsaturated fats, which have been shown to reduce levels of cholesterol in the body.

The elegant red grape, Sangiovese, makes up 75 to 90 percent of all Chianti. However, 2 to 10 percent of Chianti is made with white grapes (Trebbiano and malvasia).

It is very important to emphasize that the lasagna should be cooled at least 15 minutes after cooking, before it is served.

# Antipasto

*serves 6 (serve on salad or small dinner plates)*

| | |
|---|---|
| 1 cup | Italian vinaigrette (recipe follows) |
| 1 quart | broccoli, cut (approximately 1 bunch) |
| 2 | carrots |
| 1/2 pound | mushrooms, medium |
| 3/4 teaspoon | salt |
| 1 cup | large pitted black olives |
| 3/4 cup | green olives stuffed with pimentos |
| 2 | cornichons (sour dill pickles) |
| 1/2 pound | Italian salami, deli sliced |
| 1/3 cup | capers |

## Preparation

1. Prepare the Italian vinaigrette according to the recipe that follows and refrigerate. Prepare 2 hours ahead of time.
2. Cut the broccoli into florets about the size of a quarter; blanch them in salted boiling water for 3 minutes or until tender; drain in a colander and shock with cold running water; drain and refrigerate. **Salted boiling water:** Place enough water in the pot to cover the vegetables and add 1/4 teaspoon of salt.
3. Scrape and wash carrots; slice into 1/4-inch rounds; blanch the carrots in salted boiling water for 5 minutes or until tender; drain in a colander and shock with cold running water; drain and refrigerate.
4. Wash and slice the mushrooms in half; blanch in salted boiling water for 2 minutes or until tender; drain and refrigerate. **Note:** Do not shock with cold running water.
5. Drain the juice from the olives.
6. Cut the cornichons into 1/4-inch rounds.
7. Combine olives, cornichons, Italian salami, capers, and blanched vegetables and mushrooms; thoroughly mix with the Italian vinaigrette; cover and refrigerate for at least 1 hour.

## Ready to Serve

1. Place an equal amount on each plate and serve.

**Preparation Time:** 20 minutes

**Final Preparation Time:** 5 minutes

# Italian Vinaigrette

*serves 6*

| | |
|---|---|
| 1 | lemon |
| 1/3 cup | olive oil |
| 1/3 cup | salad oil |
| 1/4 cup | white wine vinegar |
| 1 teaspoon | thyme, dried |
| 2 teaspoons | oregano, flakes |
| 1 1/2 teaspoons | onion powder |
| 1 tablespoon | garlic, minced |
| 1 1/2 teaspoons | salt |
| 1 1/2 teaspoons | ground black pepper |

### Preparation

1. Squeeze the juice from the lemon.
2. Combine all of the ingredients in a bowl and thoroughly mix; cover and refrigerate for at least 2 hours.

**Note:** Most vinaigrettes are much better 1 to 2 days after they are made, as the time allows the flavors to mull together.

**Preparation Time:** 5 minutes

# Minestrone Soup

*serves 6 (serve in 6-ounce soup bowls)*

| | |
|---|---|
| 3 | tomatoes, large |
| 1 | yellow onion, jumbo |
| 2 tablespoons | garlic, minced |
| 1 head | romaine lettuce |
| 1 1/3 cups | parsley, chopped (approximately 1 bunch) |
| 4 | zucchini |
| 1 1/4 cups | sweet peas, frozen |
| 1 1/2 teaspoons | basil, dry |

| 1 1/4 cups | lima beans (canned) |
| 1/4 cup | olive oil |
| 3 cups | water |
| 2 tablespoons | ground black pepper |
| 3/4 cup | Parmesan cheese, grated |
| 12 slices | Italian bread (1 loaf evenly sliced) |
| 1/4 pound | sweet cream butter |

### Preparation

1. Peel the tomatoes by blanching them in boiling water for 30 seconds; peel away the thin skin and cut into a 1-inch dice; set aside.
2. Peel and cut the onion in half; slice both halves into very thin slices; set aside.
3. Peel and mince the garlic; set aside.
4. Wash, drain, and shred the romaine lettuce; set aside.
5. Wash, drain, and coarsely chop the parsley; set aside.
6. Peel and chop the zucchini; set aside.
7. Place the prepared vegetables in a large pot by layering in the following order:
   a. The bottom layer of tomatoes covered with the onions and garlic.
   b. Next, place the zucchini and the shredded romaine.
   c. Put the peas on top of the romaine and sprinkle with half of the chopped parsley and basil.
   d. Top the peas with the lima beans, sprinkle the remaining half of chopped parsley, basil, and the olive oil.

**Note:** Be sure to follow the above order and **do not stir or mix the vegetables!!**

8. Cook over a medium heat for 10 minutes or until the vegetables release their liquid.
9. Thoroughly stir the vegetables; add the water and ground pepper and simmer at 180°F for 30 minutes, frequently stirring.
10. Serve in bowls using a 6-ounce ladle and top off with 2 tablespoons of fresh grated Parmesan cheese in each bowl.
11. Put a loaf of Italian bread into a bread basket and place on the table.
12. Slice butter into 1/4-inch cuts; put on a small plate next to the bread.

**Preparation Time:** 1 hour

# Sausage and Spinach Lasagna

*serves 6*

| | |
|---|---|
| 1 pound | pork sausage |
| 3 | shallots |
| 3 tablespoons | garlic, diced |
| 1 1/2 cups | ricotta cheese |
| 4 | eggs |
| 1 teaspoon | salt |
| 1 tablespoon | ground black pepper |
| 1 package (10 ounces) | chopped spinach, frozen |
| 2 tablespoons | olive oil |
| 1/4 cup | salad oil |
| 1/2 pound | lasagna noodles |
| 1 1/2 cups | spaghetti sauce, jar prepared |
| 3 cups | mozzarella cheese, shredded |
| 1/2 cup | Parmesan cheese, grated |

## Preparation

1. Sauté the sausage over medium heat until completely cooked and reaching 155°F or higher for at least 15 seconds; place the sausage on a paper towel to absorb the grease and cool.
2. Peel and dice the shallots and garlic; set aside.
3. Combine the ricotta cheese, eggs, salt, and ground pepper in a large mixing bowl and blend with an electric mixer until smooth.
4. Thaw frozen spinach in a microwave oven, drain, and cool.
5. Place the olive oil in a sauté pan over medium heat; add the shallots and garlic and sauté for 1 minute; add the spinach and sauté for an additional 2 minutes over low heat.
6. Roughly chop the cooked sausage and add it to the spinach mixture; sauté for another 2 minutes while thoroughly mixing the sausage with the spinach, shallots, and garlic; remove from the heat and set aside.

7. Place a gallon of water and the salad oil in a large pot and bring to a boil; add the lasagna noodles and boil until *al dente*.

8. Remove the lasagna noodles when *al dente* and place in a colander; run cold water over the noodles to cool.

9. Start layering the lasagna noodles on the bottom of a 9-by-13-inch baking pan; 4 noodles across the bottom.

10. Next, place a layer of half of the ricotta and egg mixture; then half of the spinach and sausage mixture.

11. Pour 3/4 cup of spaghetti sauce over the sausage and spinach mixture; then sprinkle 1 cup of shredded mozzarella cheese.

12. Now another layer of lasagna noodles, the remaining half of the ricotta and egg mixture and the spinach and sausage mixture, 3/4 cup of spaghetti sauce, and 1 cup of shredded mozzarella cheese.

13. Top with the final layer of lasagna noodles; cover with 1 cup of shredded mozzarella cheese and 1/2 cup of grated Parmesan cheese; cover with plastic wrap and refrigerate.

**Ready to Serve**

1. Remove the plastic wrap and place on the center rack of a 325°F preheated oven for 45 minutes or until it has reached 165°F or higher for at least 15 seconds and is a nice golden brown.

2. Remove from the oven and cool for 15 minutes before cutting and serving; cut into 6 squares and serve with a spatula.

**Note:** The preparation may be done the previous evening.

**Preparation Time:** 45 minutes
**Final Cooking Time:** 1 hour

# Fried Creams

*serves 6*

| | |
|---|---|
| 3 | eggs |
| 2 cups | milk |
| 1/4 teaspoon | cinnamon |
| 1/4 cup | cornstarch |
| 2 tablespoons | flour |
| 1 cup | sugar |
| 1/2 teaspoon | vanilla extract |
| 5 | graham crackers |
| 1/3 cup | milk |
| 1 tablespoon | butter |
| 1/3 cup | brandy (optional) |
| 1/3 cup | powdered sugar |

### Preparation

1. Separate the yolks from the eggs using plastic gloves or egg separator and beat the yolks.
2. Mix the egg yolks with 2 cups of milk and the cinnamon; pour into a saucepan over medium heat.
3. Mix the cornstarch, flour, and sugar; add to the milk and egg solution; stir constantly for about 15 minutes or until the mixture becomes very thick.
4. Remove from the heat and blend in the vanilla extract.
5. Pour into a 9-by-13-inch pan and refrigerate for at least 1 hour or until very firm.

### Ready to Serve

1. Cut the cream mixture into 1-inch cubes.
2. Place graham crackers between 2 pieces of wax paper and roll with a rolling pin to create 3/4 cups of graham cracker crumbs.
3. Pour 1/3 cup of milk into a small bowl and dip each cube into the milk and then roll in the graham cracker crumbs.
4. Melt the butter in a large sauté pan over medium heat; add the cream cubes and quickly fry until they reach a light golden brown.
5. OPTIONAL . . . Pour 1 tablespoon of brandy on each dessert plate.
6. Remove the creams from the sauté pan and place on the dessert plates (optional: on top of the brandy).
7. Sprinkle with powdered sugar and serve.

**Preparation Time:** 20 minutes

**Final Preparation Time:** 10 minutes

# Backyard Barbecue

•

*Roasted Corn and Red Pepper Salad*

### *Mixed Grill:*
*Garlic and Fresh Mint Lamb Chops*
*Beer-Basted Flank Steak*
*Honey Dijon Chicken*

*Melon Surprise*

•

# Beverage Selections

No party can call itself a barbecue without **beer,** so have plenty of domestic or imported bottles on hand. Display the selections on ice in an old metal washtub if you have one, or a standard cooler will work just fine. If the party is large enough, you may want to consider a half keg (pony) or even a full one to keep the refreshment on tap.

**Microbrews,** one of the hottest beverage trends in America, come in a variety of styles and can provide some local flavor to the barbecue. Serve some of these small-batch brews as an alternative to the big commercial brands and your guests will be enjoying the freshest beer available. Widmer and Full Sail, both from the Pacific Northwest, are excellent examples of microbrews and would make welcome additions to any party.

If you really want the barbecue hot, try mixing up a big batch of **Long Island iced tea.** Not for the faint of heart, this drink consists of all the white liquors (vodka, gin, rum, and tequila) mixed with cola. The taste is remarkably similar to real iced tea, and garnished with a lemon wedge, it even has the same appearance. Be very careful with guests who are driving, though, as this is a potent drink and it's easy to overimbibe.

If your guests prefer wine, a merlot from the Napa Valley or St. Emilion in Bordeaux will hold its own against the powerful grill items. A well-made chardonnay, with at least one year of oak aging, should display a wide range of flavors that will pair perfectly with the honey dijon chicken.

## NONALCOHOLIC

If the weather is too hot for alcohol, serve **fresh-squeezed lemonade** and **sun tea.** Add strawberries for garnish and flavor. These drinks will invigorate the guests and leave room for the melon surprise.

# When to Start Cooking

*When the barbecue is at 5:00 P.M. . . . .*

| Cooking Preparation Schedule | | Cooking Times |
|---|---|---|
| 2:00 P.M. | Mixed Grill | 20 minutes |
| 2:20 | Roasted Corn and Red Pepper Salad | 45 minutes |
| 3:05 | Melon Surprise | 15 minutes |
| 3:20 | Time to set the tables. | |
| 4:00 | Time to clean up, relax a bit, double-check everything, and get ready for the barbecue. | |

**Final Cooking and Preparation Schedule**          **Serving Times**

| 4:50 P.M. | Mixed Grill | 10 minutes | 5:00 P.M. |
| 4:55 | Roast Corn and Red Pepper Salad | 5 minutes | 5:00 |
| | Beverages | | 5:00 |
| 5:15 | Melon Surprise | 5 minutes | 5:20 |

# Tips and Details

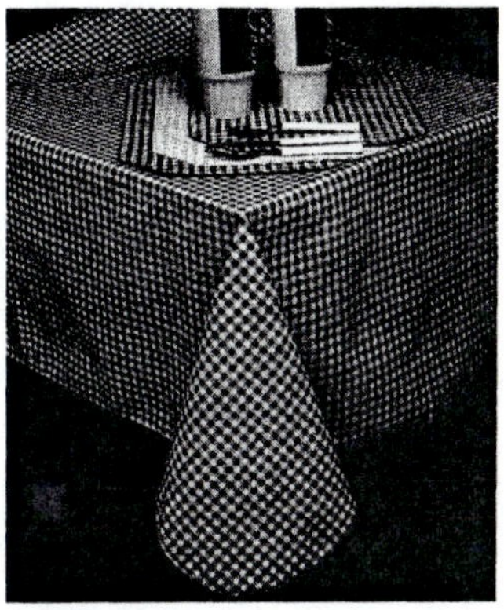

Red checked tablecloths set the stage for barbecues, but do not forget outdoor games, such as volleyball, badminton, and the classic, frisbee. (Also, remember to have plenty of napkins available and use plastic tablecloths, as shown in Fugure 6–1.)

The quality of barbecue food is in part dependent on the readiness of the coals. Coals that are too hot will result in burned food that is not fully cooked. Cool coals will require longer cooking times resulting in tougher meats.

The optimum coal for cooking should be white and powdery around the edges of the briquette. Flaring may occur when fats and juices drip onto the coals. Keep a spray bottle of water handy to extinguish small flare-ups.

If using a gas barbecue, set the flame to medium.

FIGURE 6-1
**PLASTIC TABLECLOTH**
*Courtesy of Artex International*

# Roasted Corn and Red Pepper Salad

*serves 6 (serve on a large platter)*

| | |
|---|---|
| 3 ears | corn, fresh on the cob |
| 1/4 cup | salad oil |
| 2 tablespoons | garlic, minced |
| 1 | lemon |
| 1/4 cup | balsamic vinegar |
| 1 1/2 teaspoons | salt |
| 1 tablespoon | ground black pepper |
| 1 tablespoon | sugar |
| 2 | red bell peppers |
| 3 | flour tortillas |
| 1 head | lettuce |
| 1/3 cup | cilantro, chopped (approximately 1/4 bunch) |
| 1/2 cup | green onions, chopped (approximately 1 bunch) |

## Preparation

1. Clean and wash the corn on the cob; cut the corn off the cob by holding the cob vertically and running a knife down the length. If fresh corn is not available, use 1 cup of frozen corn.

2. Place the corn into a lightly oiled shallow roasting pan; cover the pan with foil and put into a 350°F preheated oven for 20 minutes, stirring after 10 minutes.

3. Peel and mince the garlic; set aside.

4. Squeeze the juice from the lemon; set aside.

5. Combine the garlic, lemon juice, balsamic vinegar, salt, ground pepper, sugar, and 1/4 cup of salad oil; then refrigerate.

6. Cut the red bell peppers in half, removing the seeds; wash the peppers and cut into thin strips.

7. When the corn has slightly cooled, combine with the sliced peppers and the dressing; cover with plastic wrap and refrigerate.

8. Cut the flour tortillas in half; cut the halves into very thin strips and place them into a shallow roasting pan; place the pan into a 350°F preheated oven for approximately 15 minutes or until the strips become golden brown and crisp, being careful not to burn.

9. Wash and clean the lettuce; drain and tear into small bite-size pieces and refrigerate.
10. Wash, drain, and chop the cilantro and green onions; cover with plastic wrap and refrigerate.

### Ready to Serve

1. Place the lettuce on a large platter.
2. Carefully drop the tortilla strips on top of the lettuce.
3. Pour the marinated corn and peppers over the tortilla strips along with the dressing marinade.
4. Sprinkle the top with the chopped cilantro and green onions. Serve family style.

**Preparation Time:** 45 minutes
**Final Preparation Time:** 5 minutes

# Mixed Grill

*serves 6 (serve on a large platter)*

| | |
|---|---|
| 6 (1-inch-thick cut) | lamb chops |
| 6 (5-ounce) | chicken breasts, boneless, skinless |
| 1 1/2 pounds | flank steak |
| 1/4 cup | mint, chopped (approximately 1/3 bunch) |
| 2 tablespoons | garlic, minced |
| 1 teaspoon | salt |
| 1 1/2 teaspoons | ground black pepper |
| 1 tablespoon | vegetable oil |
| 1 cup | V8 vegetable juice |
| 1 cup | beer |
| 2 tablespoons | Worcestershire sauce |
| 2 tablespoons | rice wine vinegar |
| 2 tablespoons | water |
| 2 tablespoons | sage, chopped (approximately 1/4 bunch) |
| 2 tablespoons | rosemary, chopped (approximately 1/4 bunch) |
| 1 | lime |
| 1/4 cup | honey |
| 1/3 cup | Dijon mustard |

## Preparation

1. Wash, drain, and chop the mint and mince the garlic; combine with 1/2 teaspoon of salt, 1/2 teaspoon of ground pepper, and 1 tablespoon of vegetable oil.
2. Rub the marinade mix onto the lamb chops; place onto a plate, cover with plastic wrap, and refrigerate.
3. Combine the V8 juice, beer, Worcestershire sauce, rice wine vinegar, water, 1/2 teaspoon of salt, and 1 teaspoon of ground pepper in a shallow pan.
4. Lay the flank steak in the marinade; cover with plastic wrap, and refrigerate.
5. Wash, drain, and chop the fresh sage and rosemary. **Note:** Dried whole herbs may be substituted, but the flavor of the fresh cannot be duplicated.
6. Squeeze the juice from the lime.

7. Combine the honey, Dijon mustard, lime juice, and chopped sage and rosemary.
8. Marinate the chicken in this mixture.

## Ready to Grill

1. Preheat the barbecue grill on medium heat for about 5 minutes.
2. Drain (and save) the marinade from the chicken and place the breasts on the grill with the smooth side down.
3. Put the lamb chops on the grill.
4. Put the flank steak on the grill, save the marinade.
5. Turn the chicken breasts 1/4 turn to crosshatch grill marks.
6. After about 1 or 2 minutes, turn the chicken and lamb chops over; turn the flank steak 1/4 turn to create the grill marks.
7. Brush the chicken with the remaining chicken marinade.
8. Turn the flank steak over and brush with its marinade.
9. Continue to grill the chicken, reaching 165°F or higher for at least 15 seconds, and the lamb chops and flank steak, reaching 155°F or higher for at least 15 seconds or until desired doneness.

## Ready to Serve

1. Slice the flank steak into very thin cuts across the grain and place on a platter.
2. Arrange the chicken and lamb chops on the same platter and serve family style.

**Preparation Time:** 20 minutes

**Final Cooking Time:** 10 minutes

# Melon Surprise

*serves 6*

| | |
|---|---|
| 6 | cantaloupe, small |
| 3 | bananas |
| 1 cup | pineapple, diced |
| 1 pint | French vanilla ice cream |

**Preparation**

1. Lay each cantaloupe on its side and cut a flat bottom to prevent wobbling. Be careful not to cut off too much.
2. Remove the tops from the cantaloupes (like taking the top off the head of a pumpkin); remove the seeds and cut the cantaloupe into small balls by using a melon baller; set the melon balls aside along with the cantaloupe shells.
3. Slice the bananas and set aside.
4. Dice the pineapple into 1/4-inch pieces; set aside.
5. Combine the melon balls, sliced bananas, and diced pineapple in a mixing bowl; cover and refrigerate.

**Ready to Serve**

1. Fill each cantaloupe shell halfway with the melon ball mix.
2. Place a 2-ounce scoop of vanilla ice cream on top of the melon ball mix.
3. Cover the ice cream with more of the melon ball mix; place the lids back on the cantaloupes and promptly serve.

**Preparation Time:** 15 minutes
**Final Preparation Time:** 5 minutes

# Wedding Bells

*Wedding Reception serves 25*
*Buffet Service*

•

**Assortment of hors d'oeuvres buffet style**
*Fresh Vegetables and Dip*
*Fresh Fruit Platters*
*Cheese Trays and Cracker Baskets*
*Pasta Salad*
*Swedish Meatballs*
*Quiche Lorraine*
*Teriyaki Chicken Wings*
*Shrimp Rumaki*
*Stuffed Mushrooms*
*Wedding Cake (your choice)*

•

# Beverage Selections

Wedding celebrations call for three classic beverage selections: **champagne** or **sparkling wine, punch,** and **coffee.** Sparkling wine and punch should be served throughout the reception, and coffee should be available during the cake cutting ceremony.

Dom Perignon and Louis Roederer Cristal are both superb choices for this special occasion and just two of the many great champagnes from France. Whichever you choose, don't forget to reserve one bottle for the bride and groom.

If you're looking for something a little more economical, many excellent sparkling wines are available from the Loire Valley in France, Spain, or California and the Pacific Northwest. These sparklers are well made, well priced, and perfectly acceptable for service to the reception guests.

## NONALCOHOLIC

A refreshing **punch made with assorted fruit juices** (and plenty of sliced fruit wheels) is further enhanced when chilled with ice molds. **Tropical iced tea** is a good alternative to the more conventional punch.

For a special treat, go to your local coffee store and make two divergent selections. A light roast preserves some of the delicate flavor oils and is used for mild beans. This will not overwhelm the wedding cake. A second selection might be available for those who demand a strong cup of coffee. A full roast retains a rich dark brown color and produces a strong coffee with a touch of bitterness. (China service is a must.)

# When to Start Cooking

*When the wedding reception buffet service begins at 5:00 P.M. . . .*

| **Cooking Preparation Schedule** | | **Cooking Times** |
|---|---|---|
| 7:30 A.M. | Vinaigrette/Pasta Salad (refrigerate 2 hours) | 5 minutes |
| 8:30 | Set the tables and arrange the room | 1 hour |
| 9:30 | Pasta Salad | 40 minutes |
| 10:15 | Shrimp Rumaki | 1 hour |
| 11:15 | Stuffed Mushrooms | 45 minutes |
| 12:00 P.M. | Swedish Meatballs | 45 minutes |
| 12:45 | Fresh Vegetables and Dip | 25 minutes |
| 1:10 | Fresh Fruit Platters | 30 minutes |
| 1:40 | Cheese Trays | 20 minutes |
| 2:00 | Quiche Lorraine | 1 hour |

| **Final Cooking and Preparation Schedule** | | | **Buffet Serving Times** |
|---|---|---|---|
| 3:00 P.M. | Teriyaki Chicken Wings | 1 hour | 5:00 P.M. |
| 4:00 | Stuffed Mushrooms | 10 minutes | ↓ |
| 4:10 | Shrimp Rumaki | 20 minutes | |
| 4:15 | Swedish Meatballs | 25 minutes | |
| 4:40 | Quiche Lorraine | 5 minutes | |
| 4:45 | Cheese Trays and Cracker Baskets | 5 minutes | |
| 4:50 | Fresh Vegetables and Dip Fresh Fruit Platters Pasta Salad Wedding Cake | | ↓ |

**Postscript:** Order the wedding cake 2 weeks in advance . . . and do not forget to pick it up.

# Tips and Details

Be prepared for delays in the ceremony and keep the food at the appropriate temperature for service throughout the occasion: hot food at 140°F and cold food below 41°F.

Be sure to have one nice ice bucket for the traditional champagne toast. The remainder of the sparkling wine can be stored in any ice bin or refrigerator.

The cleanup for this function will be somewhat extensive. Secure as many helpers as possible and reminisce while you clean.

# Fresh Vegetables and Dip

*serves 25 (serve on 2 large platters)*

| | |
|---|---|
| 2 cups | ranch dressing |
| 5 | carrots |
| 5 stalks | celery |
| 2 pounds | jicama |
| 24 | green onions (approximately 4 bunches) |
| 3 pounds | mushrooms, small |
| 2 cups | radishes, small (approximately 2 bunches) |
| 5 | cucumbers |
| 3 | zucchini |

**Preparation**

1. Pour 1 cup of ranch dressing into each of 2 serving bowls; cover and refrigerate.
2. Scrape the carrots, wash, and cut into 2-inch sticks about 1/4 inch thick.
3. Wash the celery stalks and cut into thin 3-inch sticks.
4. Peel and wash the jicama; cut into 2-inch sticks about 1/4 inch thick.
5. Trim the green onions into 5-inch pieces and wash.
6. Cut the stems from the mushrooms and wash.
7. Remove the stems from the radishes and wash.
8. Wash the cucumbers and cut lengthwise into halves; scrape out the seeds with a spoon; place the cucumber halves, hollow side down, onto a cutting board; slice into long thin strips; then cross cut into 1 1/2-inch sticks.
9. Peel and wash the zucchini; slice at a 45-degree angle into 1/4-inch rounds.
10. Arrange all of the cut vegetables on 2 large platters with a bowl of ranch dressing in the center of each platter; cover with plastic wrap and refrigerate until ready to serve.

**Preparation Time:** 25 minutes

# Fresh Fruit Platters

*serves 25 (serve on 2 large platters)*

| | |
|---|---|
| 3 cups | plain yogurt |
| 1/3 cup | sugar |
| 2 | lemons |
| 1 | lime |
| 1 1/2 cups | mint sprigs (approximately 1 bunch) |
| 3 baskets (12 ounces each) | raspberries |
| 4 baskets (12 ounces each) | strawberries |
| 10 | oranges |
| 2 | honeydew melons |
| 2 | cantaloupes |
| 2 pounds | red seedless grapes |
| 2 pounds | green seedless grapes |
| 10 | kiwi |

## Preparation

1. Place the yogurt into a blender; add the sugar, juice from the lemons and lime, 3/4 cup of washed mint, and 1/2 a basket of washed raspberries; blend at medium speed until the ingredients become smooth; place an equal amount into 2 serving bowls, cover, and refrigerate.
2. Wash, drain, and remove the stems from the strawberries.
3. Peel the oranges and remove all the white pulp; cut each orange into six 1/4-inch slices.
4. Cut the honeydew melons and cantaloupes in half and remove the seeds with a spoon; cut the rind from the outside and slice into 1-inch wedges.
5. Wash, drain, and cut the bunches of grapes into small clusters of 6 to 8 grapes per cluster by using utility scissors.
6. Peel the kiwi and slice into 1/8-inch rings.
7. Arrange all of the fruit on 2 large platters with a bowl of raspberry yogurt dressing in the center of each platter; garnish with the remaining mint sprigs; cover with plastic wrap and refrigerate until ready to serve.

**Preparation Time:** 30 minutes

# Cheese Trays and Cracker Baskets

*serves 25 (serve on 2 round platters)*

| | |
|---|---|
| 2 pounds | cheddar cheese |
| 2 pounds | brie cheese |
| 2 pounds | Gouda cheese |
| 2 pounds | Jarlsberg cheese |
| 3 boxes (7 ounces each) | assorted crackers |
| 1 box (200 count) | frill picks (toothpicks with frill tops) |

### Preparation

1. Cut the cheddar cheese into small cubes; insert a frill pick into the center of each cube.
2. Cut the brie and Gouda into small wedges.
3. Cut the Jarlsberg into thin slices.
4. Arrange the cut cheese on 2 round trays (platters), keeping each type separate; radiate out from the center of the tray in triangle patterns (like pizza cuts); cover with plastic wrap and refrigerate until ready to serve.

### Ready to Serve

1. Place a linen napkin lying flat in each of 2 bread baskets; arrange the crackers in the baskets, keeping each type separate.
2. Place the baskets next to the cheese trays.

**Preparation Time:** 20 minutes

**Final Preparation Time:** 5 minutes

# Pasta Salad

*serves 25 (serve in a large bowl)*

| | |
|---|---|
| 1/4 cup | balsamic vinegar |
| 1/4 cup | red wine vinegar |
| 1/2 cup | olive oil |
| 2 cups | salad oil |
| 1 1/2 cups | water |
| 1 | lemon |
| 3 tablespoons | garlic, minced |
| 2 teaspoons | thyme |

| 1 teaspoon | oregano, flakes |
|---|---|
| 1 tablespoon | basil |
| 2 tablespoons | salt |
| 2 tablespoons | ground pepper |
| 2 tablespoons | sugar |
| 2 pounds | rotelli pasta (spiral) |
| 2 | yellow onions, jumbo |
| 1 | red bell pepper |
| 1/2 cup | green onions, chopped (approximately 1 bunch) |
| 1 1/2 cups | pitted black olives |
| 1/2 pound | mushrooms, medium |

## Preparation

1. Pour the balsamic vinegar, red wine vinegar, olive oil, 1 1/2 cups salad oil, water, and the juice of the lemon into a bowl; add the minced garlic, thyme, oregano flakes, basil, salt, ground pepper, and sugar and thoroughly mix; cover and refrigerate for at least 2 hours. **Note:** Most vinaigrettes taste better 1 to 2 days after they are prepared, as time allows the flavors to mull together.

2. Pour 2 gallons of water into a large pot; add 1/4 cup of salad oil and bring to a rapid boil; add the rotelli pasta and cook until tender; place a colander in the sink and drain the boiling water from the pasta; run cold water over the pasta to cool.

3. Dump the pasta into a large bowl; add 1/4 cup of salad oil and toss; cover with plastic wrap and refrigerate. **Note:** The salad oil keeps the pasta from sticking together.

4. Peel the yellow onions and cut into quarters; cut the quarters into very thin slices and set aside.

5. Cut the red bell pepper in half, remove the seeds, and wash; chop the halves into a medium dice, about the size of a dime; set aside

6. Wash and chop the green onions and set aside.

7. Drain the olives, slice into thin rings, and set aside.

8. Wash the mushrooms, cut into thin slices, and set aside.

9. Combine all of the cut ingredients together with the pasta and vinaigrette dressing in a large serving bowl; gently toss, being careful not to overmix.

10. Cover with plastic wrap and refrigerate for at least 1 hour before serving.

**Preparation Time:** 45 minutes

# Swedish Meatballs

*serves 25 (serve in a heated service bowl)*

| | |
|---|---|
| *2* | *yellow onions, jumbo* |
| *2 cups* | *bread crumbs* |
| *1/2 cup* | *milk* |
| *2* | *eggs* |
| *1/3 cup* | *Dijon mustard* |
| *2 tablespoons* | *salt* |
| *2 tablespoons* | *black pepper* |
| *4 pounds* | *ground beef, minimum fat content* |
| *2 1/2 cups* | *beef stock (using a beef base with water)* |
| *1 3/4 cups* | *sour cream* |
| *1/8 cup* | *chives, chopped (approximately 1/4 bunch)* |

## Preparation

1. Peel and mince the onions and set aside.
2. Moisten the bread crumbs with the milk; combine with the eggs and thoroughly mix.
3. Combine the moistened bread crumbs and eggs with 1/4 cup of Dijon mustard, salt, pepper, ground beef, and half of the minced onions and thoroughly mix.
4. Use a 1 1/3-ounce, number 24, scoop and scoop the mixture into 75 balls and place in a baking pan. **Note:** This may have to be done more than once depending upon the size of the baking pan.
5. Place the meatballs into a 375°F preheated oven for 10 minutes or until fully cooked, reaching 155°F or higher for at least 15 seconds; remove from the oven, drain, cool, and carefully place in a bowl; cover with plastic wrap and refrigerate until ready to serve. **Note:** Shake pan halfway through cooking time for more uniform cooking.

### Ready to Serve

1. Prepare the beef stock according to package directions and bring to a 180°F simmer; add the remaining onions and mustard and continue to simmer for 10 minutes.

2. Add the sour cream and thoroughly mix.

3. Add the meatballs and gently mix; simmer at 180°F for another 5 minutes to heat up the meatballs to 165°F or higher for at least 15 seconds, then pour into a heated service bowl.

4. Wash, drain, and chop the chives and sprinkle over the top of the meatballs.

**Preparation Time:** 45 minutes

**Final Cooking Time:** 25 minutes

# Quiche Lorraine

*serves 25*

| | |
|---|---|
| *14 strips* | *sliced bacon* |
| *1* | *yellow onion, jumbo* |
| *2 (9-inch)* | *pie shells, prepared* |
| *2 cups* | *Swiss cheese, grated* |
| *8* | *eggs* |
| *3 cups* | *half-and-half* |
| *1 1/2 teaspoons* | *ground white pepper* |
| *1 tablespoon* | *nutmeg* |

## Preparation

1. Cut the bacon into 1/4-inch pieces and place into a sauté pan over medium heat for approximately 2 minutes, bringing the temperature to 155°F or higher for at least 15 seconds.

2. Peel and mince the onion and add to the bacon in the sauté pan; continue to sauté until the bacon becomes crisp; remove the bacon and onions from the pan and place on paper towels to absorb the grease.

3. Spread an equal amount of the bacon and onions over the bottom of the 2 pie shells.

4. Sprinkle half of the grated Swiss cheese over the bacon and onion mixture.

5. Combine the eggs, half-and-half, white pepper, and nutmeg in a mixing bowl and blend until smooth; slowly pour an equal amount on top of the grated Swiss cheese in the 2 pie shells.

6. Sprinkle the remaining Swiss cheese on top of each quiche.

7. Place the 2 quiches in a 350°F preheated oven for approximately 30 minutes until reaching 145°F or higher for at least 15 seconds and the top is golden brown; remove from the oven and cool for 10 minutes before serving.

**Note:** May be served warm or cold.

## Ready to Serve

1. Cut into small pieces, yielding 12 to 13 slices per quiche.

**Preparation Time:** 1 hour

**Final Preparation Time:** 5 minutes

# Teriyaki Chicken Wings

*serves 25 (serve on a platter)*

| | |
|---|---|
| 4 pounds | chicken wings |
| 1 cup | diced pineapple, canned |
| 1 cup | teriyaki sauce, bottle prepared |
| 1/2 cup | green onions, chopped (approximately 1 bunch) |
| 1 head | red leaf lettuce |
| 3 tablespoons | sesame seeds |

## Preparation

1. Wash and drain the chicken wings.
2. Bring 2 gallons of water to a boil; add 1 tablespoon salt; remove the pot of boiling water from the stove and place the chicken wings into the piping hot water, blanching for 10 minutes; remove, drain, and cool.
3. Open the canned diced pineapple; drain the juice and add it to the teriyaki sauce, mixing well.
4. Pour the teriyaki sauce mixture over the chicken wings and toss the wings in the sauce.
5. Place the chicken wings on a baking pan. **Note:** This may have to be done more than once depending upon the size of the baking pan.
6. Place the chicken wings into a 350°F preheated oven for approximately 20 minutes or until golden brown and reaching 165°F or higher for at least 15 seconds; stir frequently with a spatula to keep chicken from sticking to the baking pan.
7. Wash, drain, and finely chop the green onions; set aside.
8. Remove the lettuce leaves from the head; wash, drain, and evenly arrange on a large tray.
9. Place the chicken wings on top of the lettuce-lined platter.
10. Sprinkle the diced pineapple, chopped green onions, and sesame seeds over the top of the chicken wings and serve.

**Note:** May be served warm or cold.

**Preparation Time:** 1 hour

# Shrimp Rumaki

*serves 25 (serve on a large oval platter)*

| | |
|---|---|
| 50 | shrimp, 21 to 25 per pound size |
| 1/2 cup | soy sauce |
| 1 cup | water chestnuts |
| 25 slices | Canadian bacon |
| 1 box | round toothpicks |

### Preparation

1. Remove the shells from the shrimp; clean and wash the shrimp under cold water and drain.
2. Pour the soy sauce over the shrimp and toss the shrimp in the soy sauce.
3. Drain the water chestnuts from the cans and slice thin.
4. Cut the bacon slices in half, creating 50 half slices.
5. Place a slice of water chestnut next to a shrimp; wrap half a slice of bacon around the shrimp and water chestnut, securing in place with a wooden pick. Repeat this procedure until all of the shrimp are wrapped.
6. Place the wrapped shrimp on a large baking pan; cover with plastic wrap and refrigerate until ready to serve.

### Ready to Serve

1. Remove the plastic wrap and place the pan into a 350°F preheated oven for approximately 10 minutes, until reaching 155°F or higher for at least 15 seconds and the bacon is crisp.
2. Remove the shrimp rumaki from the pan and place onto paper towels to absorb any grease.
3. Arrange on a large oval serving platter.

**Preparation Time:** 1 hour

**Final Cooking Time:** 20 minutes

# Stuffed Mushrooms

*serves 25 (serve on a large round platter)*

| | |
|---|---|
| 50 | mushrooms, medium |
| 1 | yellow onion, jumbo |
| 1 | green bell pepper |
| 1 | red bell pepper |
| 3/4 pound | baked ham, deli sliced |
| 1/2 cup (1 stick) | butter |
| 1 1/2 cups | dry bread crumbs |

| 1/2 cup | milk |
| 1 tablespoon | salt |
| 1 1/2 teaspoons | ground black pepper |
| 2 tablespoons | stone ground mustard |
| 1 tablespoon | Worcestershire sauce |
| 1 teaspoon | Tabasco sauce |
| 1/4 cup | Parmesan cheese |
| 1 1/2 teaspoons | paprika |

## Preparation

1. Wash and clean mushrooms; remove the stems by popping out with your thumb; discard stems.
2. Bring 1 gallon of water to a rapid boil; remove the pot of boiling water from the stove and place the mushrooms into the piping hot water, blanching for 30 seconds; remove the mushrooms to a colander to drain; chill under cold running water for about 10 seconds; remove the mushrooms and place on paper towels to dry.
3. Peel and mince the onion and set aside.
4. Cut the green and red bell peppers in half, remove the seeds, wash, and drain; chop into a fine dice and set aside.
5. Chop the ham into a fine dice and set aside.
6. Melt 1/4 cup of butter in a sauté pan over medium heat; add the onions and sauté until they become clear.
7. Combine 1 cup of dry bread crumbs with the milk.
8. Remove the sautéed onions from the pan and combine with the moistened bread crumbs, diced peppers, salt, ground black pepper, diced ham, stone ground mustard, Worcestershire sauce, and Tabasco sauce and thoroughly mix.
9. Place the mushrooms, with the cup side up, side by side in a baking pan.
10. Place an equal amount of stuffing in each mushroom.
11. Place the Parmesan cheese in a mixing bowl; add the paprika and 1/2 cup of dry bread crumbs; melt the remaining 1/4 cup of butter and thoroughly mix with the ingredients.
12. Sprinkle an even amount of the bread crumb mixture over the top of each stuffed mushroom; cover with plastic wrap and refrigerate.

## Ready to Serve

1. Remove the plastic wrap and place into a 400°F preheated oven for 5 minutes or until the bread crumbs have become golden brown.
2. Arrange the stuffed mushrooms on a large platter.

**Note:** May be served hot or at room temperature.

**Preparation Time:** 45 minutes

**Final Cooking Time:** 10 minutes

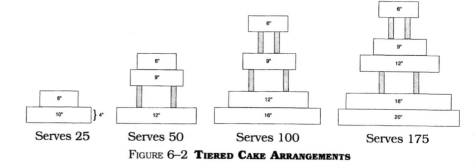

Serves 25   Serves 50   Serves 100   Serves 175

FIGURE 6–2 **TIERED CAKE ARRANGEMENTS**

FIGURE 6–3 **WEDDING CART**
*Courtesy of Bon Chef*

The wedding cake will command a lot of attention from guests and must be prepared, presented, and served exactly to the customer's request. As discussed in chapter 2, the caterer should have at least two or three specialty bakeries as sources that could be called upon to fulfill the order. Bakeries having a reputation for producing high-quality wedding cakes often require an advance order date of several weeks, depending upon the time of the year and the complexity of the cake.

The examples in Figure 6–2 are typical tiered cake arrangements that would serve different numbers of guests. The arrangements will vary according to the customer's preferences and the individual bakery's capabilities and personal presentation style. The cost of the cake can vary not only according to size, but also by the number of layers within each tier, the ingredients, and the extent of the decorating. In addition to the decorated wedding cake for large weddings, a customer may request the caterer to have several sheet cakes ready to be cut and served to guests.

The wedding cart, as shown in Figure 6–3, further enhances the visual presentation of the cake. It can be used to prominently display the cake or to roll it out at the appropriate time for photos and when the bride and groom will cut the cake with a decorative cake knife.

Immediately following the cake cutting ceremony, the caterer would have the cake cut, plated, and served to the wedding party first and then to the guests. Cakes that are 4 inches high per tier are usually cut 2 inches by 2 inches. Figure 6–4 illustrates cake cutting patterns.

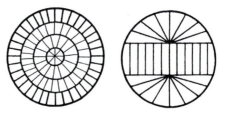

FIGURE 6–4 **CAKE CUTTING PATTERNS**

## Buffet Service

The extent to which a buffet line is set up will be determined by the number of guests attending. It is important to follow the guidelines discussed in chapter 3, from arranging the buffet tables to properly placing and displaying the food. The single-sided buffet arrangement example in Figure 6–5 will be able to comfortably accommodate 50 to 100 guests within 10 to 20 minutes.

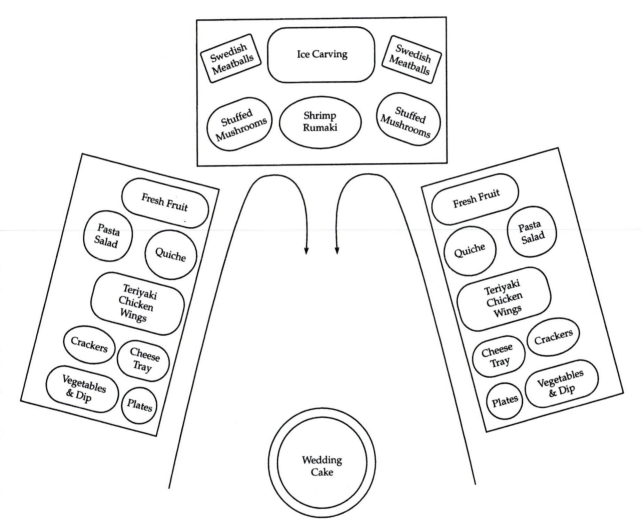

FIGURE 6–5 **SINGLE-SIDED BUFFET ARRANGEMENT**

# Flower Drum Song

*Japanese*

•

*Sunomono*
*(Marinated Cucumber and Bay Shrimp Salad on a bed of glass)*
*Vegetable Sushi, Maki Style*
*Teriyaki Salmon with Steamed Rice and Snow Peas*
*Coconut Custard with Plum Sauce*

•

# Beverage Selections

Tradition is extremely important to the Japanese, and serving traditional beverages is a must with their cuisine. **Sake, plum wine, and green tea** are all very popular and are classic offerings with the meal. For this theme night, however, you must remember that the ritual of service is as important as the beverage itself.

Sake, although it is referred to as wine, is really more similar to beer in that it's made from grain mash rather than grapes or other fruits. Japanese people drink this delicacy in small porcelain cups. It is served warm in the winter and cold in the summer. Custom calls for sake to be on the table throughout the meal, although it certainly can be enjoyed with the entrée only.

Plum wine would be an excellent choice with the custard dessert and should be served in a clear cordial glass.

## NONALCOHOLIC

Green tea is a time-honored drink for those who prefer an exquisite feast without alcohol. This is ideally presented in Japanese white porcelain and available throughout the entire meal. For the younger generation, you might serve an assortment of **chilled flavored Snapples®** in the same vessels.

# When to Start Cooking

*When dinner is served at 7:00 P.M. . . .*

| Cooking Preparation Schedule | | Cooking Times |
|---|---|---|
| 3:25 P.M. | Coconut Custard | 15 minutes |
| 3:40 | Teriyaki Salmon | 10 minutes |
| 3:50 | Snow Peas | 5 minutes |
| 3:55 | Vegetable Sushi | 45 minutes |
| 4:40 | Sunomono | 20 minutes |
| 5:00 | Time to set the tables and arrange the room. | |
| 5:30 | Time to clean up, relax a bit, double-check everything, and dress for the occasion. | |

**Final Cooking and Preparation Schedule**                   **Serving Times**

| | | | |
|---|---|---|---|
| 6:55 P.M. | Sunomono | 5 minutes | 7:00 P.M. |
| 7:00 | Teriyaki Salmon, | | |
| | Steamed Rice | 30 minutes | 7:30 |
| 7:10 | Vegetable Sushi | 5 minutes | 7:15 |
| 7:20 | Snow Peas | 10 minutes | 7:30 |
| 7:40 | Coconut Custard | 10 minutes | 7:50 |
| | with Plum Sauce | | |
| | Final Beverage | | 7:55 |

## Tips and Details

Rice is a key ingredient of Japanese cuisine. The quality of the rice will greatly affect the entire meal. If you have access to an Oriental market, that is where it is advisable to purchase the rice and other products. Many of these markets can be found in your local community due to the recent popularity of this style of food.

While you are at the specialty shop, you might want to pick up small pine boxes used for drinking cold sake. Whereas warm sake is served in porcelain cups, premium grade sake is traditionally presented in a small pine box. Some of the flavor of the wood is extracted by the sake to create a unique flavor.

# Sunomono

*serves 6 (serve in 6-ounce salad bowls)*

| | |
|---|---|
| 1/3 cup | rice wine vinegar |
| 2 tablespoons | sugar |
| 1 1/2 teaspoons | salt |
| 1 cup | water |
| 2/3 cup | soy sauce |
| 2 | cucumbers |
| 6 ounces | bean thread noodles |
| 1 1/2 cups | bay shrimp, precooked, frozen |
| 2 tablespoons | sesame seeds |
| 1 stem | green onion |

## Preparation

1. Combine the rice wine vinegar, sugar, salt, water, and soy sauce in a bowl and thoroughly mix.
2. Peel the cucumbers and cut lengthwise into halves; scrape out the seeds with a spoon; place the cucumber halves, hollow side down, onto a cutting board; cut at a 45-degree angle into very thin slices.
3. Add the thin sliced cucumbers to the dressing mix; cover and refrigerate.
4. Prepare bean thread noodles according to package directions; drain and cool.
5. Place an equal amount of noodles into 6 salad bowls (this represents the bed of glass).
6. Top off the noodles with an equal amount of marinated cucumbers (reserve the dressing mix).
7. Remove the bay shrimp from the bag and place in a colander; put the colander in a sink and run cold water over the shrimp until thawed, approximately 3 or 4 minutes. Then drop 2 ounces of shrimp over the marinated cucumber slices; refrigerate until ready to serve.

## Ready to Serve

1. Sprinkle an equal amount of sesame seeds over the shrimp.
2. Wash and mince the green onion and drop an equal amount over the shrimp and sesame seeds.
3. Ladle 1 ounce of the dressing mix over the salads and serve.

**Preparation Time:** 20 minutes

**Final Preparation Time:** 5 minutes

# Vegetable Sushi, Maki Style

*serves 6*

| | |
|---|---|
| 1 1/2 cups | short grain rice |
| 2 cups | water |
| 3 teaspoons | salt |
| 1/3 cup | rice wine vinegar |
| 2 tablespoons | sugar |
| 1 | cucumber |
| 1 | red bell pepper |
| 1/8 cup | green onions, minced (approximately 1/4 bunch) |
| 12 sheets | yaki nori (dried seaweed) |
| 1/3 cup | Oriental sweet and hot mustard* |
| 1/3 cup | soy sauce |

* *(alternative choice) wasabi, a very hot horseradish.*

**Note:** This recipe requires the use of a "sushi mat," which can be found in the Oriental section of a grocery store or at any Oriental food store. The mats are typically 10 inches square, made of bamboo, and are very inexpensive.

## Preparation

1. Place the short grain rice in a strainer and rinse with cold water until the water runs clear.
2. Place the water, 1 1/2 teaspoons of salt, and the rice in a saucepan; bring to a boil over medium heat for 1 minute; cover the pan, reduce the heat to low, and simmer for 20 minutes; remove from the pan and place in a large mixing bowl to cool.
3. Combine the rice wine vinegar, sugar, and 1 1/2 teaspoons of salt in a bowl and thoroughly mix.
4. While the rice is still warm, but not hot, add the rice wine vinegar mixture and thoroughly mix; cover and leave at room temperature during preparation.
5. Peel the cucumber and cut in half lengthwise; scrape out the seeds with a spoon; place the two halves, hollow side down, onto a cutting board; cut lengthwise into thin slices, about 1/8 inch in diameter; then crosscut into 2-inch lengths (thin sticks) and set aside.

6. Cut the red bell pepper in half, remove the seeds, and wash. Only half will be used, so save the second half for another use.

7. Cut the half into thin slices, about 1/8 inch in diameter and 2 inches long, and set aside.

8. Wash and mince the green onions and set aside.

9. Lay the sushi mat on a counter and place three pieces of yaki nori (typically measures 2 1/2 inches wide by 3 1/2 inches long) side by side, narrow ends touching, on the mat. **Note:** You will be rolling lengthwise.

10. Cover the half of the yaki nori (closest to you) with a thin layer of rice.

11. Place a small amount of sweet and hot mustard (or wasabi if you prefer the very hot) down the center of the rice, from left to right, reserving 3 teaspoons for serving.

12. Place 2 cucumber sticks and 2 red pepper slices on top of the mustard.

13. Garnish with the minced green onions on top of the cucumber and red pepper sticks.

14. Lightly dampen the edge of the yaki nori that is farthest away from you with a small amount of water.

15. While carefully holding everything else in place, roll the mat so the yaki nori and rice wrap tightly around the vegetables, keeping constant pressure on the mat until the yaki nori is sealed. Remove the mat and use to prepare the rest of the sushi.

16. Prepare 12 vegetable sushi, place on a platter; cover and set aside until ready to serve.


**Ready to Serve**

1. Place 2 sushi on each plate; garnish the plate with 1/2 teaspoon of sweet and hot mustard and 1/2 teaspoon of soy sauce for dipping.

2. Place an additional amount of mustard and soy sauce in small fruit dishes with teaspoons for additional servings. Place on the table when serving the vegetable sushi course.

**Preparation Time:** 45 minutes

**Final Preparation Time:** 5 minutes

# Teriyaki Salmon with Steamed Rice

*serves 6*

| | |
|---|---|
| 6 (8-ounce) | salmon fillets |
| 2 tablespoons | rice wine vinegar |
| 2 tablespoons | salt |
| 1 tablespoon | soy sauce |
| 1 cup | teriyaki sauce |
| 2 | oranges |
| 2 cups | short grain rice |
| 2 2/3 cups | water |

### Preparation

1. Purchase 6 (8-ounce) fresh chinook salmon fillets. Request to have as many of the bones removed as possible.
2. Combine the rice wine vinegar, 1 tablespoon of salt, soy sauce, and teriyaki sauce in a bowl and thoroughly mix.
3. Place the salmon fillets in a deep pan; pour the teriyaki marinade over the salmon fillets; cover and refrigerate for at least 1 hour.
4. Peel the oranges and remove all the white pulp; cut each orange into six 1/4-inch slices for a total of 12 slices; cover and refrigerate.

### Ready to Serve

1. Place the short grain rice in a strainer and rinse with cold water until the water runs clear.
2. Place the water, 1 tablespoon of salt, and the rice in a saucepan; bring to a boil over medium heat for 1 minute; cover the pan, reduce the heat to low, and simmer for 20 minutes; remove from the heat.
3. While the rice simmers, drain the salmon fillets and place skin side down onto a baking pan; place into a 300°F preheated oven for 15 minutes or until done; check for doneness by flaking with a fork. When the fish begins to flake and has reached 145°F or higher for at least 15 seconds, it is done.
4. Place an equal amount of rice on each plate; spread and flatten the rice.
5. Place a salmon fillet half on the rice, half off.
6. Garnish each plate with 2 orange slices and serve.

**Preparation Time:** 10 minutes

**Final Cooking Time:** 30 minutes

# Snow Peas

*serves 6*

| | |
|---|---|
| 1 pound | snow peas |
| 4 tablespoons | unsalted butter |
| 1 teaspoon | salt |
| 1/2 teaspoon | ground white pepper |
| 1 | lemon |
| 1 teaspoon | ground ginger |

## Preparation

1. Remove the stem end from the peas with a sharp paring knife and pull the string away from the flat edge of the pod; wash, drain, cover, and refrigerate.

## Ready to Serve

1. Melt the butter over medium heat in a sauté pan.
2. Add the snow peas, salt, ground white pepper, the juice from the lemon, and the ground ginger.
3. Sauté for approximately 3 or 4 minutes. The snow peas should remain crisp.
4. Place an equal amount on each plate with salmon and rice.

**Preparation Time:** 5 minutes
**Final Cooking Time:** 10 minutes

# Coconut Custard with Plum Sauce

*serves 6*

| | |
|---|---|
| 2 cups | custard, prepared mix |
| 1 | egg |
| 1/2 cup | shredded coconut |
| 1 tablespoon | butter |
| 6 | whole purple plums, canned |
| 1 | orange |
| 1 teaspoon | ground ginger |
| 1/4 cup | white wine |

## Preparation

1. Prepare the custard according to package directions adding 1 beaten egg yolk, separating egg yolk from egg white using plastic gloves or egg separator.
2. Pour into a saucepan over medium heat, constantly stirring until the mixture comes to a full rolling boil; remove from the heat and mix in the shredded coconut; lightly butter a 9-by-13-inch pan; pour the coconut custard mixture into the pan and refrigerate for at least 1 hour.

## Ready to Serve

1. Open the can of plums; drain the juice, remove the plums, place on a cutting board, and finely chop.
2. Squeeze the juice from the orange and pour into a sauté pan; add the ground ginger and white wine and mix; simmer over a medium heat for 2 minutes.
3. Add the chopped plums to the sauce; mix and simmer for 3 minutes; remove from the heat and place an equal amount onto 6 dessert plates.
4. Cut the coconut custard into 1-inch cubes; place an equal number of cubes on top of the plum sauce on each plate and serve.

**Preparation Time:** 15 minutes

**Final Cooking Time:** 10 minutes

# Fall Harvest

•

*Cream of Pumpkin Soup*
served in small hollowed-out pumpkins
*Greens of Fall with Walnut Blue Cheese*
*Stuffed Green Peppers*
*Lyonnaise Potatoes*
*Baked Apples*

•

# Beverage Selections

Rich, full-bodied **Alsatian wines** are an excellent choice to serve with an autumn theme menu. Alsace, a northeastern region of France renowned for its superb white wines, also produces some exciting cuisine when the leaves begin to fall.

Rather than pair the wines with each course, you may want to try placing two or three selections on the table for your guests to choose from. This family-style service, which is the custom in Alsace, helps set a casual and convivial mood for the evening.

The grape varieties grown in Alsace bear witness to the fact that this region was once a part of Germany. Unlike their German counterparts, however, the **Riesling, Gewürztraminer,** and **pinot gris** from Alsace are all made in a dry style. A bottle of each one of these wines on the table would perfectly match the menu and may stimulate some interesting conversation. Encourage the guests to discuss which wine pairs better with each course.

For the dessert course you might try one of the same grape varieties, however, look for those labeled either *Vendange Tardive* or *Sélection de Grains Nobles*. Although still usually dry, these late harvest wines are very fruity and flavorful and good with fruit desserts.

## NONALCOHOLIC

Several varieties of steaming **herbal teas** will also nicely match this harvest menu. **Sparkling waters** by Perrier or Vital will cleanse the palate as well as make refreshing accompaniments to the repast.

# When to Start Cooking

*When dinner is served at 7:00 P.M. . . .*

| Cooking Preparation Schedule | | Cooking Times |
|---|---|---|
| 1:50 P.M. | Baked Apples | 50 minutes |
| 2:45 | Stuffed Green Peppers | 30 minutes |
| 3:15 | Lyonnaise Potatoes | 30 minutes |
| 3:45 | Greens of Fall with Walnut Blue Cheese | 30 minutes |
| 4:15 | Time to set the tables and arrange the room. | |
| 4:45 | Time to clean up, relax a bit, double-check everything, and dress for the occasion. | |

## Final Cooking and Preparation Schedule

| Time | Dish | Duration | Serving Times |
|---|---|---|---|
| 6:00 P.M. | Cream of Pumpkin Soup | 1 hour | 7:00 P.M. |
| 6:30 | Stuffed Green Peppers | 1 hour | 7:30 |
| 7:05 | Greens of Fall with Walnut Blue Cheese | 10 minutes | 7:15 |
| 7:20 | Lyonnaise Potatoes | 10 minutes | 7:30 |
| 7:45 | Baked Apples | 2 minutes | 7:50 |
| | Final Beverage | | 7:55 |

# Tips and Details

If you prefer to substitute a wine for one of the suggested white Alsatians, you might find a hearty red wine from the Rhone Valley appetizing with the ground beef stuffed peppers. These wonderful wines from France are often a blend of grapes including the aromatic Syrah and Grenache varieties.

Although all of the greens in the salad recipe are available at your local grocery store, you may want to consider the use of a pre-mixed specialty salad. These can be found in the produce section and are of a very high quality and excellent variety.

Consider serving the baked apples with a scoop of French vanilla ice cream for those with a hearty appetite.

# Cream of Pumpkin Soup

*serves 6*

| | |
|---|---|
| *6* | *baby pumpkins* |
| *1* | *yellow onion, jumbo* |
| *1/4 cup* | *unsalted butter* |
| *1 cup* | *chicken stock (using a chicken base with water)* |
| *1 1/2 cans (16-ounce can)* | *solid pack pumpkin (puree)* |
| *1 tablespoon* | *salt* |
| *1 tablespoon* | *ground white pepper* |
| *1 1/2 teaspoons* | *ground nutmeg* |
| *3/4 cup* | *milk* |

## Preparation

1. Cut and remove the tops from the baby pumpkins; scrape out the seeds with a spoon; thoroughly rinse, drain, cover with plastic wrap, and refrigerate.
2. Peel the onion and cut in half; save half for another use; mince the remaining half and set aside.
3. Melt the butter in a large soup pot over medium heat; add the minced onions and sauté until they become clear.
4. Prepare the chicken stock according to package directions; add to the onions and simmer for 5 minutes.
5. Add the pumpkin puree; reduce the heat to low and simmer for 15 minutes.
6. Season with the salt, ground white pepper, and ground nutmeg; mix and simmer for an additional 5 minutes.

## Ready to Serve

1. Place the baby pumpkins into a 300°F preheated oven for 5 minutes.
2. Add the milk to the soup and mix; continue to simmer for 5 minutes.
3. Remove the pumpkins from the oven and individually place on salad plates; using a 5-ounce ladle, slowly pour the soup into each pumpkin; set the lids off to one side on the plates and serve.

**Preparation Time:** 45 minutes

**Final Cooking Time:** 15 minutes

# Greens of Fall
# with Walnut Blue Cheese

*serves 6*

| | |
|---|---|
| 3 | eggs |
| 1 head | red leaf lettuce |
| 2 stalks (heads) | Belgian endive |
| 1 head | radicchio (small round red cabbage lettuce) |
| 1/3 cup | walnuts, chopped |
| 3 ounces | Danish blue cheese |
| 2 cups | walnut blue cheese vinaigrette (recipe follows) (refrigerate 2 hours) |

## Preparation

1. Hard cook the eggs; cool; peel and chop; place on a plate, cover with plastic wrap, and refrigerate.
2. Wash, drain, and cut the red leaf lettuce, Belgian endive, and radicchio into bite-size pieces; mix in a large bowl, cover with plastic wrap, and refrigerate.
3. Prepare the walnut blue cheese vinaigrette (recipe follows), cover with plastic wrap, and refrigerate for at least 2 hours.

## Ready to Serve

1. Place an equal amount of the salad mix onto the salad plates.
2. Chop the walnuts into 1/4-inch bits and set aside.
3. Break the blue cheese into crumbles and set aside.
4. Ladle 2 ounces of the walnut blue cheese vinaigrette over each salad.
5. Sprinkle an equal amount of chopped eggs, chopped walnuts, and blue cheese crumbles over each salad and serve.

**Preparation Time:** 30 minutes
**Final Preparation Time:** 10 minutes

# Walnut Blue Cheese Vinaigrette

*serves 6*

| | |
|---|---|
| 1/4 cup | walnuts, fine chop |
| 3 ounces | Danish blue cheese |
| 1 | lemon |
| 2 tablespoons | water |
| 2/3 cup | salad oil |
| 1/4 cup | raspberry vinegar |
| 2 tablespoons | tomato paste |
| 2 tablespoons | sugar |
| 1 tablespoon | salt |
| 1 tablespoon | ground black pepper |

## Preparation

1. Fine chop the walnuts and set aside.
2. Make a paste from the blue cheese by mashing it with a fork in a bowl.
3. Squeeze the juice from the lemon into a small bowl.
4. Combine all the ingredients in a bowl and thoroughly mix; cover with plastic wrap and refrigerate for at least 2 hours.

**Preparation Time:** 10 minutes

# Stuffed Green Peppers

*serves 6*

| | |
|---|---|
| 6 | green bell peppers, medium |
| 6 slices | bacon |
| 1 cup | soft bread crumbs |
| 1 | yellow onion, jumbo |
| 1 pound | ground beef, minimum fat content |
| 1 teaspoon | salt |
| 1/2 teaspoon | ground black pepper |
| 3/4 cup | tomato sauce |
| 1 teaspoon | basil |
| 3 ounces | mozzarella cheese |

## Preparation

1. Cut the stem and top from each pepper; remove the seeds and tough sections by scraping out with a spoon; wash and drain.
2. Place the peppers in boiling water for 2 minutes, remove with tongs, and drain.
3. Sauté the bacon until crisp, reaching 155°F or higher for at least 15 seconds; place on paper towels to absorb grease and cool; chop into bits.
4. Remove the crusts from several slices of white bread and chop the bread into very small bits to fill 1 cup.
5. Peel the onion and cut in half; save half for another use; mince the remaining half.
6. Combine the ground beef, bread crumbs, minced onions, salt, and ground black pepper in a bowl and thoroughly mix.
7. Stand the peppers upright in a deep baking pan and sprinkle an equal amount of half of the chopped bacon bits into the pepper bottoms.
8. Scoop 3 1/4 ounces (using a number 10 scoop) of the ground beef mixture into each pepper.
9. Top each stuffed pepper with 1 ounce (using a 1-ounce ladle) of tomato sauce, a pinch of basil, and the remaining chopped bacon bits evenly distributed; cover with plastic wrap and refrigerate until ready to bake.

## Ready to Serve

1. Remove the plastic wrap and place into a 350°F preheated oven for 45 minutes.
2. Remove from the oven and place a 1/2-ounce slice of mozzarella cheese on the top of each green pepper.
3. Return to the oven and bake for an additional 15 minutes, reaching 155°F or higher for at least 15 seconds; remove and serve.

**Preparation Time:** 30 minutes

**Final Cooking Time:** 1 hour

# Lyonnaise Potatoes

*serves 6*

| | |
|---|---|
| *2 pounds* | *potatoes* |
| *1* | *yellow onion, jumbo* |
| *1/3 cup* | *butter* |
| *1/2 teaspoon* | *salt* |
| *1/2 teaspoon* | *ground white pepper* |

## Preparation

1. Peel, wash, and boil potatoes over medium heat for 20 minutes, being careful not to overcook; drain, cool, and chop into 1/4-inch dice; place in a bowl, cover, and refrigerate.
2. Peel and cut the onion in half; save half for another use (or use the half saved from the stuffed green peppers recipe); mince the remaining half and place in a small bowl, cover and refrigerate.

## Ready to Serve

1. Melt the butter in a sauté pan over medium heat; add the minced onions and sauté until they become clear.
2. Add the chopped potatoes, salt, and ground white pepper; continually turn the potatoes until all sides are nicely browned; remove and place a 5-ounce portion next to each stuffed green pepper.

**Preparation Time:** 30 minutes
**Final Cooking Time:** 10 minutes

# Baked Apples

*serves 6*

| | |
|---|---|
| 6 | red delicious apples |
| 2 | lemons |
| 1/3 cup | grenadine syrup |
| 1/2 cup | brown sugar |
| 1/2 cup | golden raisins |
| 1 1/2 teaspoons | ground allspice |
| 1 1/2 teaspoons | cinnamon powder |
| 1 1/2 teaspoons | whole cloves |

## Preparation

1. Wash the apples and remove the cores with an apple corer.
2. Place the apples upright in a baking pan.
3. Combine the grenadine syrup, juice from the lemons, brown sugar, golden raisins, ground allspice, cinnamon powder, and whole cloves in a bowl and thoroughly mix.
4. Pour the sauce mixture over the tops of the apples, filling up the core holes.
5. Cover the pan with aluminum foil; punch a few holes in the foil so steam can escape.
6. Place the pan in a 325°F preheated oven for 20 minutes; lift the foil and baste the apples with the sauce; recover and bake for an additional 20 minutes or until tender, basting every 10 minutes.
7. Remove from the oven.

**Note:** May be served hot or cold.

## Ready to Serve

1. Place apples on individual dessert plates, baste with the remaining sauce, and serve.

**Preparation Time:** 50 minutes
**Final Preparation Time:** 2 minutes

# New England Seafood Festival

•

*New England Clam Chowder*
*Parkerhouse Rolls and Butter*
*Shrimp and Crab Stuffed Avocado*
*Scallops and Tomatoes*
*Duchess Potatoes*
*Boston Cream Pie*

•

# Beverage Selections

**Sauvignon blanc** is the ideal wine to serve with shellfish. Bottlings from California, the Loire Valley, Australia, or New Zealand are all wonderful choices to accompany this meal. These wines are noted for their grassy and herbaceous aroma and lively acidity. (This grape variety is often labeled Fumé Blanc in California in an effort to mimic Pouilly-Fumé of the Loire Valley.)

Try offering sauvignon blancs from different regions of the world with each of the first three courses. It will be interesting for guests to note how the same grape variety produces slightly different results when made in unique climate zones by a diverse group of vintners.

**Hot apple cider** (with or without a splash of rum) is a hearty and tasty companion for the Boston cream pie.

### NONALCOHOLIC

In place of the wine, you might substitute **cranberry juice.** This beverage is not overly sweet and provides some of the acid that is also found in wine. **Mineral water** will further add zest and sparkles when mixed with the cranberry juice.

# When to Start Cooking

*When dinner is served at 6:00 P.M. . . .*

| Cooking Preparation Schedule | | Cooking Times |
|---|---|---|
| 2:00 P.M. | Boston Cream Pie | 1 hour |
| 3:00 | Duchess Potatoes | 1 hour |
| 3:15 | Shrimp and Crab Stuffed Avocado | 30 minutes |
| 4:00 | Time to set the tables and arrange the room. | |
| 4:30 | Time to clean up, relax a bit, double-check everything, and dress for the occasion. | |

**Final Cooking and Preparation Schedule**          **Serving Times**

| | | | |
|---|---|---|---|
| 5:15 P.M. | New England Clam Chowder | 45 minutes | 6:00 P.M. |
| 5:55 | Parkerhouse Rolls and Butter | 5 minutes | 6:00 |
| 6:05 | Scallops and Tomatoes | 25 minutes | 6:30 |
| 6:10 | Shrimp and Crab Stuffed Avocado | | 6:15 |
| 6:15 | Duchess Potatoes | 15 minutes | 6:30 |
| 6:45 | Boston Cream Pie | 5 minutes | 6:50 |
| | Final Beverage | | 6:55 |

## *Tips and Details*

Depending upon the time of the year, the quality of avocados may vary, therefore you may want to substitute papaya or mango. Both of these are a nice complement to the seafood and provide a good variation to the menu.

Oyster crackers are a good accent to a clam chowder. They add texture and tradition to this dish.

Many white wines will be appropriate with this meal. Plan 1/3 to 1/2 bottle per person and your wine needs will be met.

This menu offers a recipe for Boston cream pie, but if time is limited, you could purchase one from a local bakery.

# New England Clam Chowder

*serves 6*

| | |
|---|---|
| 1 | yellow onion, jumbo |
| 2 stalks | celery |
| 2 | potatoes |
| 2 (6 1/2-ounce cans) | minced clams |
| 3/4 cup (1 1/2 sticks) | unsalted butter |
| 3/4 cup | flour |
| 1 teaspoon | salt |
| 1/2 teaspoon | ground white pepper |
| 1 quart | half-and-half |
| 2 tablespoons | red wine vinegar |

## Preparation

1. Peel and mince the onion.
2. Wash, drain, and mince the celery.
3. Peel, wash, and chop the potatoes into bite-size pieces.
4. Place the onions, celery, and potatoes in a saucepan over medium heat.
5. Drain the juice from the clams and pour it over the onions, celery, and potatoes; add water (just enough) to cover the vegetables; cover the saucepan and simmer at 180°F for 20 minutes or until vegetables become tender.
6. Melt the butter in a large saucepan over medium heat; add the flour, salt, and pepper and stir it in with a wire whip; add half-and-half and continue to stir until thick and smooth.
7. Pour in the cooked vegetables (liquid included); add the minced clams and red wine vinegar and bring to a low boil; remove from the stove and serve with a 6-ounce ladle.

**Preparation Time:** 45 minutes

# Parkerhouse Rolls and Butter

*serves 6*

| 6 to 8 | parkerhouse rolls |
|--------|-------------------|
| 1/4 pound | butter |

**Preparation**

1. Purchase parkerhouse rolls from your local bakery. Allow for the guest who may request an additional roll.
2. Cut the butter into 1/2-ounce slices. **Note:** Most 1/4-pound bricks of butter are marked for 1/2-ounce cutting.
3. Place 1 roll and a 1/2-ounce slice of butter on each bread and butter plate.

**Final Preparation Time:** 5 minutes

# Shrimp and Crab Stuffed Avocado

*serves 6*

| | |
|---|---|
| 3 | avocados, ripe |
| 3 | lemons |
| 1/2 pound | crab meat |
| 1/2 pound | bay shrimp, precooked, frozen |
| 3 tablespoons | mayonnaise |
| 1 teaspoon | Dijon mustard |
| 1 head | lettuce |
| 6 | pitted black olives |

## Preparation

1. Cut the avocados in half and remove the pits; then peel off the skin and cut a small amount off the round side of the avocados to prevent wobbling, allowing the avocados to sit flat.

2. Squeeze the juice from 2 lemons and dip the avocado halves in the lemon juice. This will enhance the flavor and keep the avocados green.

3. Chop the crab meat into bite-size pieces about the size of a dime.

4. Remove the bay shrimp from the bag and place in a colander; put the colander in a sink and run cold water over the shrimp until thawed, approximately 3 or 4 minutes; drain and place the shrimp in a mixing bowl along with the chopped crab meat.

5. Mix the mayonnaise and Dijon mustard together in a separate bowl; add the mixture to the shrimp and crab meat and gently mix.

6. Equally stuff the avocado shells with the shrimp and crab mixture.

7. Wash and drain the lettuce, then slice into a very fine shred. This is referred to as "chiffonade."

8. Slice black olives into thin rings.

9. Cut the remaining lemon into 6 wedges.

10. Place an equal amount of chiffonade onto each salad plate; set a stuffed avocado into the center of the chiffonade; top off by layering 3 or 4 black olive rings over the top of the shrimp and crab mixture; garnish with a lemon wedge and refrigerate until ready to serve.

**Preparation Time:** 30 minutes

# Scallops and Tomatoes

*serves 6*

| | |
|---|---|
| *4* | *tomatoes, medium* |
| *1/3 cup* | *parsley, chopped (approximately 1/4 bunch)* |
| *3 pounds* | *scallops, medium* |
| *1 1/2 cups* | *flour* |
| *1/2 cup* | *olive oil* |
| *1 teaspoon* | *salt* |
| *1/2 teaspoon* | *ground black pepper* |
| *1 teaspoon* | *garlic, minced* |
| *1* | *lemon* |

**Preparation**

1. Peel the tomatoes by blanching them in boiling water for 30 seconds; peel away the thin skin and cut into a 1/2-inch dice; set aside.
2. Wash, drain, and finely chop the parsley and set aside.
3. Roll the scallops in the flour.
4. Pour the olive oil into a large sauté pan over medium heat; place the scallops into the pan and sauté all sides, continually turning, for approximately 4 or 5 minutes or until nicely browned and reaching 145°F or higher for at least 15 seconds.
5. Add the diced tomatoes, salt, ground black pepper, minced garlic, chopped parsley, and the juice from the lemon; stir with a wooden spoon and sauté for another 2 or 3 minutes; then serve by placing 8 ounces onto each dinner plate.

**Preparation Time:** 25 minutes

# Duchess Potatoes

*serves 6*

| | |
|---|---|
| 6 | russet potatoes, medium |
| 2 | eggs |
| 2 tablespoons | butter |
| 1/3 cup | milk |
| 1 teaspoon | salt |
| 1/2 teaspoon | ground white pepper |
| 1/2 teaspoon | nutmeg |

## Preparation

1. Thoroughly wash potatoes, dry, and place in a 375°F preheated oven for 45 minutes or until done.
2. Remove potatoes from the oven and cut in half; allow to cool for a few minutes; scoop out the inside of the potatoes with a tablespoon.
3. Separate the egg yolks from the whites using plastic gloves or egg separator.
4. Whip the potatoes while adding the egg yolks, butter, milk, salt, ground white pepper, and nutmeg; whip until the potatoes are a soft fluffy mixture.
5. Place the potato mixture into a pastry bag with a large rose tip and squeeze out 18 equal amounts onto a baking pan, resembling 18 small cones; carefully cover with plastic wrap and refrigerate.

## Ready to Serve

1. Remove the plastic wrap and place the pan into a 375°F preheated oven for 10 to 12 minutes or until the potatoes reach 165°F or higher for at least 15 seconds and are lightly browned; remove with a spatula and promptly serve 3 per plate.

**Preparation Time:** 1 hour
**Final Cooking Time:** 15 minutes

# Boston Cream Pie

*serves 6 to 10*

| | |
|---|---|
| 1 cup | cake flour |
| 1 1/2 teaspoons | baking soda |
| 1/4 teaspoon | salt |
| 2 | eggs |
| 1 cup | sugar |
| 1 1/2 teaspoons | lemon juice |
| 1/3 cup | hot water |

**Custard Filling**

| | |
|---|---|
| 2 cups | custard, prepared mix |
| 1 | egg |

**Frosting**

| | |
|---|---|
| 3/4 cup | chocolate chips |

### Preparation

1. Mix the cake flour with baking soda and salt; sift into a bowl and set aside.
2. Crack the eggs into a bowl and whip with an electric mixer until the eggs become thick and light; gradually add the sugar and continue to mix; add the lemon juice and slowly add the hot water, mixing until thick.
3. Fold in flour mixture in small amounts.
4. Lightly butter two 8-inch round cake pans; pour an equal amount of batter into each pan; place the pans in the center of a 350°F preheated oven for 30 minutes or until the cakes are done. **Note:** Test for doneness by inserting a wooden pick into the center of each cake. If it comes out clean, then cake is done.
5. Remove the cakes from the oven and place on wire racks to cool; do not remove the cakes from the pans for about 10 minutes or until totally cooled.
6. Carefully run a knife around the edges of the cakes while still in the pans; invert the pans onto the wire racks and carefully remove from the cakes; allow cakes to cool for an additional 5 to 10 minutes.

**Custard Filling** (prepare while the cakes are baking)

1. Prepare custard filling according to package directions, adding 1 beaten egg yolk, separating egg yolk from egg white using plastic gloves or egg separator.
2. Pour into a saucepan over medium heat, constantly stirring until the mixture comes to a full rolling boil; pour the custard into a bowl and refrigerate for about 45 minutes to cool and thicken.

**Time to Put It Together**

1. Place one cake layer on a cake platter.
2. Evenly spread the custard filling over the top of the cake by using a spatula.
3. Place the second cake layer over the top of the custard filling.
4. Put the chocolate chips in a small bowl and place into the microwave oven for short bursts (10 to 15 seconds), frequently stirring, until the chocolate has melted evenly. **Caution:** Be careful not to overheat.
5. Evenly spread the melted chocolate over the top of the cake by using a spatula; refrigerate until ready to serve.

**Ready to Serve**

1. Slice and serve on dessert plates.

**Note:** Alternative for those in a hurry . . . purchase a Boston cream pie from your local bakery or a prepared frozen pie that can be easily thawed and ready to serve.

**Preparation Time:** 1 hour
**Final Preparation Time:** 5 minutes

# For the Holidays

*Thanksgiving/Christmas*

•

*Sage Roasted Turkey with Apple-Walnut Stuffing*
*Brown Sugar Glazed Sweet Potatoes*
*Mashed Potatoes and Gravy*
*Honey Glazed Beets*
*Brandied Carrots*
*Pumpkin Raisin Pie*

•

# Beverage Selections

The holidays are a very festive time of year. Serving **sparkling wines** or **apple cider** when friends and family gather can only make the mood even brighter. Excellent domestic versions of both are available at most stores and are sure to please grandparents and children alike.

If you prefer **still wine,** select a bottle of dry rosé. Rosé is made from red grapes. Vintners harvest, crush, and then press the juice from the skins and seeds before much color or harsh tannin has interacted with the juice. The resulting wine is light, fresh, and fruity.

Rosé is always a good complement to fowl and will add color to your holiday repast. Just remember to stay away from the sweet rosés. These are often not high quality, and the abundant sugar will interfere with your enjoyment of the food.

### NONALCOHOLIC

It's a good idea to have **eggnog** on hand to complete the meal (or as a starter). Although available in stores, it might be fun to make your own. In a large bowl, whisk together 4 eggs (pasteurized), 2 teaspoons vanilla, 1/4 cup of sugar, and 1 cup of milk until the sugar is dissolved and the mixture is well blended. Next, add 1 quart of milk, whisking constantly. Finish by grating some nutmeg onto each cup of eggnog as it is served.

# When to Start Cooking

*When dinner is served at 4:00 P.M. . . .*

| Cooking Preparation Schedule | | Cooking Times |
|---|---|---|
| 11:00 A.M. | Pumpkin Raisin Pie | 1 hour |
| 12:00 P.M. | Sage Roasted Turkey | 3 hours |
| 12:15 | Brandied Carrots | 30 minutes |
| 12:40 | Brown Sugar Glazed Sweet Potatoes | 20 minutes |
| 1:00 | Time to set the tables and arrange the room. | |
| 1:30 | Time to clean up, relax a bit, double-check everything, and dress for the occasion. | |

**Final Cooking and Preparation Schedule**        **Serving Times**

| Time | Dish | Duration | Serving Time |
|------|------|----------|--------------|
| 3:00 P.M. | Apple-Walnut Stuffing | 1 hour | 4:00 P.M. |
| 3:05 | Brown Sugar Glazed Sweet Potatoes | 55 minutes | |
| 3:15 | Mashed Potatoes | 45 minutes | |
| 3:25 | Gravy | 15 minutes | |
| 3:40 | Sage Roasted Turkey | 10 minutes | |
| 3:45 | Honey Glazed Beets | 15 minutes | |
| 3:50 | Brandied Carrots | 10 minutes | |
| 4:25 | Pumpkin Raisin Pie | 5 minutes | 4:30 |
| | Final Beverage | | 4:40 |

# Tips and Details

Decorate with festive winter holiday colors of greens and reds. Quilts and blankets coupled with copper pots and pans create a beautiful holiday setting. This is also the time to pull out the best linens, china, and crystal.

The use of pine wreaths and centerpieces accent the occasion by stimulating your vision and providing a wonderful aromatic atmosphere.

Mulled wine punch is a nice alternative for the winter holidays. For á serving of 8, simmer 2 cups of water, 3/4 cups of sugar, lemon and lime peels, 3 whole cloves, 1 cinnamon stick, and 3 whole allspice berries for about 10 minutes in a saucepan. In a separate pan, heat 4 cups of red wine, 1/2 cup of orange juice, and 1/4 cup of crème de cassis. Strain the spice mixture and add to the wine. If you wish, garnish with whole cloves or cinnamon sticks.

# Sage Roasted Turkey

*serves 6*

| | |
|---|---|
| 2 | carrots |
| 4 stalks | celery |
| 1 | yellow onion, jumbo |
| 2 cups | chicken stock (using a chicken base with water) |
| 3 leaves | bay leaves |
| 1/3 cup | sage, chopped (approximately 1/2 bunch) |
| 10- to 12-pound | fresh turkey (follow package directions for oven preparedness) |

## Preparation

1. Roughly chop the carrots, celery, and onion; mix and spread over the bottom of a roasting pan.
2. Prepare the chicken stock by mixing a chicken base with water according to package directions; add the bay leaves, mix, and pour over the chopped carrots, celery, and onion.
3. Wash and finely chop the sage leaves; rub the inside of the turkey with the chopped sage and place the turkey on top of the vegetables in the roasting pan.
4. Place the turkey in a 325°F preheated oven and bake for approximately 10 to 15 minutes per pound or until the turkey has reached an internal temperature of 165°F or higher for at least 15 seconds, using a thermometer.
5. Baste the turkey 3 or 4 times with the stock from the roasting pan while the turkey is baking. **Note:** If the turkey begins to get too dark, cover with foil.
6. When the turkey is done, remove from the oven, cover with foil, and set aside for 20 minutes or until ready to carve. Reserve drippings for gravy.

## Ready to Serve

1. Carefully remove both breasts of the turkey and place on a cutting board. Slice each breast into 1/2-inch cuts and serve 3 per plate.
2. Remove the legs and wings, and with the remaining turkey breast, decoratively arrange on a platter. A guest may request a leg, wing, or additional portion of breast.

**Preparation Time:** 2 1/2 to 3 hours

**Final Preparation Time:** 10 minutes

# Apple-Walnut Stuffing

*serves 6*

| | |
|---|---|
| *1 stalk* | *celery* |
| *1* | *yellow onion, jumbo* |
| *18 slices, 1/2 inch* | *French bread (approximately 1 loaf)* |
| *2* | *Granny Smith apples* |
| *1/3 cup* | *unsalted butter* |
| *1/2 cup* | *chopped walnuts* |
| *1 tablespoon* | *salt* |
| *1 tablespoon* | *ground black pepper* |
| *2 teaspoons* | *sage* |
| *1 teaspoon* | *garlic powder* |
| *1 cup* | *chicken stock (using a chicken base with water)* |

## Preparation

1. Wash, drain, and mince the celery and set aside.
2. Peel and cut the onion in half; mince half of the onion and set aside; save the other half for another use.
3. Cut the French bread into 1/2-inch cubes and set aside. **Note:** Older bread is easier to cut and makes better stuffing.
4. Peel and remove the core from the apples; chop into 1/4-inch dice and set aside.
5. Melt 1/4 cup of butter in a pot over medium heat; add the minced celery and onions and sauté until they become transparent.
6. Add the chopped apples and chopped walnuts and sauté for approximately 3 minutes.
7. Add the cut bread, salt, ground black pepper, sage, and garlic powder and thoroughly mix.
8. Prepare the chicken stock by mixing a chicken base with water according to package directions; add the chicken stock to the bread mixture and thoroughly mix; cover the pot, reduce the heat to low, and simmer for 5 minutes.
9. Spread the remaining butter over the bottom and sides of a deep baking pan.
10. Remove the pot from the stove and place the dressing into the baking pan.
11. Place the pan into a 325°F preheated oven and bake for approximately 45 minutes or until the dressing becomes golden brown on the top; set aside until ready to serve with a 3 1/4-ounce, number 10 scoop.

**Preparation Time:** 1 hour

**Final Preparation Time:** 5 minutes

# Brown Sugar Glazed Sweet Potatoes

*serves 6*

| | |
|---|---|
| 2 pounds | sweet potatoes |
| 3 | oranges |
| 3/4 cup | brown sugar |
| 1 teaspoon | ground cloves |
| 1 1/2 teaspoons | ground allspice |
| 1 1/2 teaspoons | ground ginger |
| 2 tablespoons | Dijon mustard |
| 1/2 cup | golden raisins |

## Preparation

1. Peel, wash, and cut sweet potatoes into 1-inch dice; boil for approximately 8 minutes or until tender; drain and cool.
2. Squeeze the juice from the oranges; add the brown sugar, ground cloves, ground allspice, ground ginger, and Dijon mustard and thoroughly mix.
3. Place the sweet potatoes into a shallow roasting pan; cover with the orange spice marinade; sprinkle the golden raisins on top; cover with foil and refrigerate.

## Ready to Serve

1. Place the foil-covered pan into a 325°F preheated oven for 30 minutes; then remove the foil and put back into the oven for another 15 minutes, reaching 165°F or higher for at least 15 seconds.
2. Remove from the oven and place on a wire rack to cool for 10 minutes; gently stir and serve with a 3-ounce spoon.

**Preparation Time:** 20 minutes
**Final Cooking Time:** 55 minutes

# Mashed Potatoes and Gravy

*serves 6*

| | |
|---|---|
| 4 | *russet potatoes, large* |
| *1/3 cup* | *milk* |
| *2 teaspoons* | *salt* |
| *1/2 cup (1 stick)* | *butter* |
| *1* | *egg, pasteurized* |
| *1/2* | *ground white pepper* |
| *1/8 teaspoon* | *nutmeg* |

## Preparation

1. Peel, wash, slice, and boil potatoes in salted water (1 teaspoon of salt per gallon of water) for approximately 20 to 30 minutes or until fork tender.
2. Heat the milk in the microwave for 1 minute.
3. Mash the potatoes; add butter, milk, egg, salt, ground white pepper, and nutmeg and whip until fluffy; then serve with a 3 1/4-ounce, number 10 scoop.

**Preparation Time:** 45 minutes

# Turkey Gravy

*serves 6*

| | |
|---|---|
| 1/2 cup (1 stick) | unsalted butter |
| 1/2 cup | flour |
| 2 cups | chicken stock (using a chicken base with water) |
| 1 leaf | bay leaf |
| 1/2 tablespoon | salt |
| 1 1/2 teaspoon | ground black pepper |
| 1 cup | drippings from roast turkey |

**Preparation**

1. Melt the butter in a sauté pan over medium heat; add the flour and stir it in well with a wooden spoon; continue to heat and stir until it becomes a light golden color. This is called a "roux." Set aside.

2. Prepare the chicken stock by mixing a chicken base with water according to package directions; add the bay leaf, salt, and ground pepper in a saucepan over medium heat and bring it to a boil.

3. After the turkey is finally cooked, drain 1 cup of drippings from the roasting pan; add the drippings to the chicken stock and mix.

4. Slowly add the roux to the boiling stock; thoroughly mix with a wire whip. **Note:** Add only enough roux to thicken the gravy to the desired consistency.

5. Strain the gravy through a mesh strainer; place in a gravy dish for guests to serve themselves for potatoes and turkey or ladle 1 ounce onto each serving of potatoes and 1 ounce onto each serving of turkey.

**Preparation Time:** 15 minutes

# Honey Glazed Beets

*serves 6*

| | |
|---|---|
| *1* | *orange* |
| *1/3 cup* | *honey* |
| *1/4 cup* | *brown sugar* |
| *3 cups* | *sliced beets, canned* |

## Preparation

1. Squeeze the juice from the orange; mix with the honey and brown sugar in a sauté pan over medium heat; continue to heat and stir for 2 minutes.

2. Drain the juice from the sliced beets; add the beets to the orange and honey glaze and thoroughly mix; cook for 5 minutes; remove from the stove and serve with a 3-ounce spoon.

**Preparation Time:** 15 minutes

# Brandied Carrots

*serves 6*

| | |
|---|---|
| 18 | baby carrots |
| 1/4 cup (1/2 stick) | unsalted butter |
| 1/4 cup | sugar |
| 3 tablespoons | brandy |

## Preparation

1. Scrape and wash the baby carrots.
2. Place the baby carrots into a pot of water and bring to a boil; cook for 20 minutes or until the carrots are tender, being careful not to overcook.
3. Remove the carrots from the stove; place a colander in the sink and drain the carrots; run cold water over them to prevent further cooking; place in a covered bowl and refrigerate.

## Ready to Serve

1. Melt the butter in a sauté pan over medium heat; add the sugar, stir, and sauté for approximately 2 minutes.
2. Add the baby carrots and mix well with the butter and sugar; sauté for approximately 2 minutes.
3. Remove the pan from the stove; pour the brandy over the carrots; carefully put the pan back onto the stove, at arm's distance for the brandy will flame. After the flame has gone out, continue to sauté for another minute; serve 3 per plate.

**Preparation Time:** 30 minutes
**Final Cooking Time:** 10 minutes

# Pumpkin-Raisin Pie

*serves 6*

| | |
|---|---|
| 1 (9-inch) | pie crust, prepared |
| 2 | eggs |
| 1 can (16 ounces) | solid pack pumpkin |
| 3/4 cup | raisins |
| 3/4 cup | sugar |
| 1/2 teaspoon | salt |
| 1 teaspoon | ground cinnamon |
| 1/2 teaspoon | ground ginger |
| 1/2 teaspoon | ground cloves |
| 1 1/2 cups | evaporated milk |

## Preparation

1. Place the pie crust into a 9-inch pie pan and set aside.
2. Crack the eggs into a large bowl and gently beat.
3. Add the solid pack pumpkin, raisins, sugar, salt, ground cinnamon, ground ginger, ground cloves, and evaporated milk and thoroughly mix.
4. Pour the mixture into the pie crust and place in a 425°F preheated oven for 15 minutes, then reduce the temperature to 350°F and bake for an additional 45 minutes or until done. **Note:** Test for doneness by inserting a wooden pick into the center of the pie. If it comes out clean, then the pie is done.
5. Remove the pie from the oven and place on a wire rack to cool.

## Ready to Serve

1. Cut into 6 slices and serve.

**Note:** Alternative for those in a hurry . . . purchase a pumpkin-raisin pie from your local bakery or a prepared frozen pie that can be easily baked and ready to

**Preparation Time:** 1 hour
**Final Preparation Time:** 5 minutes

# Superbowl Sunday

•

*Beer Sausage with Smoked Gouda*
*Meat Loaf with Walnut Stuffing*
*Sliced Baked Potatoes*
*Cloverleaf Rolls and Butter*
*Apple Cobbler with Ice Cream*

•

# Beverage Selections

Before kickoff, consider serving **hot buttered rum** (sugar, water, clove, rum, butter, and nutmeg) to welcome your guests in from the cold. This classic winter warmer will help set a lively mood. For nondrinkers, some **hot spiced cider** would be an excellent alternative.

Once the game begins, have plenty of **beer** and **soda** on hand to quench the sports fans' thirst. Many small microbreweries now exist, and it might be fun to see if you can find beers from each of the participating teams' hometowns to serve. In any event, choose a variety of styles to offer.

As always, be careful to ensure that the alcohol drinkers do not overdo it prior to leaving for home. This sometimes awkward subject can be handled successfully by being prepared should a potential situation arise.

## NONALCOHOLIC

As the game reaches halftime, set out a **coffee bar,** which will be fun for guests and take their minds away from alcohol. The presentation should be attractive. Cream and whipped cream should be placed in glass bowls set in ice containers to keep them cold. Granulated sugar should be offered in a glass bowl. Cinnamon, nutmeg, and chocolate should be grated or tendered in shakers. Orange and lime peels as well as almond slivers will complete the table.

# When to Start Cooking

*When dinner is served at 6:00 P.M. . . .*

| Cooking Preparation Schedule | | Cooking Times |
|---|---|---|
| 12:00 P.M. | Apple Cobbler | 1 hour |
| 12:15 | Meat Loaf with Walnut Stuffing | 20 minutes |
| 12:35 | Beer Sausage with Smoked Gouda | 30 minutes |
| 1:05 | Time to set the tables and get ready to watch the game. | |

## Final Cooking and Preparation Schedule

| | | | Serving Times |
|---|---|---|---|
| 4:50 P.M. | Meat Loaf with Walnut Stuffing | 1 hour 40 min. | 6:30 P.M. |
| 6:00 | Beer Sausage and Smoked Gouda | | 6:00 |
| 6:00 | Sliced Baked Potatoes | 30 minutes | 6:30 |
| 6:25 | Cloverleaf Rolls and Butter | 5 minutes | 6:30 |
| 6:45 | Apple Cobbler with Ice Cream | 5 minutes | 6:50 |
| | Final Beverage | | 6:55 |

## Tips and Details

Create a sports bar atmosphere by placing bowls of assorted nuts and pretzels in strategic locations. If possible, hook up the television to a stereo for better audio.

To make the day a little more interesting, ask each guest to contribute some sports memorabilia with a predetermined value, say $10. Award all of the items to the person who best predicts the final score. This will spice up the day without adding the specter of hard gambling.

Make sure the food is served buffet style so that the guests may enjoy it throughout the entire afternoon. You may want to use paper plates to reduce cleanup and eliminate the possibility of an overenthusiastic fan breaking expensive china.

# Beer Sausage with Smoked Gouda

*serves 6*

| | |
|---|---|
| 1/4 cup | honey |
| 1/2 cup | Dijon mustard |
| 1 1/2 pounds | pork sausage (regular, medium, or hot)) |
| 1 bottle (12 ounces) | beer |
| 1 head | lettuce |
| 1 | Granny Smith apple |
| 1 | red delicious apple |
| 1/4 cup | lemon juice |
| 9 ounces | smoked Gouda cheese |

**Preparation**

1. Combine the honey and Dijon mustard in a bowl and thoroughly mix; cover and refrigerate.
2. Cut the sausage into 12 silver dollar–size patties; place the patties in a sauté pan over medium heat and brown, reaching 155°F or higher for at least 15 seconds; add the beer just before the sausage is completely cooked; reduce heat to low and simmer for 5 minutes; remove the sausage and place on paper towels to drain. **Note:** Purchase sausage according to taste: regular, medium, or hot.
3. Wash and drain the lettuce; spread the lettuce leaves (as a liner) over a large platter.
4. Wash the apples and cut each into 6 wedges using a paring knife or apple cutter; dip into the lemon juice to enhance the flavor and reduce browning.
5. Cut the cheese into 1/4-inch sticks.
6. Pour the honey mustard sauce in a fruit dish; place the fruit dish in the center of the lettuce-lined platter; arrange the sausage, sliced apples, and smoked Gouda cheese sticks around the platter in a decorative manner; cover with plastic wrap and refrigerate until ready to serve.

**Preparation Time:** 30 minutes

**Final Preparation Time:** 2 minutes

# Meat Loaf with Walnut Stuffing

*serves 6*

| | |
|---|---|
| 1 | yellow onion, jumbo |
| 1 | green bell pepper |
| 1 cup | soft bread crumbs (white bread) |
| 1 1/2 pounds | ground beef, minimum fat content |
| 1 tablespoon | Worcestershire sauce |

| 1 teaspoon | salt |
| 1/2 teaspoon | ground black pepper |
| 1/2 cup | milk |
| 2 | eggs |
| 1 tablespoon | vegetable shortening |
| 2 stalks | celery |
| 1/2 cup | chopped walnuts |
| 1/4 cup (1/2 stick) | butter |
| 2 cups | soft bread crumbs (whole wheat bread) |
| 1/4 cup | water |

## Preparation

1. Peel and cut the onion in half; mince half of the onion, saving the other half for another use.
2. Cut the green bell pepper in half, remove the seeds and wash; mince half of the pepper, saving the other half for another use.
3. Remove the crusts from several slices of bread and chop into very small bits (use same proceedure for whole wheat bread crumbs in step 10).
4. Combine the ground beef, minced onion, minced green pepper, Worcestershire sauce, white bread crumbs, salt, ground black pepper, milk, and 1 egg in a bowl and thoroughly mix.
5. Using the vegetable shortening, lightly grease the bottom and sides of a 9-by-13-inch baking pan.
6. Press half of the ground beef mixture into the bottom of the pan.
7. Wash and dice the celery.
8. Finely chop the walnuts.
9. Melt the butter in a microwave oven.
10. Combine the whole wheat bread crumbs, diced celery, chopped walnuts, 1 egg, melted butter, and water and thoroughly mix; spread on top of the meat mixture in the pan.
11. Press the other half of the ground beef mixture on top of the stuffing; cover with plastic wrap and refrigerate until ready to bake.

## Ready to Serve

1. Remove the plastic wrap and place in a 350°F preheated oven for 1 1/2 hours, reaching 155°F or higher for at least 15 seconds.
2. Remove from the oven and cool for 5 minutes; slice into 6- or 8-ounce portions and serve.

**Preparation Time:** 20 minutes

**Final Cooking Time:** 1 hour 35 minutes

# Sliced Baked Potatoes

*serves 6*

| | |
|---|---|
| *6* | *russet potatoes, medium* |
| *1/3 cup* | *butter* |
| *1 1/2 teaspoons* | *garlic salt* |
| *1/2 teaspoon* | *lemon pepper* |
| *1/8 cup* | *chives, chopped (approximately 1/4 bunch)* |
| *1/3 cup* | *grated cheddar cheese* |
| *2 tablespoons* | *grated Parmesan cheese* |

## Preparation

1. Peel and wash potatoes.
2. Place the potatoes on a cutting board; cut the potatoes into 1/4-inch slices, being careful not to cut all the way through. **Note:** Place the handle of a wooden spoon next to the potatoes while cutting. This will serve as a safety guide and will prevent the knife from cutting all the way through the potatoes.
3. Place the potatoes onto a microwave-safe plate.
4. Melt the butter in the microwave oven and pour over the potatoes.
5. Sprinkle the garlic salt and lemon pepper over the potatoes.
6. Wash, drain, and chop the chives into 1/4-inch pieces; sprinkle over the potatoes.
7. Microwave potatoes at high power for 15 minutes; remove from the microwave and cool for 2 or 3 minutes.
8. Sprinkle the grated cheddar cheese over the potatoes.
9. Sprinkle the Parmesan cheese over the cheddar cheese.
10. Microwave at high power for 5 minutes or until the cheeses are melted and the potatoes are fully cooked; remove and serve with a 3-ounce spoon.

**Preparation Time:** 30 minutes

# Cloverleaf Rolls and Butter

*serves 6*

| 6 to 12 | *cloverleaf rolls* |
| 1/4 pound | *butter* |

## Preparation

1. Purchase cloverleaf rolls from your local bakery. Allow for the guest who may request an additional roll or two.
2. Cut butter into 1/2-ounce slices. **Note:** Most 1/4-pound bricks of butter are marked for 1/2-ounce cutting.
3. Place 1 roll and a 1/2-ounce slice of butter on each bread and butter plate.

**Final Preparation Time:** 5 minutes

# Apple Cobbler with Ice Cream

*serves 6*

| | |
|---|---|
| 2 | Granny Smith apples |
| 4 | red delicious apples |
| 1 | lemon |
| 1 1/2 quarts | water |
| 1 cup | sugar |
| 1 stick | cinnamon stick |
| 3/4 cup (1 1/2 sticks) | unsalted butter |
| 1 1/2 cups | graham cracker crumbs (10 graham crackers) |
| 1 tablespoon | cinnamon powder |
| 1 tablespoon | ground cloves |
| 1/4 cup | brown sugar |
| 1 quart | vanilla ice cream |

## Preparation

1. Peel the apples and remove the cores; slice the apples into a 1/2-inch dice and set aside.
2. Cut the lemon in half and squeeze out the juice into a small bowl.
3. Combine the water, juice from the lemon, 1/3 cup of white sugar, and the cinnamon stick in a large saucepan; place the diced apples into the water solution and simmer for approximately 5 minutes or until the apples are just tender; drain the apples and set aside.
4. Melt the butter in a microwave oven and set aside.
5. Combine the graham cracker crumbs, cinnamon powder, ground cloves, the remaining white sugar, and the brown sugar and thoroughly mix; add the melted butter and mix until well blended. **Note:** Place graham crackers between 2 pieces of wax paper and roll with a rolling pin to create the graham cracker crumbs.
6. Sprinkle half of the graham cracker mixture into the bottom of a 9-by-13-inch baking pan; do not pack it down.
7. Cover the graham cracker mixture with the cooked apples.
8. Cover the top of the apples with the remaining graham cracker mixture; do not pack it down.

**9.** Place in a 300°F preheated oven for approximately 45 minutes or until the crust becomes golden brown; remove from the oven and cool before serving.

### Ready to Serve

**1.** Serve 6-ounce portions of the cobbler in soup bowls; top off with a 4-ounce scoop of vanilla ice cream and serve. **Note:** Remove the ice cream from the freezer approximately 5 minutes before serving to allow for easier scooping.

**Preparation Time:** 1 hour
**Final Preparation Time:** 5 minutes

# Orient Express

•

*Chicken Spring Rolls*
*Oriental Barbecued Pork*
*Stir-fried Bok Choy with Pork and Shrimp*
*over Steamed Rice*
*Peppermint Ice Cream and Fortune Cookies*

•

# Beverage Selections

The dry and full-bodied nature of **Gewürztraminer** makes it an ideal "food wine." For this theme night, its floral aroma and slightly spicy flavor make it the perfect complement to the Chinese meal. Be careful to select a dry style of this wine though, as many Gewürztraminers produced outside of France and the Pacific Northwest are cheap and overly sweet imitations of the real thing.

## NONALCOHOLIC

There are more than 3000 different varieties of tea, each with its own flavor, body, color, and aroma. Like wines, they often take their name from the area where the leaves are grown. **Darjeeling, oolong,** and **green teas,** served hot or even iced, make dependable companions for a Chinese meal.

**Note:** If possible, serve the wine in green stems (clear glass bowls), reminiscent of Alsace, and the tea in Oriental porcelain, in the style of the tea flavor.

# When to Start Cooking

*When dinner is served at 7:00 P.M. . . .*

| Cooking Preparation Schedule | | Cooking Times |
|---|---|---|
| 2:00 P.M. | Oriental Barbecued Pork | 10 minutes |
| 2:10 | Chicken Spring Rolls | 30 minutes |
| 2:40 | Stir-fried Bok Choy with Pork and Shrimp | 30 minutes |
| 3:10 | Time to set the tables and arrange the room. | |
| 4:00 | Time to clean up, relax a bit, double-check everything, and dress for the occasion. | |

| Final Cooking and Preparation Schedule | | | Serving Times |
|---|---|---|---|
| 6:15 P.M. | Oriental Barbecued Pork | 1 hour | 7:15 P.M. |
| 6:40 | Chicken Spring Rolls | 20 minutes | 7:00 |
| 7:00 | Steamed Rice | 25 minutes | 7:30 |
| 7:05 | Stir-fried Bok Choy with Pork and Shrimp | 25 minutes | 7:30 |
| 7:45 | Peppermint Ice Cream and Fortune Cookies | 5 minutes | 7:50 |
| | Final Beverage | | 7:55 |

# Tips and Details

Spring rolls are a classic Chinese dish. For their best quality, it is very important that they be deep-fried in oil at 375°F. If the oil is too cold the spring rolls will absorb the oil and become greasy. If the oil is too hot, they will cook too quickly, becoming dark brown and not fully cooked inside.

Ginger is a key component in Oriental cuisine. It offers a wonderful background flavor and a very cleansing effect on the palate. For the stir-fry, you may choose to substitute fresh sliced ginger in place of the ground ginger. The resulting taste will be a true essence of ginger without the bitterness sometimes associated with this spice in its dried, ground form.

If you prefer a red wine with your Chinese food, a California zinfandel can be quite pleasing. Its spicy, berrylike, and brambly qualities match admirably with the Orient Express menu.

Encourage your guests to use chopsticks. These can be purchased at your local grocery store or Oriental specialty shop. They are available in a wide variety of styles and prices. Porcelain sticks are washable and impressive for your guests.

# Chicken Spring Rolls

*serves 6 (serve on small salad or bread and butter plates)*

| | |
|---|---|
| 2 (5-ounce) | chicken breasts, boneless, skinless |
| 1 1/2 teaspoons | garlic, minced |
| 1/8 cup | green onions, sliced (approximately 1/4 bunch) |
| 2 tablespoons | sherry |
| 2 tablespoons | soy sauce |
| 1 tablespoon | cornstarch |
| 1 1/2 teaspoons | oyster sauce |
| 1 1/2 teaspoons | ground ginger |
| 1 1/2 teaspoons | sugar |
| 2 | eggs |
| 12 | won ton skins |
| 3 cups | vegetable oil |
| 1/3 cup | soy sauce |
| 1/3 cup | Oriental sweet and hot mustard |

## Preparation

1. Chop the chicken breasts into 1/8-inch strips.
2. Peel and mince the garlic.
3. Wash, drain, and cut the green onions into very thin slices.
4. Combine the chicken strips, minced garlic, sliced green onions, sherry, 2 tablespoons of soy sauce, cornstarch, oyster sauce, ground ginger, and sugar in a bowl and thoroughly mix; place in the refrigerator for 15 minutes.
5. Separate the egg whites from the yolks using plastic gloves or egg separator; beat the whites until smooth.
6. Place the won ton skins on a clean flat surface; brush all 4 edges of each won ton skin with the egg wash.
7. Place an equal amount of the chicken mixture in the center of each won ton skin.
8. Roll each won ton around the chicken mixture forming a cylinder shape; roll the bottom up and fold the sides inward, making sure that the won tons form a good seal around the chicken mixture stuffing. **Note:** The egg wash helps the won ton skins to stick together.
9. Place the chicken spring rolls on a plate, cover with plastic wrap, and refrigerate until ready to cook.

## Ready to Serve

1. Pour 3 cups of vegetable oil into a saucepan over medium heat.
2. Carefully place the chicken spring rolls into the hot oil; cook for about 15 minutes or until the rolls become golden brown, reaching 165°F or higher for at least 15 seconds; remove from the oil and place on paper towels to drain. **Caution:** Be very careful with this procedure, for the oil is very hot.
3. Place 2 chicken spring rolls on each salad plate.
4. Pour 1/3 cup of soy sauce into a small fruit dish; pour Oriental sweet and hot mustard into a small fruit dish; place on the table with a teaspoon next to each dish for guests to serve themselves. **Note:** Refill the dishes if necessary and serve with the next course of Oriental barbecued pork.

**Preparation Time:** 30 minutes
**Final Cooking Time:** 20 minutes

# Oriental Barbecued Pork

*serves 6 (serve on salad plates)*

| | |
|---|---|
| 2 tablespoons | garlic, minced |
| 1 tablespoon | Dijon mustard |
| 1/3 cup | soy sauce |
| 1/2 cup | brown sugar |
| 1 tablespoon | ground ginger |
| 1/4 cup | grenadine syrup |
| 1/4 cup | oyster sauce |
| 1/4 cup | tomato paste |
| 3 pounds | pork tenderloins |
| 1 head | lettuce |
| 1/8 cup | green onions, sliced (approximately 1/4 bunch) |
| 1 tablespoon | sesame seeds |
| 6 pieces | crystallized ginger |

## Preparation

1. Peel and mince the garlic.
2. Combine the minced garlic, Dijon mustard, soy sauce, brown sugar, ground ginger, grenadine syrup, oyster sauce, and tomato paste in a bowl and thoroughly mix.
3. Trim any excess fat from the pork and place tenderloins in a deep pan; pour the marinade over the tenderloins, making sure they are fully covered; cover with plastic wrap and refrigerate for 4 hours.

**Ready to Serve**

1. Remove the plastic wrap and place the pork tenderloins on a rack set inside of a roasting pan; place into a 300°F preheated oven for 1 hour or until completely cooked, reaching 155°F or higher for at least 15 seconds; spoon the marinade over the tenderloins every 15 minutes.

2. Remove from the oven and cut into 1/2-inch slices.

3. Wash and drain the lettuce leaves; place lettuce leaf liners on 6 salad plates.

4. Place an equal number of pork tenderloin slices on top of each lettuce liner.

5. Wash, drain, and cut the green onions into very thin slices; sprinkle on top of the sliced tenderloins.

6. Sprinkle sesame seeds over the top of the sliced green onions.

7. Garnish with a piece of crystallized ginger set off to the side of the tenderloins.

**Preparation Time:** 10 minutes

**Final Cooking Time:** 1 hour

# Stir-fried Bok Choy with Pork and Shrimp

*serves 6*

| | |
|---|---|
| *1 head* | bok choy |
| *1 pound* | pork tenderloin |
| *3/4 pound* | bay shrimp, precooked, frozen |
| *1* | red bell pepper |
| *1/2 pound* | mushrooms, medium |
| *1* | yellow onion, jumbo |
| *2 tablespoons* | garlic, chopped |
| *2 tablespoons* | vegetable oil |
| *2 tablespoons* | sesame oil |
| *1 1/2 teaspoons* | ground ginger |
| *2 tablespoons* | soy sauce |
| *1 tablespoon* | oyster sauce |
| *1 cup* | chicken stock (using a chicken base with water) |
| *1/4 cup* | sherry |
| *1 1/2 teaspoons* | Chinese five spice |
| *1 1/2 teaspoons* | salt |
| *1 tablespoon* | ground black pepper |

## Preparation

1. Cut the leaves from the head of bok choy, leaving very little stem; wash, drain, and cut the leaves into long strips approximately 3/4-inch wide; put into a bowl, cover, and refrigerate.

2. Trim any excess fat from the pork tenderloins and cut into 1/2-inch cubes; place in a bowl, cover, and refrigerate.

3. Remove the bay shrimp from the bag and place in a colander; put the colander in a sink and run cold water over the shrimp until thawed, approximately 3 or 4 minutes; put into a bowl, cover, and refrigerate.

4. Cut the red bell pepper in half, remove the seeds, and wash; cut into 1/8-inch wide strips; put into a bowl, cover, and refrigerate.

5. Wash and cut the mushrooms into 1/8-inch slices; put into a bowl, cover, and refrigerate.

6. Peel the onion and cut in half; slice each half into 1/8-inch slices; put into a bowl, cover, and refrigerate.

7. Peel and chop the garlic; put into a bowl, cover, and refrigerate.

**Ready to Serve**

1. Pour the vegetable oil and sesame oil into a wok or very large sauté pan over medium heat.

2. Remove all of the previously prepared ingredients from the refrigerator and uncover.

3. Carefully drop the sliced onions, red pepper strips, and chopped garlic into the hot oil and fry for 1 or 2 minutes or until the onions are golden in color, constantly stirring.

4. Add the pork and fry for 3 or 4 minutes or until cooked on all sides, reaching 155°F or higher for at least 15 seconds, constantly stirring.

5. Add the shrimp and cook for another 2 or 3 minutes, constantly stirring.

6. Add the ground ginger, soy sauce, and oyster sauce and thoroughly mix.

7. Add the bok choy and sliced mushrooms and thoroughly mix.

8. Prepare the chicken stock according to package directions; add to the mixture along with the sherry and thoroughly mix.

9. Add the Chinese five spice, salt, and ground black peppper and thoroughly mix.

10. Cover the wok or sauté pan with a lid or aluminum foil and cook for 10 minutes; remove from the stove and serve a 6-ounce portion (using a 6-ounce ladle) over steamed rice.

**Preparation Time:** 30 minutes
**Final Cooking Time:** 25 minutes

# Steamed Rice

*serves 6*

2 cups            *short grain rice*

2 2/3 cups       *water*

1 teaspoon       *salt*

### Preparation

1. Place the short grain rice in a strainer and rinse with cold water until the water runs clear.
2. Place the water, salt, and rice in a saucepan; bring to a boil over medium heat for 1 minute; cover the pan, reduce the heat to low, and simmer for 20 minutes; remove from the heat and serve.

**Preparation Time:** 25 minutes

# Peppermint Ice Cream and Fortune Cookies

*serves 6*

*(serve the ice cream in small fruit dishes
and the fortune cookies in a bowl)*

1 quart             *peppermint ice cream*

6                   *fortune cookies\**

*\*(Fortune cookies may be purchased at an Oriental grocery store.)*

### Preparation

1. Place a single 2-ounce scoop of peppermint ice cream in the center of a small fruit dish and promptly serve. **Note:** Remove the ice cream from the freezer approximately 5 minutes before serving to allow for easier scooping.
2. Place 6 fortune cookies in a bowl and place in the center of the table to allow guests to randomly select their fortunes.

**Preparation Time:** 5 minutes

# Oktoberfest

•

Hot German Potato Salad
Grilled Bratwurst
Juniper Spiced Sauerkraut
Potato Pancakes
Fresh Applesauce
Fraulein Katherine's White Chocolate Cake

•

# Beverage Selections

Serving good **beer** is an absolute must with any Oktoberfest menu. Choose a light **pilsner** or **kolsch** variety for the aperitif. **Hefeweizen,** an unfiltered wheat beer, would be a superb choice with the entrée. Unfiltered beer is a traditional German style that yields a heightened sense of body or "mouth feel" and a distinctive yeasty aroma. This stylish, opaque beverage is best described as fresh and should be served with a lemon wedge to properly accent the yeast. Any number of strong, **dark beers** would be a fitting finale and complement the rich chocolate dessert.

If **wine** is preferred, a Gewürztraminer or dry Riesling from Germany will not overpower the food and will retain its own integrity and quality. Late harvest Riesling is best saved for the dessert course. Germany has a ranking system that lists wine according to the sugar content of the grape at harvest. General consensus says that the later the harvest the higher the quality of the wine. A *beerenauslese* or *trockenbeerenauslese* is expensive but well worth the price. *Eiswein* (or icewine) is wine made from grapes that were literally frozen on the vine.

For the dessert course, you can substitute these pricey German wines with **late harvest Rieslings** from America.

### NONALCOHOLIC

**Nonalcohol beers** may serve as a substitute for the real thing. Other than this, your only choice would be **ice water,** for fear of tainting this heavy menu.

# When to Start Cooking

*When dinner is served at 6:00 P.M. . . .*

| Cooking Preparation Schedule | | Cooking Times |
|---|---|---|
| 2:15 P.M. | Fraulein Katherine's Cake | 1 hour 10 minutes |
| 3:30 | Potato Pancakes | 10 minutes |
| 3:40 | Fresh Applesauce | 20 minutes |
| 4:00 | Time to set the tables and arrange the room. | |
| 4:30 | Time to clean up, relax a bit, double-check everything, and dress for the occasion. | |

## Final Cooking and Preparation Schedule

| Time | Dish | Duration | Serving Times |
|------|------|----------|---------------|
| 5:00 P.M. | Hot German Potato Salad | 30 minutes | 6:00 P.M. |
| 5:40 | Juniper Spiced Sauerkraut | 30 minutes | 6:10 |
| 5:50 | Grilled Bratwurst | 20 minutes | 6:10 |
| 6:00 | Potato Pancakes | 10 minutes | 6:10 |
| 6:10 | Fresh Applesauce | | 6:10 |
| 6:25 | Fraulein Katherine's Cake | 5 minutes | 6:30 |
| | Final Beverage | | 6:35 |

# Tips and Details

Juniper is a primary seasoning component in the sauerkraut. The juniper berry's pungent flavor is also the main flavoring ingredient in gin. *Genever* is Dutch for juniper, from which gin gets its name.

Less than 15 percent of all wine produced in Germany is red. *Spätburgunder*, a light form of pinot noir, and *Trollenger*, are seldom imported into America, but can be found at wine specialty shops.

Potato pancakes are a very special item served during this festive holiday. To ensure the authenticity of this dish, cook the pancakes slowly, forming a nice golden brown crust on the outside, keeping the inside moist. Do not rush the cooking time.

The applesauce, as described in this recipe, is served cold. However, other styles of applesauce may be served warm. You may further want to experiment by leaving the apples a little on the coarse (chunky) side.

# Hot German Potato Salad

*serves 6*

| | |
|---|---|
| 3 pounds | red potatoes, small |
| 1/2 pound | bacon |
| 1 | red onion |
| 1 tablespoon | caraway seeds |
| 3 tablespoons | sugar |
| 1 tablespoon | salt |
| 1 tablespoon | ground black pepper |
| 1/4 cup | vegetable oil |
| 1/3 cup | malt vinegar |
| 1/4 cup | water |
| 2 tablespoons | cornstarch |
| 1/3 cup | parsley, chopped (approximately 1/4 bunch) |

## Preparation

1. Wash the red potatoes, scrape off any dark spots, and boil for approximately 20 minutes or until fork tender, being careful not to overcook.

2. Remove the potatoes from the water and allow to cool at room temperature.

3. Sauté the bacon over medium heat until light golden brown and reaching 155°F for at least 15 seconds; place onto paper towels to absorb grease (save the grease in the pan); chop the bacon into a 1/2-inch dice.

4. Peel the onion, cut in half, and slice into 1/8-inch strips.

5. Pour 1/4 cup of bacon grease into a clean pan, add the sliced onions, and sauté over low heat until the onions become tender; add the caraway seeds and sauté for an additional 2 minutes, while slowly adding the sugar, salt, ground black pepper, vegetable oil, and malt vinegar.

6. Place the water and cornstarch in a bowl and thoroughly mix; pour into a saucepan and bring to a boil.

7. Pour a small amount of the cornstarch mixture into the pan with the sliced onions, thoroughly mixing with a wire whip while adding the rest until a smooth consistency is reached.

8. Add the chopped bacon to the hot dressing.

9. Cut the potatoes into 1/4-inch slices; pour the hot dressing over the potato slices and toss until well mixed.

10. Put the potato salad into a casserole dish, cover with foil, and place in the oven to keep it warm until ready to serve.

### Ready to Serve

1. Wash, drain, and finely chop the parsley; sprinkle over the top of the potato salad; serve family style or serve 6-ounce portions with a serving spoon.

**Preparation Time:** 30 minutes

**Final Preparation Time:** 5 minutes

# Grilled Bratwurst

*serves 6*

| | |
|---|---|
| 6 | *bratwurst* |
| *1/4 cup* | *water* |
| *1/3 cup* | *stone ground mustard* |

### Preparation

1. Place the bratwurst in a sauté pan over medium heat; add the water; cover the pan and cook for 5 minutes.
2. Remove the cover and continue to sauté for an additional 10 minutes or until fully cooked, reaching 155°F or higher for at least 15 seconds, and golden brown on all sides.
3. Serve over sauerkraut (recipe follows) and garnish with a tablespoon of stone ground mustard over the bratwurst.

**Preparation Time:** 20 minutes

# Juniper Spiced Sauerkraut

## serves 6

| | |
|---|---|
| 2 1/4 cups | sauerkraut, jar prepared |
| 1 | red onion |
| 1/4 cup (1/2 stick) | unsalted butter |
| 1 ounce | juniper berries* |
| 1 teaspoon | salt |
| 1 1/2 teaspoons | ground black pepper |
| 1 leaf | bay leaf |
| 1 cup | chicken stock (using a chicken base with water) |
| 2 tablespoons | sugar |
| 1/4 cup | white wine |

*(Juniper berries are typically available at health food stores or specialty markets.)*

## Preparation

1. Place the prepared sauerkraut in a colander in the sink and rinse with cool water.
2. Peel the onion, cut in half, and cut into very thin slices.
3. Melt the butter in a large sauté pan over medium heat; add the sliced onions and sauté until they become clear.
4. Add the washed sauerkraut, juniper berries, salt, ground black pepper, and bay leaf and sauté for 1 or 2 minutes.
5. Prepare the chicken stock according to package directions; add to the sauerkraut mixture along with the sugar and white wine; continue to sauté until most of the liquid has evaporated.
6. Remove the juniper berries and bay leaf and promptly serve with a 3-ounce slotted spoon.

**Preparation Time:** 30 minutes

# Potato Pancakes

*serves 6*

| | |
|---|---|
| 2 | *russet potatoes, large* |
| 1 | *yellow onion, jumbo* |
| 2 | *eggs* |
| 2 tablespoons | *water* |
| 1 1/2 teaspoons | *salt* |
| 1 1/2 teaspoons | *ground black pepper* |
| 1 1/2 teaspoons | *dried parsley flakes* |
| 1/3 cup | *all-purpose flour* |
| 2 tablespoons | *vegetable oil* |

## Preparation

1. Peel and wash the potatoes; coarsely grate, using a hand grater.
2. Peel the onion and cut in half; save half for another use; hand grate the remaining half into a coarse grate.
3. Crack the eggs into a bowl; add the water, salt, ground black pepper, dried parsley flakes, and flour and thoroughly mix.
4. Combine the grated potatoes and onions with the egg mixture and thoroughly mix; cover and refrigerate for 1 hour.

## Ready to Serve

1. Place the vegetable oil in a large sauté pan over medium heat.
2. Spoon 6 equal-size pancakes and flatten them to 1/2-inch thickness.
3. Grill on both sides for 3 or 4 minutes or until they are golden brown; remove and serve.

**Preparation Time:** 10 minutes
**Final Cooking Time:** 10 minutes

# Fresh Applesauce

*serves 6*

| | |
|---|---|
| 3 | Granny Smith apples |
| 2 cups | water |
| 1/2 cup | sugar |
| 1 stick | cinnamon |
| 1 1/2 teaspoons | whole cloves |
| 1 | lemon |

## Preparation

1. Peel the apples and remove the core using a paring knife; cut into a 1-inch dice.
2. Combine the water, sugar, cinnamon stick, and whole cloves in a saucepan over medium heat.
3. Place the diced apples into the sugar-water solution and simmer for about 10 minutes or until the apples are tender.
4. Place a colander in the sink and drain the apples; remove the cinnamon stick and cloves.
5. Place the apples into a food processor or blender and puree until they reach the desired consistency, smooth or chunky.
6. Squeeze the juice from the lemon and thoroughly mix with the applesauce; refrigerate until ready to serve using a 3-ounce spoon.

**Note:** Alternative for those in a hurry . . . purchase a jar of applesauce!

**Preparation Time:** 20 minutes

# Fraulein Katherine's
# White Chocolate Cake

*serves 6 to 12 (three-layer cake)*

| | |
|---|---|
| 2 1/2 cups | cake flour |
| 1 teaspoon | baking soda |
| 1 cup (2 sticks) | unsalted butter |
| 1 1/2 cups | sugar |
| 4 | eggs |
| 3/4 cup | white chocolate chips |
| 1/2 teaspoon | vanilla extract |
| 1 cup | buttermilk |
| 1 cup | shredded coconut |
| 1 cup | pecan bits |

## Frosting

| | |
|---|---|
| 1/2 cup (1 stick) | unsalted butter |
| 1 cup | evaporated milk |
| 1 cup | sugar |
| 3 | eggs |
| 1/2 teaspoon | vanilla extract |
| 1 cup | shredded coconut |
| 1 cup | pecan bits |

## Preparation

1. Mix the cake flour with the baking soda and sift into a bowl; set aside.
2. Allow the butter to soften; cut into pieces and place in a large mixing bowl; slowly whip with an electric mixer while adding the sugar; mix until thoroughly blended.
 3. Separate the egg yolks from the whites using plastic gloves or egg separator; set the whites aside; slowly add the egg yolks to the butter mixture; mix until thoroughly blended.
4. Put the white chocolate chips in a small bowl and place into the microwave oven for short bursts (10 to 15 seconds), frequently stirring until the chocolate has melted evenly. **Caution:** Be careful not to overheat.
5. Add the melted chocolate and vanilla extract to the butter mixture and thoroughly blend.
6. Blend in 1/3 of the sifted flour mixture and 1/3 of the buttermilk to the butter and chocolate mixture; add the second 1/3 of the flour and buttermilk and blend; add the final 1/3 of flour and buttermilk while thoroughly blending the cake batter.
7. Fold in the shredded coconut and pecan bits with a spatula and set aside.

8. Beat the egg whites with an electric mixer until they form stiff peaks.

9. Add 1/2 of the egg whites to the cake batter and thoroughly blend; fold (gently mix) in the remaining egg whites with a spatula.

10. Thoroughly butter three 8-inch round cake pans; pour an even amount of batter into each pan; place the pans in the center of a 350°F preheated oven for 30 to 40 minutes or until the cakes are done. **Note:** Test for doneness by inserting a wooden pick into the center of each cake. If it comes out clean, then cakes are done.

11. Remove the cakes from the oven and place on wire racks to cool; do not remove the cakes from the pans for about 10 minutes or until totally cooled.

12. Carefully run a knife around the edges of the cakes while still in the pans; invert the pans onto the wire racks and carefully remove from the cakes; allow cakes to cool for an additional 5 to 10 minutes.

**Frosting** (prepare while the cakes are baking)

1. Cut the butter into chips and place in a saucepan over medium heat; add the evaporated milk and sugar and mix.

2. Separate the egg yolks from the whites using plastic gloves or egg separator; add the yolks to the butter and milk mixture; simmer at 180°F for 8 to 10 minutes while constantly stirring.

3. Remove from the stove and add the vanilla extract, shredded coconut, and pecan bits and thoroughly mix.

4. Pour the frosting mixture into a small steel bowl; place the small bowl into a larger bowl that is filled with ice; stir the frosting until it thickens and cools.

**Time to Put It Together**

1. Place one cake layer on a cake platter.

2. Evenly spread 1/4 of the frosting over the top of the cake by using a spatula.

3. Place the second cake layer over the top of the frosting and spread another 1/4 of the frosting on top of the cake layer.

4. Top off with the third cake layer and spread the remaining frosting over the top and sides, covering all areas; set aside until ready to cut and serve; do not refrigerate. **Note:** Coconut lovers may want to sprinkle additional shredded or shaved coconut over the top and sides of the cake.

**Ready to Serve**

1. Slice and serve on dessert plates.

**Preparation Time:** 1 hour 10 minutes

**Final Preparation Time:** 5 minutes

# Snows of Leningrad

•

*Marinated Herring with Capers and Onions*
*Cold Borscht*
*Roast Pork with Potato Dumplings*
*Boiled Cabbage Wedges with Toasted Caraway*
*Mazourka (Walnut Cake)*

•

# Beverage Selections

You have to fit **vodka** in someplace during the evening, so why not with the first course. The guests will know your intentions are honorable when you present the marinated herring with a chilled shot of premium Russian vodka.

Russia produces a great deal of wine, however, little of it is palatable. A domestic **chardonnay** or **pinot noir** will work well with the pork.

The classical **Russian cocktail** (1 ounce vodka, 1/2 ounce gin, 1/2 ounce white crème de Cacao) would add an aromatic accent to the entrée course and spice up this traditional fare.

### NONALCOHOLIC

Brewed **hot coffee** will conclude the meal nicely, but if you want to wow your guests, serve a **kaphe balalaika.** To make this traditional Russian drink, combine coffee and sugar in a glass (add vodka if preferred). Pour heavy cream over the back of a rounded spoon so that it falls down in layers on top of the coffee. For that touch of authenticity use metal holders for your glasses.

# When to Start Cooking

*When dinner is served at 7:00 P.M. . . .*

| Cooking Preparation Schedule | | Cooking Times |
|---|---|---|
| 3:00 P.M. | Mazourka (Walnut Cake) | 45 minutes |
| 3:30 | Roast Pork | 20 minutes |
| 4:00 | Time to set the tables and arrange the room. | |
| 4:30 | Time to clean up, relax a bit, double-check everything, and dress for the occasion. | |

| Final Cooking and Preparation Schedule | | | Serving Times |
|---|---|---|---|
| 5:30 P.M. | Roast Pork | 1 3/4 hours | 7:20 P.M. |
| 6:35 | Potato Dumplings | 45 minutes | 7:20 |
| 6:50 | Marinated Herring | 10 minutes | 7:00 |
| 7:05 | Cold Borscht | 5 minutes | 7:10 |
| 7:10 | Boiled Cabbage Wedges | 10 minutes | 7:20 |
| 7:35 | Mazourka (Walnut Cake) | 5 minutes | 7:40 |
| | Final Beverage | | 7:45 |

# Tips and Details

Many people think that vodka is made from potatoes. This may be true, however, most vodka is made from grain. Malt is added to change the starch into a form of sugar, and the resultant mash is fermented and distilled several times, resulting in a clear, potent beverage.

Marinated herring can be purchased at your local grocery store. It comes in two forms, one in a cream marinade, the other in white wine, neither of which has a very strong fish flavor, but both are influenced by pickling. The choice is yours.

# Marinated Herring
# with Capers and Onions

*serves 6 (serve on salad plates)*

| | |
|---|---|
| *1* | *red onion* |
| *1 head* | *lettuce* |
| *1 1/4 pounds* | *marinated herring* |
| *1/4 cup* | *capers* |
| *18 slices* | *cocktail rye bread* |

### Preparation

1. Peel and cut the red onion in half; save half for another use; cut the remaining half into 6 even slices.
2. Remove 6 lettuce leaves from the head; wash and drain; place one large leaf on each of 6 salad plates.
3. Place a 3-ounce portion of marinated herring on top and slightly off to one side of the lettuce liner on each plate.
4. Place 1 onion slice leaning on the herring on each plate.
5. Sprinkle an equal amount of capers over the herring and onion slice.
6. Place 3 slices of cocktail rye bread on each plate and serve.

**Preparation Time:** 10 minutes

# Cold Borscht

*serves 6 (serve in 6-ounce soup bowls)*

| | |
|---|---|
| *1 quart* | *borscht, jar prepared, chilled* |
| *1/2 cup* | *sour cream* |

## Preparation

1. Refrigerate borscht; fill 6 soup bowls with an equal amount of chilled borscht.
2. Top each of the bowls with 1 tablespoon of sour cream and serve.

**Preparation Time:** 5 minutes

# Roast Pork

*serves 6*

| | |
|---|---|
| *1* | *yellow onion, jumbo* |
| *2 stalks* | *celery* |
| *2* | *carrots* |
| *2 leaves* | *bay leaves* |
| *1/3 cup* | *garlic, minced* |
| *1 tablespoon* | *salt* |
| *1 tablespoon* | *ground black pepper* |
| *1 tablespoon* | *rosemary* |
| *3 pounds* | *pork roast* |
| *1 1/2 cups* | *chicken stock (using a chicken base with water)* |

## Preparation

1. Rough chop the onion, celery, and carrots; mix and spread over the bottom of a roasting pan along with the bay leaves.
2. Peel and mince the garlic.
3. Combine the minced garlic with the salt, ground black pepper, and rosemary; thoroughly mix to form a paste.
4. Rub the outside of the pork roast with the garlic paste and place roast on top of the chopped vegetables in the roasting pan; cover with plastic wrap and refrigerate.

## Ready to Serve

1. Prepare the chicken stock by mixing a chicken base with water according to package directions; pour the chicken stock into the pan over the chopped vegetables.
2. Place the roast into a 325°F preheated oven for 1 hour, basting every 20 minutes with the stock in the pan.
3. Remove the roast from the oven and invert (turn upside down) and continue to roast and baste for another 30 to 45 minutes or until it reaches 155°F or higher for at least 15 seconds.
4. Remove from the oven and slice into 6-ounce portions; save the juice in the pan to pour over the potato dumplings.

**Preparation Time:** 20 minutes

**Final Cooking Time:** 1 hour 45 minutes

# Potato Dumplings

*serves 6*

| | |
|---|---|
| 2 | *russet potatoes, medium* |
| 3 strips | *bacon* |
| 4 | *eggs* |
| 1 1/2 teaspoons | *salt* |
| 1 1/2 teaspoons | *ground nutmeg* |
| 3 tablespoons | *all-purpose flour* |

## Preparation

1. Boil the potatoes in the skin for 20 minutes or until fork tender; drain and cool.

2. Sauté the bacon over medium heat until light golden brown, reaching 155°F or higher for at least 15 seconds; place onto paper towels to absorb grease (save the grease); chop the bacon into 1/4-inch dice.

3. Remove the skin from the potatoes and whip the potatoes with an electric mixer until smooth.

4. Add the chopped bacon, eggs, salt, ground nutmeg, 2 tablespoons of bacon grease, and the flour and thoroughly mix.

5. Make 12 balls from the potato dough; place into a large pan of boiling water over medium heat; simmer the dumplings for 5 minutes or until they all float on the surface of the water; remove, drain for 1 minute, and serve 2 per plate. Ladle 1 ounce of the roast pork pan juice over each serving of dumplings.

**Preparation Time:** 45 minutes

# Boiled Cabbage Wedges
# with Toasted Caraway

*serves 6*

| | |
|---|---|
| *1 head* | *green cabbage* |
| *2 tablespoons* | *caraway seeds* |

## Preparation

1. Cut the head of cabbage in half; lay each half flat side down on a cutting board and cut 3 equal wedges from each half.
2. Place the cabbage wedges into a large pot of boiling water for 4 or 5 minutes or until tender; remove and drain.
3. Place the caraway seeds into a sauté pan over medium heat; continually shake the pan as the caraway seeds quickly toast.
4. Place a cabbage wedge on each plate and sprinkle with the toasted caraway seeds.

**Preparation Time:** 10 minutes

# Mazourka (Walnut Cake)

*serves 6 to 12*

| | |
|---|---|
| 9 | eggs |
| 2 cups | sugar |
| 1 pound | walnuts |
| 1/2 pound | dried fruit mix |
| 2 | lemons |
| 3 cups | flour |
| 1/4 cup | powdered sugar |

## Preparation

1. Separate the egg yolks from the whites using plastic gloves or egg separator; set the egg whites aside; place the egg yolks in a bowl and beat with an electric mixer; add the sugar and thoroughly blend.
2. Beat the egg whites in a separate bowl with an electric mixer until they form stiff peaks; fold into the egg yolk mixture.
3. Chop the walnuts and dried fruit mix into a very fine grind.
4. Squeeze the juice from the lemons.
5. Add the ground walnuts, ground dried fruit mix, lemon juice, and flour to the egg mixture, gently mixing.
6. Thoroughly butter an 8-by-12-inch baking pan; pour the cake batter into the pan; place into a 325°F preheated oven for 30 minutes or until the cake is done. **Note:** Test for doneness by inserting a wooden pick into the center of the cake. If it comes out clean, then the cake is done.
7. Remove the cake from the oven and place on a wire rack to cool.
8. Dust the top of the cake with powdered sugar and cut into 2-inch squares.

## Ready to Serve

1. Place two or three 2-inch squares on each dessert plate and serve.

**Preparation Time:** 45 minutes

**Final Preparation Time:** 5 minutes

# Breakfast at Tiffany's

*brunch*

•

*Chocolate Waffles*
*Poached Eggs on Apple Rings*
*Peppered Bacon*
*Spanish Potatoes*
*Fresh Fruit Platter*
*Whole Wheat Toast and Bagels*

•

# Beverage Selections

A magnificent brunch requires an equally superb beverage menu. Start guests off with a **mimosa cocktail** (champagne and orange juice) or simply with **fresh-squeezed juice.**

If the brunch is somewhat informal, buy "splits" (small, single-serving bottles equal to 1/10 of a regular bottle) of **sparkling wine** rather than champagne. Display these on ice near your buffet or main table. Cordon Negro is an excellent producer from Spain, and splits of their wine can be found in many stores.

If you prefer not to mix your sparkler, serve it with a whole strawberry. A slice of kiwi or peach is also a nice touch.

## NONALCOHOLIC

Distinctive **espresso-based drinks** are ideal with breakfast. (If you do not have an espresso machine, select a strong coffee to brew in its place.) **Café au lait** has given many a Frenchman that morning jumpstart with a touch of class (2 cups scalded or steamed milk, 2 cups strong coffee, and cinnamon powder to yield 4 cups). **Bayrischer kaffee** (Bavarian coffee) is also delicious with breakfast foods (4 egg yolks, 6 teaspoons sugar, 2 cups strong coffee, and 1 cup steamed milk to yield 4 cups).

Homemade **crème chantilly** is wonderful to add to your coffee drinks. This sweet and flavored whipped cream is made by adding 4 teaspoons of sugar to 1 cup of heavy cream before beating. Beat the cream and sugar by moving the beater around in a mixing bowl allowing lots of air into the cream. If you like, add vanilla, cocoa, or liqueur for additional flavor.

Excellent teas to serve include English Breakfast, Assam, and Darjeeling. Garnish with a lemon wedge and serve in decorative china.

# When to Start Cooking

*When brunch is served at 10:00 A.M. . . .*

| Cooking Preparation Schedule | | Cooking Times |
|---|---|---|
| 8:00 A.M. | Spanish Potatoes | 30 minutes |
| 8:30 | Fresh Fruit Platter | 10 minutes |
| 8:40 | Time to set the tables and arrange the room, relax a bit, and double-check everything. | |

**Final Cooking and Preparation Schedule**        **Serving Times**

| | | | |
|---|---|---|---|
| 9:30 A.M. | Chocolate Waffles | 25 minutes | 10:00 A.M. |
| 9:40 | Peppered Bacon | 15 minutes | |
| 9:45 | Poached Eggs on Apple Rings | 15 minutes | |
| 9:50 | Spanish Potatoes | 10 minutes | |
| 9:55 | Whole Wheat Toast and Bagels | 5 minutes | |
| 10:00 | Fresh Fruit Platter Beverage | | |

# Tips and Details

This menu is a gala brunch extravaganza. Take the opportunity to display the wide variety of menu items on silver platters.

Seasonal availability will dictate what items go on your fruit platter. It is always a good idea to use what is fresh and in season to ensure the highest quality and lowest price. Always remember to use as many colorful items as possible.

# Chocolate Waffles

*serves 6 (serve on a round platter)*

| | |
|---|---|
| *1/4 cup* | *chocolate chips* |
| *2 cups* | *all-purpose baking mix* |
| *1 1/3 cups* | *milk* |
| *1* | *egg* |
| *2 tablespoons* | *vegetable oil* |
| *1 cup* | *maple syrup* |
| *3 tablespoons* | *powdered sugar* |

**Preparation**

**1.** Put the chocolate chips in a small bowl and place into the microwave oven for short 10-second bursts until the chocolate has melted evenly, stirring at the end of each microwave time. **Caution:** Be careful not to overheat.

2. Combine the baking mix, milk, egg, vegetable oil, and melted chocolate in a mixing bowl and beat with a wire whip until completely blended.

3. Pour approximately 1/3 of the batter onto the center of a hot 9-inch square waffle iron and bake until steaming stops and the waffles are done; carefully remove and place on a round platter; sprinkle with powdered sugar and serve (or place each in a low-heat oven and cover until all the waffles are prepared).

4. Pour maple syrup into a small syrup pitcher and place next to the platter of waffles.

**Preparation Time:** 25 minutes

# Poached Eggs on Apple Rings

*serves 6 (serve on a warm platter)*

| 2 | *red delicious apples, large* |
| 2 tablespoons | *vegetable oil* |
| 6 | *eggs* |

**Preparation**

1. Wash the apples and remove the cores with a paring knife; slice into 1/2-inch rings. Each ring should have 1 1/2-inch diameter opening at the core.

2. Place the vegetable oil into a sauté pan over low heat; sauté the apple rings for 2 or 3 minutes on each side.

3. Place an egg in the center of each apple ring; cover the pan and continue to cook until the eggs are firm. Remove with a spatula and place onto a warm platter and serve.

**Note:** The platter can be heated by placing in a warm oven for 3 or 4 minutes.

**Preparation Time:** 15 minutes

# Peppered Bacon

*serves 6 (serve on a rectangular platter)*

1 pound                  peppered bacon

### Preparation

1. Sauté the bacon over medium heat until light golden brown, reaching 155°F or higher for at least 15 seconds; place onto paper towels to absorb grease.
2. Arrange the bacon strips lengthwise onto a rectangular platter and serve.

**Preparation Time:** 15 minutes

# Spanish Potatoes

*serves 6 to 8 (serve on a round platter)*

| | |
|---|---|
| 1 1/2 pounds | potatoes |
| 1 | yellow onion, jumbo |
| 1 | green bell pepper |
| 1/2 pound | baked ham |
| 1/4 cup (1/2 stick) | butter |
| 3 tablespoons | chopped pimento, prepared |
| 1 1/2 teaspoons | salt |
| 1 teaspoon | ground black pepper |
| 3/4 teaspoon | paprika |

### Preparation

1. Peel, wash, and boil potatoes for 20 minutes or until fork tender; drain, cool, and cut into 1/2-inch cubes; cover and refrigerate.
2. Peel the onion and cut in half; save half for another use; mince the remaining half, place in a bowl, cover, and refrigerate.

3. Cut the green pepper in half; save half for another use; scrape out the seeds, wash and dice the remaining half; place in a bowl, cover, and refrigerate.
4. Chop baked ham into a 1/2-inch dice; place in a bowl, cover, and refrigerate.

**Ready to Serve**

1. Melt the butter in a large sauté pan over medium heat; add the minced onions, diced green pepper, and chopped pimento and sauté until light brown.
2. Add the diced potatoes, diced ham, salt, ground black pepper, and paprika and sauté for 5 minutes, reaching 165°F or higher for at least 15 seconds, occasionally turning; remove from the pan and serve on a large round platter.

**Preparation Time:** 30 minutes
**Final Cooking Time:** 10 minutes

# Fresh Fruit Platter

*serves 6 (serve on an oval platter)*

| | |
|---|---|
| 4 | *oranges* |
| 2 | *grapefruits* |
| 6 | *bananas (unpeeled)* |

**Preparation**

1. Peel the skin from the oranges and grapefruits; carefully section and remove any excess skin fragments.
2. Arrange the grapefruit sections down the center of an oval platter, the orange sections down the sides.
3. Place 3 bananas at the top and 3 bananas at the bottom of the platter; cover and refrigerate until ready to serve.

**Preparation Time:** 10 minutes

# Whole Wheat Toast and Bagels

*serves 6 (serve in a bread basket )*

| | |
|---|---|
| 9 slices | *whole wheat bread* |
| 6 | *bagels* |
| 5 tablespoons | *sweet orange marmalade* |
| 5 tablespoons | *strawberry preserves* |
| 4 ounces | *cream cheese* |
| 4 ounces (1 stick) | *butter* |

## Preparation

1. Toast the whole wheat bread; cut each slice diagonally; arrange in one side of a round bread basket.
2. Cut the bagels in half; keep the two halves together and arrange in the other side of the bread basket.
3. Place the sweet orange marmalade and strawberry preserves in separate fruit dishes with serving spoons; place the fruit dishes next to the bread basket.
4. Place a 4-ounce square of cream cheese onto a bread and butter plate; lay a butter spreader on the side of the plate; place the plate next to the bread basket.
5. Place a 4-ounce stick of butter onto a bread and butter plate; lay a butter spreader on the side of the plate; place the plate next to the bread basket.

**Note:** Arrange the fruit dishes and bread and butter plates along the front side of the bread basket for guests to reach easily.

**Preparation Time:** 5 minutes

# Appendix A
## ChefTec Software

Accurate, up-to-date costing is a critical factor for the foodservice operator and caterer. Success in obtaining catering contracts is often determined by the most competitive bid. Therefore, the caterer that can quickly identify the cost of each recipe, determine a total menu cost, assign a profit margin, and then price the menu will be in a superior competitive position by having prompt customer price quotations.

The *Chef*Tec program—developed by Culinary Software Services—has been designed to be flexible, friendly, and very easy to use. Throughout *Chef*Tec, the screens, drop-down menus, and icons are all consistent and clear. Comprehensive online help is also available throughout the program.

The commercial (complete) *ChefTec Software* package will enable the user to

—Keep constant records of unlimited recipes and provide convenient printouts at any time.

—Cost recipes, menus, functions, or complete catering events within minutes.

—Instantaneously see the effect of price increases on current costs and margins.

—Enter a price once with the result that every recipe using the item automatically reflects the change.

—Ask "What if" questions to analyze food cost, profit margins, and pricing.

—Rescale recipes at the click of a button.

—Add photographs and diagrams to recipes.

—Write recipes with customizable fonts: type, size, and color.

—Calculate nutritional data instantly, based on USDA guidelines.

—Track supplier bids.

—Interface with suppliers' online ordering systems to instantly download bids and prices.

—Create physical inventory worksheets, based on actual locations including shelf order.

—Generate orders automatically and fax them directly from *ChefTec*.

—Be informed of the price fluctuations of inventory items.

—Be able to identify the supplier that offers the lowest product cost.

Culinary Software Services is a software developer that has consistently provided the foodservice industry with functional software backed by telephone technical support and training. For more information on the full *ChefTec* program, call Culinary Software Services in Boulder, Colorado, at 303.447.3334 or 1.800.447.1466 or visit their Web site online at www.culinarysoftware.com.

## System Requirements

To use the *ChefTec* program, you must meet the following system requirements:

IBM PC or compatible

Windows 98, Windows 95, Windows NT 4.0, or later

486 processor

16 mb RAM

18 mb hard disk space

800 by 600 VGA

Recommended, Pentium Processor

## Installing ChefTec

*ChefTec* is very easy to install on your computer through the following steps:

1. Insert CD-ROM into the CD-ROM drive.
2. (a) After approximately one minute, the program will automatically load and provide instruction prompts, OR
   (b1) Click on the Start Button, Select Run . . .
   (b2) Type D:\SETUP (where D: refers to CD-ROM drive) and press <Enter>.
3. Follow the instructions on the screen.

## ChefTec Tutorial Program

The *ChefTec* Tutor software program accompanies this book, *Catering Solutions: For the Culinary Student, Foodservice Operator, and Caterer,* and it has been adapted for use with the text. This software will allow the reader/user to understand how to use this type of information technology to control costs better, thus increasing profitability and competitiveness. The program functions include recipe scaling, recipe and menu costing, recipe photographs, and recipe nutritional analysis for the recipes contained in this text.

For a functionally directed guide through the program, please see the heading "How to Get Started Using *Chef*Tec" in the online help Chapter 1, "Introducing *Chef*Tec."

The example that follows is a complete menu theme, "Rites of Spring," taken from Chapter 6 of this text, which demonstrates the software application. The recipes have been scaled to quantities of 150. The preparation instructions and preparation and cooking times remain the same as for the original recipe quantities. (The software does not have the capacity to adjust the instructions and times.) The costing function of the software allows the user to enter product costs within his or her local market. The nutrition facts for each recipe are based on USDA guidelines.

**Illustrative Example**

◆❄◆ *ChefTec Software*

# Chilled Lemon Soup

Catering Solutions

| | |
|---|---|
| **Author** | Catering Solutions |
| **Categories** | Rites of Spring |
| **Tools** | |
| **Locations** | |

| | | | |
|---|---|---|---|
| **Yield** | 56.25 lb | **Prep** | 15 minutes |
| **Portion** | 6 oz | **Cooking** | 5 minutes |
| **Num Portions** | 150 | **Finish** | |
| | | **Shelf** | |

## Ingredients

| | | |
|---|---|---|
| 1.953 | gal | sour cream |
| 6 1/4 | cup | sugar |
| 0.78 | cup | salt |
| 6 1/4 | fl oz | half-and-half |
| 3 1/8 | gal | chicken stock (using a chicken base with water) |
| 1.563 | cup | Worcestershire sauce |
| 100 | ea | lemons |
| 6 1/4 | cup | water |

**Preparation**

1. Combine 1 cup of sour cream, 2 tablespoons of sugar, and the salt in a bowl and thoroughly mix with a whip until smooth and creamy.

2. Slowly blend in the half-and-half, chicken stock (make the chicken stock by mixing a chicken base with water according to package directions), and Worcestershire sauce; cover the bowl with plastic wrap and refrigerate.

3. Wash and remove the rind from 1 lemon and cut the rind into very thin slices.

4. Cut the 4 lemons in half and squeeze out the juice into a bowl and set aside.

5. Combine the water with the remaining 2 tablespoons of sugar in a saute pan over low heat; bring to a boil, which creates a simple syrup.

6. Add the thin slices of lemon rind to the simple syrup and simmer for 2 minutes; set aside to cool.

7. Remove the chilled soup from the refrigerator and fold in the fresh lemon juice, cover and refrigerate until ready to serve.

**Ready to Serve**

1. Ladle (using a 5-ounce ladle) into soup bowls and place a teaspoon of sour cream into each bowl.

2. Top off with some of the poached lemon rind.

**ChefTec Software**

# Chilled Lemon Soup

Catering Solutions

**Author** Catering Solutions

**Categories** Rites of Spring

**Tools**

**Locations**

| | | |
|---|---|---|
| **Yield** | 56.25 lbs | **Prep** 15 minutes |
| **Portion** | 6 oz | **Cooking** 5 minutes |
| **Num Portions** | 150 | **Finish** |
| | | **Shelf** |

| Ingredients | | | Cost | % of Total |
|---|---|---|---|---|
| 1.953 | gal | sour cream | $17.12 | 39.2% |
| 6 1/4 | cup | sugar | $1.16 | 2.7% |
| 0.78 | cup | salt | $0.07 | 0.5% |
| 6 1/4 | fl oz | half-and-half | $0.23 | 0.5% |
| 3 1/8 | gal | chicken stock (using a chicken base with water) | $3.13 | 7.2% |
| 1.563 | cup | Worcestershire sauce | $1.26 | 2.9% |
| 100 | ea | lemons | $20.54 | 47.0% |
| 6 1/4 | cup | water | $0.00 | |
| | | | $43.50 | |

**ChefTec Software**

## Chilled Lemon Soup

Catering Solutions

**Author**      Catering Solutions
**Categories**  Rites of Spring
**Tools**
**Locations**

| | | | |
|---|---|---|---|
| **Yield** | 56.25 lb | **Prep** | 15 minutes |
| **Portion** | 6 oz | **Cooking** | 5 minutes |
| **Num Portions** | 150 | **Finish** | |
| | | **Shelf** | |

# Nutrition Facts

Serving Size   6 oz (170g)
Servings Per Container   150

**Amount Per Serving**

**Calories** 234  Calories From Fat 146

| | % Daily Value |
|---|---|
| **Total Fat** 16g | 24% |
| Saturated Fat  10g | 44% |
| **Cholesterol** 38mg | 13% |
| **Sodium** 982mg | 41% |
| **Total Carbohydrates** 18g | 6% |
| Dietary Fiber  2g | 7% |
| **Protein** 7g | |

| | | | |
|---|---|---|---|
| Vitamin A | 12% | Vitamin C | 55% |
| Calcium | 12% | Iron | 4% |

*Percent Daily Values are based on a 2000 calorie diet.

**ChefTec Software**

# Seasonal Greens w/Mustard Poppy Seed Dressing

Catering Solutions

| | |
|---|---|
| **Author** | Catering Solutions |
| **Categories** | Rites of Spring |
| **Tools** | |
| **Locations** | |

| | | | |
|---|---|---|---|
| | | **Prep** | 15 minutes |
| **Yield** | 150 | **Cooking** | 5 minutes |
| **Portion** | 1 | **Finish** | |
| **Num Portions** | 150 | **Shelf** | |

## Ingredients

| | | |
|---|---|---|
| 12 1/2 | heads | red leaf lettuce |
| 50 | heads | Belgian endive |
| 12 1/2 | heads | romaine lettuce |
| 25 | heads | radicchio lettuce |
| 1.563 | gal | mayonnaise |
| 1.563 | pt | Dijon mustard |
| 25 | tbl | poppy seeds |
| 25 | tbl | sugar |
| 1.563 | cup | white wine vinegar |

**Preparation**

1. Wash, drain, and cut the red leaf lettuce, Belgian endive, romaine, and radicchio into bite-size pieces; mix in a large salad bowl, cover with plastic wrap, and refrigerate.
2. Place the mayonnaise in a mixing bowl and mix to a smooth even consistency.
3. Add the Dijon mustard and poppy seeds to the mayonnaise and mix.
4. In a separate bowl, mix the sugar and white wine vinegar together; slowly add to the mayonnaise mixture, tasting along the way until the desired flavor is achieved; cover with plastic wrap and refrigerate until ready to serve.

**Ready to Serve**

1. Place an equal amount of the salad mix onto the salad plates.
2. Ladle 1 ounce of the mustard poppy seed dressing over each salad and serve.

◆❖◆ *ChefTec Software*

# Seasonal Greens w/Mustard Poppy Seed Dressing

Catering Solutions

---

| | |
|---|---|
| **Author** | Catering Solutions |
| **Categories** | Rites of Spring |
| **Tools** | |
| **Locations** | |

| | | | | |
|---|---|---|---|---|
| | | | **Prep** | 15 minutes |
| **Yield** | 150 | | **Cooking** | 5 minutes |
| **Portion** | 1 | | **Finish** | |
| **Num Portions** | 150 | | **Shelf** | |

| **Ingredients** | | | **Cost** | **% of Total** |
|---|---|---|---|---|
| 12 1/2 | heads | red leaf lettuce | $10.25 | 8.4% |
| 50 | heads | Belgian endive | $46.84 | 38.3% |
| 12 1/2 | heads | romaine lettuce | $7.68 | 6.3% |
| 25 | heads | radicchio lettuce | $42.04 | 34.4% |
| 1.563 | gal | mayonnaise | $12.30 | 10.1% |
| 1.563 | pt | Dijon mustard | $1.38 | 1.1% |
| 25 | tbl | poppy seeds | $1.21 | 1.0% |
| 25 | tbl | sugar | $0.29 | 0.2% |
| 1.563 | cup | white wine vinegar | $0.31 | 0.3% |
| | | | $122.30 | |

**ChefTec Software**

# Seasonal Greens w/Mustard Poppy Seed Dressing

Catering Solutions

| | | | |
|---|---|---|---|
| **Author** | Catering Solutions | | |
| **Categories** | Rites of Spring | | |
| **Tools** | | | |
| **Locations** | | | |
| | | **Prep** | 15 minutes |
| | | **Cooking** | 5 minutes |
| **Yield** | 150 | **Finish** | |
| **Portion** | 1 | **Shelf** | |
| **Num Portions** | 150 | | |

## Nutrition Facts

Serving Size   1
Servings Per Container   150

Amount Per Serving

**Calories** 188  Calories From Fat 120

| | % Daily Value |
|---|---|
| **Total Fat** 13g | 20% |
| Saturated Fat 2g | 9% |
| **Cholesterol** 10mg | 3% |
| **Sodium** 286mg | 12% |
| **Total Carbohydrates** 17g | 6% |
| Dietary Fiber 3g | 13% |
| **Protein** 3g | |

| | | | |
|---|---|---|---|
| Vitamin A | 53% | Vitamin C | 37% |
| Calcium | 9% | Iron | 8% |

*Percent Daily Values are based on a 2000 calorie diet.

### Nutrition Descriptors

Low Cholesterol

✦✦✦ *ChefTec Software*

# Grilled Salmon

Catering Solutions

| | |
|---|---|
| **Author** | Catering Solutions |
| **Categories** | Rites of Spring |
| **Tools** | |
| **Locations** | |

| | | | |
|---|---|---|---|
| | | **Prep** | 10 minutes |
| **Yield** | 75 lb | **Cooking** | 8–10 minutes |
| **Portion** | 8 oz | **Finish** | |
| **Num Portions** | 150 | **Shelf** | |

## Ingredients

| | | |
|---|---|---|
| 150 | ea | 8-oz salmon fillets |
| 3 1/8 | qt | mayonnaise |
| 1.563 | cup | lemon juice |
| 1.563 | cup | white wine |
| 0.52 | cup | salt |
| 4.167 | fl oz | Worcestershire sauce |

### Preparation

**1.** When purchasing the salmon fillets, ask to have as many of the bones removed as possible.

**2.** Combine the mayonnaise, lemon juice, white wine, salt, and Worcestershire sauce in a bowl and thoroughly mix.

**3.** Spread an equal amount of the mayonnaise mixture over both sides of the salmon fillets; cover with plastic wrap and refrigerate for at least 1 hour.

### Ready to Grill

### Barbecue Method (the preferred way to cook salmon)

**1.** Preheat the barbecue grill on medium heat for about 15 minutes.

**2.** Place the salmon on the grill with the skin side up; grill for approximately 3 minutes and then with a spatula lift and quarter turn each fillet; grill for another 2 minutes.

**3.** Turn the salmon fillets over onto the skin side and cover with a large piece of aluminum foil formed into a tent shape; grill for another 3 to 4 minutes while checking for doneness by flaking with a fork. When the fish begins to flake and has reached a minimum 145°F or higher for at least 15 seconds, it is done.

### Oven Method

**1.** Place an oiled baking pan into a 325°F preheated oven for approximately 5 minutes. (**Note:** Spread a thin layer of vegetable oil over the surface of the pan.)

**2.** Place the salmon fillets on top of the hot oiled baking pan with the skin side up and bake for approximately 4 minutes.

**3.** Turn the salmon fillets over and continue to bake for an additional 4 minutes. Check for doneness by flaking with a fork. When the fish begins to flake and has reached 145°F or higher for at least 15 seconds, it is done.

**ChefTec Software**

# Grilled Salmon

Catering Solutions

| | |
|---|---|
| **Author** | Catering Solutions |
| **Categories** | Rites of Spring |
| **Tools** | |
| **Locations** | |

| | | | | |
|---|---|---|---|---|
| | | **Prep** | 10 minutes | |
| | | **Cooking** | 8–10 minutes | |
| **Yield** | 75 lb | **Finish** | | |
| **Portion** | 8 oz | **Shelf** | | |
| **Num Portions** | 150 | | | |

| Ingredients | | | Cost | % of Total |
|---|---|---|---|---|
| 150 | ea | 8-oz salmon fillets | $248.25 | 96.0% |
| 3 1/8 | qt | mayonnaise | $6.15 | 2.4% |
| 1.563 | cup | lemon juice | $0.97 | 0.4% |
| 1.563 | cup | white wine | $2.81 | 1.1% |
| 0.52 | cup | salt | $0.03 | 0.0% |
| 4.167 | fl oz | Worcestershire sauce | $0.42 | 0.2% |
| | | | $258.63 | |

◆◆◆ *ChefTec Software*

**Grilled Salmon**

Catering Solutions

---

**Author**      Catering Solutions

**Categories**  Rites of Spring

**Tools**

**Locations**

| | | |
|---|---|---|
| **Yield** | 75 lb | **Prep** | 10 minutes |
| **Portion** | 8 oz | **Cooking** | 8 to 10 minutes |
| **Num Portions** | 150 | **Finish** | |
| | | **Shelf** | |

**Prep** 10 minutes

**Cooking** 8 to 10 minutes

**Finish**

**Shelf**

# Nutrition Facts

Serving Size   8 oz (227g)
Servings Per Container   150

**Amount Per Serving**

**Calories** 16          Calories From Fat 7

| | % Daily Value |
|---|---|
| **Total Fat** 1g | 1% |
| Saturated Fat  0g | 1% |
| **Cholesterol** 5mg | 2% |
| **Sodium** 315mg | 13% |
| **Total Carbohydrates** 0g | 0% |
| Dietary Fiber 0g | 0% |
| **Protein** 2g | |

| | | | |
|---|---|---|---|
| Vitamin A | 0% | Vitamin C | 0% |
| Calcium | 0% | Iron | 0% |

*Percent Daily Values are based on a 2000 calorie diet.

**Nutrition Descriptors**

Low Calorie

Low Fat

Low Saturated Fat

Low Cholesterol

**✦✦✦ ChefTec Software**

# Potatoes on the Half Shell

Catering Solutions

| | |
|---|---|
| **Author** | Catering Solutions |
| **Categories** | Rites of Spring |
| **Tools** | |
| **Locations** | |

| | | | |
|---|---|---|---|
| | | **Prep** | 1 hour |
| | | **Cooking** | 15 minutes |
| **Yield** | 150 ea | **Finish** | |
| **Portion** | 1 ea | **Shelf** | |
| **Num Portions** | 150 | | |

## Ingredients

| | | |
|---|---|---|
| 150 | ea | medium potatoes |
| 6 1/4 | cup | butter |
| 0.52 | cup | salt |
| 6 1/4 | tsp | ground white pepper |
| 1.563 | qt | milk |
| 1.563 | pt | Parmesan cheese, grated |

**Preparation**

1. Thoroughly wash potatoes, dry, and place in a 375°F preheated oven for 45 minutes or until done.
2. Cut into halves lengthwise.
3. Scoop out the insides of the potatoes with a tablespoon, being careful not to break the shells.
4. Whip potatoes while adding butter, salt, ground white pepper, and milk; whip until the potatoes are a soft fluffy mixture.
5. Spoon the potatoes back into the half shells in a piled-up manner. Do not pat down and smooth.
6. Sprinkle with grated Parmesan cheese.
7. Place the half shells on a baking pan, cover with plastic wrap, and refrigerate.

**Ready to Serve**

1. Remove plastic wrap and place the potatoes into a 375°F preheated oven for 10 to 12 minutes until the potatoes are lightly browned and reach 165°F or higher for at least 15 seconds.
2. Remove and promptly serve 2 half shells per plate.

**◆❋◆ ChefTec Software**

## Potatoes on the Half Shell

Catering Solutions

| | |
|---|---|
| **Author** | Catering Solutions |
| **Categories** | Rites of Spring |
| **Tools** | |
| **Locations** | |

| | | | | |
|---|---|---|---|---|
| | | | **Prep** | 1 hour |
| **Yield** | 150 ea | | **Cooking** | 15 minutes |
| **Portion** | 1 ea | | **Finish** | |
| **Num Portions** | 150 | | **Shelf** | |

### Ingredients

| | | | Cost | % of Total |
|---|---|---|---|---|
| 150 | ea | medium potatoes | $14.94 | 68.0% |
| 6 1/4 | cup | butter | $3.28 | 14.9% |
| 0.52 | cup | salt | $0.03 | 0.1% |
| 6 1/4 | tsp | ground white pepper | $0.26 | 1.2% |
| 1.563 | qt | milk | $1.21 | 5.5% |
| 1.563 | pt | Parmesan cheese, grated | $2.25 | 10.2% |
| | | | $21.97 | |

**ChefTec Software**

## Potatoes on the Half Shell

Catering Solutions

**Author** Catering Solutions

**Categories** Rites of Spring

**Tools**

**Locations**

| | | | |
|---|---|---|---|
| **Yield** | 150 ea | **Prep** | 1 hour |
| **Portion** | 1 ea | **Cooking** | 15 minutes |
| **Num Portions** | 150 | **Finish** | |
| | | **Shelf** | |

# Nutrition Facts

Serving Size 1 ea
Servings Per Container 150

**Amount Per Serving**

**Calories** 172   Calories From Fat 78

% Daily Value

| | |
|---|---|
| **Total Fat** 9g | 13% |
| Saturated Fat 5g | 24% |
| **Cholesterol** 24mg | 8% |
| **Sodium** 432mg | 18% |
| **Total Carbohydrates** 21g | 7% |
| Dietary Fiber 2g | 8% |
| **Protein** 4g | |

| | | | |
|---|---|---|---|
| Vitamin A | 6% | Vitamin C | 37% |
| Calcium | 5% | Iron | 5% |

*Percent Daily Values are based on a 2000 calorie diet.

◆❖◆ *ChefTec Software*

# Carrots Vichy
Catering Solutions

**Author**      Catering Solutions
**Categories**  Rites of Spring
**Tools**
**Locations**

| | | | |
|---|---|---|---|
| **Yield** | 50 lb | **Prep** | 30 minutes |
| **Portion** | 5.33 oz | **Cooking** | 5 minutes |
| **Num Portions** | 150 | **Finish** | |
| | | **Shelf** | |

## Ingredients

| | | |
|---|---|---|
| 50 | lb | carrots |
| 6 1/4 | cup | butter |
| 6 1/4 | cup | sugar |
| 8 1/4 | cup | chopped parsley |

**Preparation**

1. Thoroughly scrape and wash carrots; slice crosswise into very thin cuts and place in a saute pan over medium heat.
2. Cover with cold water.
3. Add the butter and sugar; boil for approximately 20 minutes or until the water has almost evaporated and the carrots are tender.
4. Wash, drain, and chop parsley and sprinkle over the carrots.
5. Place in a bowl, cover with plastic wrap, and refrigerate.

**Ready to Serve**

1. Microwave on high for 1 or 2 minutes until reaching 190°F for at least 15 seconds, then serve.

**ChefTec Software**

# Carrots Vichy

Catering Solutions

| | |
|---|---|
| **Author** | Catering Solutions |
| **Categories** | Rites of Spring |
| **Tools** | |
| **Locations** | |

| | | | |
|---|---|---|---|
| | | **Prep** | 30 minutes |
| **Yield** | 50 lb | **Cooking** | 5 minutes |
| **Portion** | 5.33 oz | **Finish** | |
| **Num Portions** | 150 | **Shelf** | |

## Ingredients

| | | | Cost | % of Total |
|---|---|---|---|---|
| 50 | lb | carrots | $12.00 | 61.6% |
| 6 1/4 | cup | butter | $3.28 | 16.8% |
| 6 1/4 | cup | sugar | $1.16 | 5.9% |
| 8 1/4 | cup | chopped parsley | $3.05 | 15.7% |
| | | | $19.49 | |

**◆ ChefTec Software**

## Carrots Vichy
Catering Solutions

**Author**      Catering Solutions
**Categories**  Rites of Spring
**Tools**
**Locations**

| | | | |
|---|---|---|---|
| **Yield** | 50 lb | **Prep** | 30 minutes |
| | | **Cooking** | 5 minutes |
| **Portion** | 5.33 oz | **Finish** | |
| **Num Portions** | 150 | **Shelf** | |

**Nutrition Descriptors**

Low Sodium

## Nutrition Facts

Serving Size   5 oz (151g)
Servings Per Container   150

Amount Per Serving

**Calories** 165      Calories from Fat 72

% Daily Value

| | |
|---|---:|
| **Total Fat** 8g | 12% |
| Saturated Fat  5g | 22% |
| **Cholesterol** 21mg | 7% |
| **Sodium** 132mg | 6% |
| **Total Carbohydrates** 24g | 8% |
| Dietary Fiber  5g | 20% |
| **Protein** 2g | |

| | | | |
|---|---|---|---|
| Vitamin A | 858% | Vitamin C | 28% |
| Calcium | 5% | Iron | 5% |

*Percent Daily Values are based on a 2000 calorie diet.

**◆ ChefTec Software**

# Fresh Fruit Tarts

Catering Solutions

| | | |
|---|---|---|
| **Author** | Catering Solutions | |
| **Categories** | Rites of Spring | |
| **Tools** | | |
| **Locations** | | |

| | | | | |
|---|---|---|---|---|
| | | | **Prep** | 30 minutes |
| | | | **Cooking** | 3 minutes |
| **Yield** | 150 ea | | **Finish** | |
| **Portion** | 1 ea | | **Shelf** | |
| **Num Portions** | 150 | | | |

## Ingredients

| | | |
|---|---|---|
| 150 | ea | frozen prepared tartlet shells |
| 50 | ea | Hershey chocolate bars |
| 50 | ea | bananas |
| 25 | basket | strawberries |
| 25 | ea | cantaloupe |
| 150 | ea | fresh peaches |
| 1.172 | gal | strawberry jelly |

### Preparation

1. Purchase the tartlet shells frozen prepared. If not available, then purchase puff pastry and follow the package directions for making tartlet shells.
2. Break the chocolate bars into small pieces and place in a bowl; put into the microwave for short bursts (10 to 15 seconds), frequently stirring, until the chocolate has melted evenly. **CAUTION:** Be careful not to overheat.
3. Brush a thin layer of melted chocolate into the tartlet shells.
4. Slice bananas and evenly place into the tartlet shells on top of the chocolate.
5. Wash and remove the tops from the strawberries, then cut strawberries into quarters.
6. Cut the cantaloupe in half and remove the seeds; remove the cantaloupe from the rind by using a melon baller.
7. Wash and remove the skin from the peaches and slice into bite-size pieces.
8. Mix the strawberries, cantaloupe balls, and peach slices and evenly place into the tartlet shells.
9. Place the strawberry jelly into a small saucepan over low heat. When the jelly becomes liquid, pour an equal amount over the top of the fruit; promptly refrigerate until ready to serve.

### Ready to Serve

1. Individually plate and serve.

**Note:** To further enhance the plate presentation, a small amount of chocolate syrup may be drizzled on each plate.

**ChefTec Software**

# Fresh Fruit Tarts

Catering Solutions

| | |
|---|---|
| **Author** | Catering Solutions |
| **Categories** | Rites of Spring |
| **Tools** | |
| **Locations** | |

| | | | | |
|---|---|---|---|---|
| | | | **Prep** | 30 minutes |
| **Yield** | 150 ea | | **Cooking** | 3 minutes |
| **Portion** | 1 ea | | **Finish** | |
| **Num Portions** | 150 | | **Shelf** | |

| Ingredients | | | Cost | % of Total |
|---|---|---|---|---|
| 150 | ea | frozen prepared tartlet shells | $123.75 | 40.6% |
| 50 | ea | Hershey chocolate bars | $29.50 | 9.7% |
| 50 | ea | bananas | $6.25 | 2.1% |
| 25 | basket | strawberries | $30.73 | 10.1% |
| 25 | ea | cantaloupe | $50.17 | 16.5% |
| 150 | ea | fresh peaches | $49.80 | 16.4% |
| 1.172 | gal | strawberry jelly | $14.25 | 4.7% |
| | | | $304.45 | |

**ChefTec Software**

## Fresh Fruit Tarts

Catering Solutions

**Author**     Catering Solutions

**Categories**     Rites of Spring

**Tools**

**Locations**

| | |
|---|---|
| **Prep** | 30 minutes |
| **Cooking** | 3 minutes |
| **Finish** | |
| **Shelf** | |

**Yield**     150 ea

**Portion**     1 ea

**Num Portions**     150

## Nutrition Facts

Serving Size   1
Servings Per Container   150

Amount Per Serving

**Calories** 161      Calories From Fat 7

% Daily Value

| | |
|---|---|
| **Total Fat** 1g | 1% |
| Saturated Fat  2g | 7% |
| **Cholesterol** 0mg | 0% |
| **Sodium** 13mg | 1% |
| **Total Carbohydrates** 41g | 14% |
| Dietary Fiber  7g | 29% |
| **Protein** 2g | |

| | | | |
|---|---|---|---|
| Vitamin A  62% | | Vitamin C  128% | |
| Calcium  7% | | Iron | 9% |

*Percent Daily Values are based on a 2000 calorie diet.

**Nutrition Descriptors**

Low Fat

Low Cholesterol

Very Low Sodium

# Appendix B

## Blank Forms

This appendix includes the following blank forms:

—Catering Contract
—Entertainment Contract
—Food Production and Portion Control Chart
—Order Sheet

They may be photocopied and used to complete chapter exercises, or they may be used in an actual foodservice or catering operation.

# CATERING CONTRACT

*(Name, address, phone, fax and e-mail of catering company)*

Name of Organization _____

Name of Contact Person _____

Phone _____ Fax _____ E-mail _____

Address _____

## Menu Details

Menu Theme _____  ❑ Full Service  ❑ Buffet

Menu Selection _____
_____
_____
_____
_____

Special Cake _____
_____

Beverage Selection *(Alcoholic/Non-Alcoholic)* _____

Portable Bar:  ❑ Open  ❑ Cash  ❑ Combination

## Accessory Details

❑ Linen
   Tablecloths _____
   Napkins _____
   Skirting _____
   Chair Cover(s) _____
❑ Floral Decor *(real or artificial silks)*
   Centerpieces _____ Sprays _____
   Baskets _____ Canopy _____
   Plants _____ Trees _____
❑ Decorations
   Table _____
   Room _____
❑ Sound System _____
   Microphone(s):  ❑ Cordless  ❑ Lavaliere (neck)
   ❑ Standing  ❑ Lectern  ❑ Table
❑ Background Music _____
❑ Printing
   Menus _____
   Invitations _____
❑ Ice Sculpture(s) _____
❑ Beverage Fountain(s) _____
❑ Valet Parking _____
❑ Limousine Service _____
❑ Other _____
❑ Entertainment *(Band, solo instrumental, singer, etc.)* _____ _____
_____
_____

❑ Computer Requirements _____
_____

❑ Head Table
❑ Table Numbers/Names
❑ Candles
❑ Coatroom Checking
❑ Registration Desk
❑ Speaker Podium
❑ Lectern
❑ Notebook & Marker
❑ Stage
❑ Flags
❑ Exhibits
❑ Tripod
❑ Easel
❑ Projector, Screen, VCR
❑ Lighting Effects
❑ Invitation Collection
❑ Dance Floor
❑ Piano
❑ Costumes
❑ Balloons
❑ Photography
❑ Videography
❑ Tenting
❑ Room Temperature

### Function Information

Date _____ Day _____ Time _____

Location _____

Type of Function _____

### Time Schedule

Arrival time _____

Cocktails served _____

Hors d'oeuvres served _____

Food served _____

Bar time  from _____ to _____

Entertainment  from _____ to _____

Speaker(s)  from _____ to _____

Dancing  from _____ to _____

Photography  from _____ to _____

Videography  from _____ to _____

Departure time _____

### Guest Count

Approximate number _____

Guaranteed number _____

*Date for final guarantee* _____

Confirmed number _____

### Floor Plan

Table Arrangements _____
_____

Seating Assignments _____
_____

*Diagram Space*

*(See attached if needed)*

### Special Instructions

_____
_____
_____
_____
_____
_____

## Agreement of Charges    Date _____

Guaranteed guest count of _____ at a $_____ per guest for a total of ............... $ _____

*(The final charge will be for the guaranteed guest count or confirmed guest count, whichever is greater.)*

Accessory Charges: _____  _____
_____  _____
_____  _____

**48 HOUR NOTICE REQUIRED ON CANCELLATIONS**

Caterer will be prepared to accommodate _____ % over the number of guaranteed guest count.

| | |
|---|---|
| Gratuities | _____ |
| Subtotal | _____ |
| Tax | _____ |
| Total | _____ |

_____ _____
*Customer's Signature*  *Date*

_____ _____
*Caterer's Signature*  *Date*

Due Date _____ Deposit (-) _____

Due Date _____ Balance $ _____

# ENTERTAINMENT CONTRACT

*(Name, address, phone, fax and e-mail of catering company)*

Name of band/entertainer(s)_____

Name of contact person _____ Federal Tax ID _____

Phone _____ Fax _____ E-mail _____

Address _____

*The band/entertainer(s) and catering company agree*
*to the following terms set forth in this contract:*

Date _____ Day _____ Time _____

Location _____

Type of function_____

Type of music or songs that will be played or sung _____

_____

_____

_____

Mode of dress *(entertainers)* _____ *(guests)* _____

| **Time Schedule** | | **Requirements** | |
|---|---|---|---|
| Arrival Time | _____ | Stage | _____ |
| Start Time | _____ | Seating | _____ |
| Break Times | _____ | Lighting | _____ |
| Length of Breaks | _____ | Electrical | _____ |
| *Designated Break Area* | | Sound System | _____ |
| | | Microphone(s) | _____ |
| _____ | | Other | _____ |
| End Time | _____ | | |

## Special Instructions

_____

_____

_____

_____

**Authorized:**   ❑ Photos   ❑ Videotaping   ❑ Audiotaping

## Food & Beverages

The band/entertainer(s) may be provided with food and beverages at break time according to the following schedule: _____

_____

_____

*The band/entertainer(s) further agree that no alchoholic beverages*
*will be consumed or drugs used during the event.*

## 30 Day Notice Required on Cancellations

Total   $ _____

Overtime charge will be billed at a rate of $_____ per hour

for each additional hour beyond contracted time . . . . . . . . . . . Overtime charge _____

Subtotal _____

Tax _____

_____   Total _____
*Entertainer's Signature*          *Date*

Due Date _____  Deposit (-) _____

_____   Due Date _____  Balance  $ _____
*Caterer's Signature*          *Date*

# Food Production and Portion Control Chart

NAME OF FUNCTION _____

PREPARED BY _____

GUARANTEED GUEST COUNT _____

AMOUNT TO PREPARE COUNT_____

❑ FULL SERVICE  ❑ BUFFET

CONFIRMED COUNT _____

PAGE _____ OF _____

DATE _____

DAY _____

FOOD SERVED TIME _____

| MENU ITEMS | QUANTITY PREPARED | PORTION SIZE | POSSIBLE NUMBER | AMOUNT LEFT | AMOUNT USED |
|---|---|---|---|---|---|
| | ____/ | | | Weight / Portions | |
| | ____/ | | | | |
| | ____/ | | | | |
| | ____/ | | | | |
| | ____/ | | | | |
| | ____/ | | | | |
| | ____/ | | | | |
| | ____/ | | | | |
| | ____/ | | | | |
| | ____/ | | | | |
| | ____/ | | | | |
| | ____/ | | | | |
| | ____/ | | | | |
| | ____/ | | | | |
| | ____/ | | | | |
| | ____/ | | | | |
| | ____/ | | | | |
| | ____/ | | | | |
| | ____/ | | | | |

# Order Sheet

### Grocery Items

_____
_____
_____
_____
_____
_____

### Spices & Seasonings

_____
_____
_____
_____
_____
_____

### Bakery

_____
_____
_____
_____
_____

### Beverage

_____
_____
_____
_____
_____

### Meat/Fish/Poultry

_____
_____
_____
_____
_____
_____

### Produce

_____
_____
_____
_____
_____
_____

### Dairy

_____
_____
_____
_____
_____

### Frozen

_____
_____
_____
_____
_____

### Miscellaneous

_____
_____
_____

# Cooking Terms

**AL DENTE:** Cooking food to a firm bite, typically pasta or vegetables.

**BLANCH:** A very fast cooking method that requires a liquid to cook the product. It is used for the purpose of precooking a food. It is not used to fully cook foods. Blanching involves the "boiling" process to quickly and partially cook items.

**BOIL:** A moist method of cooking. Boiling is a very fast procedure that requires a large volume of liquid (usually water) in order to maintain a high temperature throughout the cooking process. Water boils at 212°F at sea level and comes to a boil much faster if the pot is covered.

This process is most commonly used with starches and vegetables (potatoes, rice, tomatoes, broccoli, pasta, etc.).

Salt may be added to the cooking liquid to add flavor and to raise the water boiling point. When cooking pasta, vegetable oil can be added to the water in addition to the salt. The oil helps to keep the pasta from sticking and keeps the water from boiling over.

**BRAISE:** A moist-heat cooking process that combines the moisture of a stock in a pan or a pot that can be covered. The pan is then placed into the oven. The oven supplies the heat while the stock prevents the food from becoming dry. An alternative method would be to place the covered pan or pot on the stove over low heat.

This method often starts with the food being "seared" on all sides to seal in the moisture and to add the desirable brown color. During cooking, the liquid is used to baste the food for a deeper color and as an enhancement to the flavor.

Braising is a method of cooking that is used with red meats, poultry, starches, and vegetables. This is a slow process that should not be rushed. It is an excellent way of cooking meat items that may be a little on the tough side, as the combination of low heat, moisture, and longer cooking times works toward tenderizing the meat.

**DICE:** Cut into small cubes, 1/4 to 1/2 inch in size.

**FOLD:** A method used to mix light ingredients into heaver ingredients.

**FORK TENDER:** When a fork will slide into the food with very little resistance.

**FRY:** This is done with oil at high temperatures. It can be in the form of a deep-fat fryer or pan frying with a shallow amount of oil. This process develops a nice even browning on the food. Frying is most often done with breaded foods.

The oil needs to be at approximately 375°F and can be tested by taking a small cube of bread and dropping it into the hot oil to see how quickly it cooks. Too hot an oil will result in an overbrowning to the outside and an undercooked product inside. Too cool an oil will result in a very greasy, spongy consistency with a poor color on the outside.

**GRILL:** This is a dry heat process using a piece of equipment called a grill, broiler, or barbecue. This method of cooking requires time and must not be rushed. The foods being cooked in this manner should have distinctive "grill marks" from the rack or the bars that they are cooked on. The food should have a browning (caramelization) on the outside and be moist and tender on the inside.

This method of cooking lends itself to all types of meats, poultry, firm seafood (salmon, halibut, shark, etc.), and even some vegetables and potatoes. Foods can be marinated, dry seasoned, basted, or smoked to enhance the flavors.

This style of cooking is associated with a barbecue or an outdoor function such as a picnic or garden party.

**MINCE:** Cut into very small pieces.

**POACH:** A moist heat cooking process where the product or container holding the food is placed into a water-bath or flavorful liquid and is cooked at a low temperature until the desired doneness is attained. The temperature range for poaching is between 160°F and 180°F. Bubbles should not appear in the poaching liquid. If this happens, then the temperature has risen too high and must be turned down. Poaching should not be rushed. The poaching process is a method that delivers a moist, tender product that is not mushy or broken down.

**ROAST:** A dry-heat cooking method that is done in the oven at a wide variety of temperatures depending upon the items being cooked. The term "roasting" is usually associated with meat products (chicken, beef, duck, lamb, etc.). The cooking method known as "baking" is in fact the same procedure as roasting and is associated with dough or batter items (cakes, cookies, breads, etc).

Roasting of food should produce a browning on the outside with a moist interior. Items being roasted are sometimes "seared" on the outside to seal the moisture in and add color and flavor to the outside.

**SAUTÉ:** Sautéing is a dry-heat cooking method. Translated from French, sauté has two meanings:

1. "To jump" ... this is to say that the pan is so hot that the food must be continually moved in the pan or it will burn due to the high heat.

2. "To jump" ... in this meaning refers to the fact that the pan is so hot that as soon as the food is placed into the pan, the food will begin to move or "jump" on its own.

Sautéing is a high heat, low fat process that requires not overcrowding the pan. The object is to gain some desirable browning on the outside, while keeping the inside moist and tender. The pan that is used for this process is round with a single handle. The side is sloped so that the product in the pan may be flipped by rolling it up the side of the pan and with a slight backward motion the foods will turn over.

*Note: This cooking method requires some practice.*

**SHOCK:** The instant cooling of food after the blanching or boiling process. It is most effectively done with ice and water. The cooked item is plunged directly into the ice water, stopping the cooking process.

# Index